THE ODYSSEY OF STYLE IN

ULYSSES

THE ODYSSEY OF STYLE IN
ULYSSES

Karen Lawrence

PRINCETON UNIVERSITY PRESS

PRINCETON, NEW JERSEY

To my mother and father,
and to Peter,
with love and thanks

CONTENTS

ACKNOWLEDGMENTS

I would like to thank some outstanding teachers and scholars who were more than willing to help a new Joycean get started. First as a dissertation adviser at Columbia, and then as a reader of the book manuscript, Michael Wood offered his guidance, encouragement, and superb critical talents. His insight and subtlety as a critic have helped me immeasurably in understanding *Ulysses* and in clarifying my own approach to the text. I'd also like to thank Joseph Mazzeo, my second dissertation reader, for his support and advice. I would urge anyone writing a dissertation on Joyce to have such a Renaissance man on his committee.

The transformation of a dissertation into a book can be a difficult and sometimes unsuccessful process. I was fortunate to encounter a number of people who helped make the process both enjoyable and productive.

To three deservedly well-known Joyceans—A. Walton Litz, Fritz Senn, and Michael Groden—I would like to extend my appreciation for their astute criticism, their support, and their help in getting the book published. Walt Litz read part of the manuscript and encouraged me to submit it to Princeton University Press. Fritz Senn and Mike Groden were the kind of scrupulous readers whom any aspiring author would hope to have—demanding but encouraging, critical but sympathetic.

I also benefited greatly from discussions with friends and colleagues whom I expect will be the next generation of prominent scholars and teachers. For the last five years, I have profited from an ongoing, sometimes long-distance, dialogue on Joyce with Betsy Seifter, whose intelligence and time have been much appreciated. I would like to

Acknowledgments

thank Henry Staten, my friend and colleague at the University of Utah, who offered his talent for argument and analysis, and provided support while challenging me to clarify and prove my assertions. My thanks also to Vivian Sobchack, who offered perceptive comments and editorial suggestions right up until the manuscript was cast in cement, and to Barry Weller for help in the final stages of manuscript preparation.

I also want to thank Jerry Sherwood and Cathy Thatcher, my editors at Princeton, who have made it a pleasure to work with their press, and Karen Donahue at the University of Utah, for the meticulous care and intelligence she displayed in typing the manuscript in its various incarnations. Finally, my special thanks to my husband, Peter, for being the only surgical resident I know capable of such understanding, interest, and support during his own trial by fire.

I would like to thank Madame Marcel Duchamp, who very kindly allowed me to reprint Constantin Brancusi's *Portrait of James Joyce*, 1929, now in Madame Duchamp's private collection. For permission to quote from the works of James Joyce, I am indebted to the Society of Authors as the literary representatives of the Estate of James Joyce and to the Executors of the James Joyce Estate (*Dubliners* and *A Portrait of the Artist as a Young Man*), and to the following publishers: Random House and The Bodley Head (*Ulysses*), The Viking Press (*Letters of James Joyce*, *Selected Letters of James Joyce*, *Dubliners*, and *A Portrait of the Artist as a Young Man*), and Jonathan Cape Ltd. (*Dubliners* and *A Portrait of the Artist as a Young Man*).

In a different form, this book was a dissertation submitted for the degree of Doctor of Philosophy in English Literature at Columbia University. Two chapters of the book, since revised, have appeared as articles: "Aeolus: Interruption and Inventory" appeared in *The James Joyce Quarterly* 17 (Summer 1980): 389-405, and "Style and Narrative in

Acknowledgments

the 'Ithaca' Chapter of Joyce's *Ulysses*" appeared in *English Literary History* 47 (Fall 1980): 559-574. I wish to acknowledge The Johns Hopkins University Press as copyright holder for the latter article. My work during the summer of 1978 was made possible by a Faculty Development Grant from the University of Utah College of Humanities.

THE ODYSSEY OF STYLE IN
ULYSSES

Introduction

Until well into the 1970s, most book-length studies of *Ulysses* paid little attention to its radical stylistic changes. Critics and teachers tended to focus on character, symbol, and myth rather than style.[1] In part, this focus represented various attempts to come to terms with one of the major difficulties that critics perceived in the book: its narrative discontinuity. Leopold Bloom, Plumtree's Potted Meat, Ulysses—character, symbol, and myth—offered the critic certain patterns to offset the gaps in the narrative. During the first fifty years of *Ulysses* criticism, this focus was re-

[1] Of course, there are exceptions, such as Anthony Burgess, Arnold Goldman, and Hugh Kenner. Burgess displays a novelist's interest in style in *Re Joyce* (New York: W. W. Norton & Co., Inc., 1965) and later in *Joysprick: An Introduction to the Language of James Joyce* (London: André Deutsch, 1973). Goldman, a particularly fine literary critic, anticipates the direction of subsequent Joyce criticism in one section of his book *The Joyce Paradox: Form and Freedom in His Fiction* (London: Routledge & Kegan Paul, 1966). Kenner, who has written on Joyce's style more often and more provocatively than almost anyone else, discusses style at length in *Dublin's Joyce* (1956; reprint ed., Boston: Beacon Press, 1962). The following books published in the 1970s all include some discussion of style: David Hayman, *Ulysses: The Mechanics of Meaning* (Englewood Cliffs, N.J.: Prentice Hall, Inc., 1970); Marilyn French, *The Book as World: James Joyce's Ulysses* (Cambridge, Mass.: Harvard University Press, 1976); C. H. Peake, *James Joyce: The Citizen and the Artist* (Stanford: Stanford University Press, 1977); and Hugh Kenner, *Joyce's Voices* (Berkeley: University of California Press, 1978). Since the writing of this book, two new studies that include discussions of language have been published: Hugh Kenner, *Ulysses* (London: Allen & Unwin, Ltd., 1980), and Roy K. Gottfried, *The Art of Joyce's Syntax in Ulysses* (Athens: University of Georgia Press, 1980).

flected in two main critical approaches that, in different
ways, attempted to make sense of the narrative discontinuity
in the text: the novelistic and the "spatial" or structural
approaches.

One of the finest examples of the novelistic approach to
Ulysses is S. L. Goldberg's *The Classical Temper: A Study
of James Joyce's Ulysses*. For Goldberg, the discontinuity
of the narrative is bridged by the continuity of character
development. His interpretive model is the Jamesian novel
of character and dramatic conflict; he praises the technical
innovations in *Ulysses* that contribute to the development
of plot and character and criticizes the rhetorical experiments that impede this development.[2] Erwin Steinberg's
The Stream of Consciousness and Beyond in Ulysses is another critical study that discusses narrative discontinuity in
reference to character development and deliberately eschews
analysis of the more radical, less character-based experiments in the latter half of *Ulysses*.[3]

More prevalent from the 1920s to the 1970s was the
"spatial" or structural approach to *Ulysses*, articulated most
fully by Joseph Frank in 1945. In his "Spatial Form in
Modern Literature," Frank offered almost a manifesto for
the spatial approach to modern literature in general. Re-
sponding to the narrative discontinuity in modern fiction,
Frank proposed a "spatial" or nonsequential reading previously reserved for the study of poetry. Citing *Ulysses* as
one of his major examples, Frank claimed that modern novels are like imagist poems, which work at "frustrating the
reader's normal expectation of a sequence and forcing him
to perceive the elements of the poem as juxtaposed in space
rather than unrolling in time."[4] In order to perceive this

[2] S. L. Goldberg, *The Classical Temper: A Study of James Joyce's Ulysses*
(London: Chatto and Windus, 1961).

[3] Erwin R. Steinberg, *The Stream of Consciousness and Beyond in Ulysses*
(Pittsburgh: University of Pittsburgh Press, 1973).

[4] Joseph Frank, "Spatial Form in Modern Literature," *Sewanee Review* 53
(1945). Revised in *The Widening Gyre: Crisis and Mastery in Modern Literature*
(Bloomington: Indiana University Press, 1963), p. 10.

juxtaposition in space, the reader must have the entire book in his mind; he must see the beginning in terms of the end. Consequently, modern fiction, like modern poetry, cannot be "read" but only "reread," so that the reader can discover the "pattern of relationships" woven into the text. What Joseph Frank and others did for the readers of works like *Ulysses* was to give them a model of intelligibility, the imagist poem, that helped to explain the discontinuity of the fiction. If this modernist fiction deliberately destroyed narrative continuity, it replaced the unity of narrative with a unity of what Frank called "aesthetic form."[5]

Later critics like William York Tindall continued to read *Ulysses* as a kind of gigantic poem. Whereas Frank concerned himself with the details and allusions in *Ulysses* that had to be fit together like the pieces of a jigsaw puzzle, Tindall was equally interested in symbolic and allegorical parallels within the work. Although he leads his reader through *Ulysses* chapter by chapter in his *A Reader's Guide to James Joyce*, Tindall portrays *Ulysses* as a system of cross-references, a spatial, symbolic poem.[6]

Both the novelistic and the spatial approaches to the book refused to deal with its most strikingly original and disorienting aspect: its radical stylistic and modal changes. In reading *Ulysses* as a dramatic novel or as an imagist poem, these critics lost the sense of it as a work that deliberately changes, develops, transforms itself. One could say that the novelistic readings of *Ulysses* express the wish that all of

---

[5] Recently, there has been much debate on the concept of spatial form, particularly in *Critical Inquiry*, which has provided a forum for discussions of space versus time in literature. In recent essays, Frank has buttressed his thesis on space versus time in modern literature with arguments from structuralism and linguistics. See "Spatial Form: An Answer to Critics," *Critical Inquiry* 4 (Winter 1977): 231-252, and "Spatial Form: Some Further Reflections," *Critical Inquiry* 5 (Winter 1978): 275-290. Anyone interested in the entire debate, including some convincing rebuttals to Frank, should consult *Critical Inquiry* 4 (Winter 1977), and Frank Kermode's "Reply to Joseph Frank," in *Critical Inquiry* 4 (Spring 1978): 579-588.

[6] William York Tindall, *A Reader's Guide to James Joyce* (New York: Farrar, Straus & Giroux, 1959).

Ulysses resembled its early chapters; the spatial readings ignore the fact that it doesn't.[7] In regarding the book as a map spread out before the reader, the "spatial" critics, especially, ignore both the stylistic progression in the narrative and the process of confirmation and disconfirmation of expectations in the reader's experience.

In this book I offer a reading that focuses on style instead of plot and structure and that restores the notion of temporal process to the reading of *Ulysses* in two ways: by regarding the changes in style as rhetorical experiments that move in certain general directions and by regarding the effects of these experiments on the reader's expectations. One can describe *Ulysses* as a book that changes its mind as it progresses and forces a corresponding change of mind in the reader. The segmented quality of *Ulysses*—the discontinuity of the narrative as it dons various stylistic "masks"—can be treated as successive breaks in "narrative contracts" and successive rhetorical experiments rather than segments in a spatial whole. The reader of *Ulysses* comes to each chapter with expectations that are contingent upon what he has experienced not only in other novels but also in the preceding chapters of this one. These expectations are frustrated and altered as the book progresses. The narrative contract we form at the beginning of the book—the implicit agreement between the writer and the reader about the way the book is to be read—is broken. No one who has read *Ulysses* can deny his increasing struggle to cope with the wealth of detail and with the protean transformations of style. This sense of increasing difficulty may be mentioned in a discussion of structure, but in a sequential or linear reading of *Ulysses*, this struggle forms one of the major concerns.

My interest in the process of reading and the problems of interpretation converges, in part, with such reader-ori-

---

[7] See *Joyce's Voices* (pp. 1-2) for Hugh Kenner's remarks on T. S. Eliot's famous essay "*Ulysses*, Order and Myth," which was one of the earliest structural or spatial approaches to *Ulysses*.

ented critics as Stanley Fish, in his general criticism,[8] and Marilyn French, whose book, *The Book as World: James Joyce's Ulysses*, contains a reader-oriented approach to *Ulysses*. French and I both attempt to document the breaking of narrative contracts and the attendant confusion this process creates in the reader. But like the spatial critics whom in other ways she would oppose, French posits some kind of final revelation for the reader. She treats *Ulysses* as an heuristic text, a text that brings the reader to a final revelation of Bloom's *caritas* or humanity. As I hope to show, *Ulysses* is deliberately antirevelatory, a book that ultimately subverts the notion of an "ideal reader" who arrives at a single truth. We do learn something about novels during the course of our reading, but we do not arrive at even a Pisgah sight of meaning. Or, to put it differently, Joyce presents possibilities of meaning rather than a final revelation. I question both Frank's belief in "a unified spatial apprehension"[9] and French's belief in a final vision for the reader at the end of his Odyssean journey through the text. Thus it is not only a different focus but a different interpretation of *Ulysses* for which I am arguing. An analysis of the rhetorical experiments in the book leads, I believe, to an interpretation that calls into question the typological or teleological readings offered by Frank and French.[10] In addition, Marilyn French's focus on the struggle and heroism of the reader on his journey eclipses both the struggle of the book to continue and the verbal heroics involved in this task. The element of performance and exhibition in the

---

[8] See Stanley E. Fish, *Self-Consuming Artifacts: The Experience of Seventeenth-Century Literature* (Berkeley: University of California Press, 1972).

[9] Frank, "Spatial Form in Modern Literature," p. 19.

[10] Frank explicitly applies the vocabulary of a figural interpretation to modern texts in quotation from Gérard Genette's *Figures II* (Paris, 1969), pp. 45-46: "One may say, then, that the space of a book, like that of a page, is not passively subject to the time of a linear reading; so far as the book reveals and fulfills itself completely, it never stops diverting and reversing such a reading, and, thus, in a sense, abolishes it." See Frank, "Spatial Form: Some Further Reflections," p. 290.

writing itself is too great to allow the reader to receive all the applause.

It should be clear from my discussion of discontinuity that by "linearity" I do not refer to a neat progression in theme or in style. I do refer, however, to a movement in the book away from both the conventions of the novel form and from a stylistic norm. Probably the most significant change in the style of narration is the abandonment, roughly halfway through the book, of the third-person narrative style with which *Ulysses* begins. The authoritative narrative voice that tells the story in the early chapters (beginning the novel with the words "Stately, plump Buck Mulligan came from the stairhead . . .") is largely replaced by a series of stylistic masks. This movement of style reflects a change in the idea of style as the "signature" of the writer to one of style as, to quote Roland Barthes, "a citational process, a body of formulae, a memory, a cultural and not an expressive inheritance."[11] This "citational" quality, the opacity and history of language, dominates the second half of the narrative. Somewhere in the middle of *Ulysses*, style goes "public," as language is flooded by the memory of its prior use.

One of Joyce's distinctions among modern writers is that he created and then abandoned what we normally think of as a personal or authentic style, and *Ulysses* itself records that process. T. S. Eliot's famous observation that Joyce "had many voices but no 'style' "[12] is not, I think, totally accurate, although it identifies what makes Joyce different from his contemporaries. *Ulysses* does begin in an identifiable "style," one that Joyce developed out of the narrative experiments of *Dubliners* and *A Portrait* and that can be identified as his signature style. This is the style whose absence we feel when it is replaced by a series of rhetorical masks.

These masks in the second half of *Ulysses* both reveal and

[11] Roland Barthes, "Style and Its Image," in *Literary Style: A Symposium*, ed. Seymour Chatman (New York: Oxford University Press, 1971), p. 9.

[12] T. S. Eliot, "Lettre d'Angleterre: Le Style dans la prose anglaise contemporaine," *La Nouvelle Revue Française* 19 (July-Dec., 1922): 751-756.

disguise the author. Joyce's masks in *Ulysses* are quite different from those of other writers—Virginia Woolf, for example. In the disembodied narrative voices in *To The Lighthouse*, one feels that Woolf is neither as exhibitionistic nor as completely disguised as Joyce is in *Ulysses*. One senses in Woolf's novels the author's vulnerability in her writing; it is as if the umbilical cord between writer and writing has not been severed. *Ulysses*, on the other hand, is a work that prides itself on being "hatched" rather than fathered forth. In its own way illustrating that "paternity may be a legal fiction," the text deliberately acts as if it were cut off from any single creating consciousness.

A comment made by Stanislaus Joyce about his brother in his diary of 1904 is apposite to the mixture of revelation and disguise in *Ulysses*. Stanislaus wrote: "Jim is thought to be very frank about himself, but his style is such that it might be contended that he confesses in a foreign language."[13] The rhetorical masks that Joyce created in *Ulysses* allowed the writing to be both the "me" and the "not me" of the writer.

This series of rhetorical masks leads us to doubt the authority of any particular style. As the narrative norm is abandoned during the course of the book and is replaced by a series of styles, we see the arbitrariness of all styles. We see the styles as different but not definitive ways of filtering and ordering experience. This view of style obviates a "spatial apprehension" of the book: one cannot see *through* the various styles to an ultimate Platonic pattern of meaning. Style in *Ulysses* is not what Flaubert called "an absolute manner of seeing things";[14] it is, rather, a choice among relative possibilities.

The breakdown of the authority of style is accompanied

---

[13] *The Dublin Diary of Stanislaus Joyce*, ed. George Harris Healey (London: Faber and Faber, 1962), p. 81.

[14] Letter to Louise Colet, 16 January 1852, in *The Selected Letters of Gustave Flaubert*, trans. and ed. Francis Steegmuller; reprinted in *Madame Bovary*, ed. Paul de Man (New York: W. W. Norton—Norton Critical Edition, 1965), pp. 309-310.

by a parallel destruction of the conventions of relevance and significance of detail involved in the creation of plot and theme. As the styles and forms of the chapters proliferate, so do the "facts" included in the narrative. The book becomes an encyclopedia of possibilities of plot as well as style, deliberately breaking the conventions of selectivity and relevance upon which most novels are based. The surplus of facts and styles in *Ulysses* has the effect of making the text exceptionally resistant to critical attempts to force it into a statement of meaning. Instead of plot as we know it, the text gives us an overwhelming number of facts, not all of which can be assimilated into a single pattern; instead of narrative authority, it gives us styles that interpret reality in different ways. If, as Dorothy Van Ghent claims in her discussion of the English novel, fiction "tries to isolate the principle of coherence in events,"[15] *Ulysses* is a book that is, in this sense, an antifiction. It is a book that refuses to conclude, a book that presents us with a set of "fictions" but not a "fiction" itself.

Another way to express this would be to say that the different modes of ordering experience are also different modes of ordering a novel. The chapters of *Ulysses* provide possible organizations for the telling of a story. If the first half of the book (with the exception of "Aeolus") reads more or less like a novel (and a more complex sequel to Joyce's previous work), the second half reads like a series of aesthetic experiments. Each chapter poses a new rhetorical situation to be explored. It is as if Joyce had asked himself, "What if I write everything in two styles?" ("Cyclops"); "What if I write only in clichés?" ("Eumaeus"); "What if I 'imitate' music in language?" ("Sirens"). Part way through *Ulysses* we witness the breakdown of the novel as a form and the creation of an encyclopedia of narrative choices. The resources of subliterature (journalism, magazine fiction, mel-

[15] Dorothy Van Ghent, *The English Novel: Form and Function* (New York: Harper & Row, 1953), p. 16.

odrama) and nonliterature (science) are plumbed by Joyce and used for his own purposes. And the resources of the book's first half are pillaged and reused in the second half. In the process, style, plot, narrator, and genre are all in one way or another revealed as fictions employed in the creation of novels.

Thus, as recent critics have remarked, *Ulysses* is about novel writing and novel reading.[16] It is about its own process of creation. But part of the greatness of *Ulysses*, it seems to me, is that it is not only about writing (and reading) novels but also about living life. Although Joyce plays with the conventions of realism in the text (most notably in the "Circe" chapter), the dramatic action of the novel is still very much rooted in "the real world." This fidelity to fact, this basic realism of the text, is twofold. First, it is exemplified in the novel's more traditional aspect of realism: we can determine generally what happens in the story no matter how bizarre the verbal machinations of the style. Although certain "gaps" may occur in the narrative,[17] *Ulysses*, unlike *Finnegans Wake*, retains the specificity of place and event. "I want . . . to give a picture of Dublin so complete that if the city one day suddenly disappeared from the earth it could be reconstructed out of my book," Joyce told Frank Budgen,[18] and the meticulous documentation of geography and time does much to establish this realistic substratum. As James Maddox observes: "In his art, Joyce can allow himself such a long tether and can wander into the most

[16] See Marilyn French, *The Book as World: James Joyce's Ulysses*; Wolfgang Iser, *The Implied Reader: Patterns of Communication in Prose Fiction from Bunyan to Beckett* (Baltimore: The Johns Hopkins University Press, 1974), Chapter Eight; and A. Walton Litz, "The Genre of *Ulysses*," in *The Theory of the Novel: New Essays*, ed. John Halperin (New York: Oxford University Press, 1974), pp. 109-120.

[17] See Hugh Kenner's recent work on the significant omissions in the text, in "The Rhetoric of Silence," *James Joyce Quarterly* 14 (Summer 1977): 382-394.

[18] Quoted in Frank Budgen, *James Joyce and the Making of Ulysses* (1934); reprint ed., Bloomington: Indiana University Press, 1960), pp. 67-68.

Introduction

Byzantine of stylistic distortions because the narrative has its very roots in objects and facts."[19]

The tension between this traditional rooting of the realistic text in objects and facts and the *surplus* of detail in *Ulysses* creates the second kind of realism in the text—an imitation of the wealth of life. In *Ulysses*, Joyce abjures the notion of closure and shape to which fictions usually submit; the details of the text overflow all neat aesthetic patterns, signifying the arbitrariness and plurasignificance of life. *Ulysses* is both spectacularly artificial and, in its own way, realistic. A bizarre form of exaggeration and experiment, the book nevertheless reminds the reader of all the "facts" of life that cannot be assimilated to the literary purposes of the novel form or to any "fiction" as Dorothy Van Ghent describes it.

The book does not abandon its interest in the characters and their stories, but one can locate a shift of attention from the dramatic action of the plot to the drama of the writing, as the primary function of style shifts from the presentation of character to the verbal display in the writing. In the early chapters of *Ulysses*, the narrative largely devotes itself to exposing the quality of the characters' minds. In the second half of the book, style is no longer an expression of the sensibility of the character (with the exception of "Nausicaa" and "Penelope"—retrogressive chapters in this respect). Beginning in "Aeolus" with the intrusion of the headings and the rhetorical figures in the narration, and continuing in the linguistic games of "Sirens," the writing of the text begins to dominate our attention. Language begins a kind of insurrection, as style becomes increasingly opaque and self-dramatizing.

The tension in the book between an emphasis on the telling of the story and an emphasis on the story itself, between the rhetorical and the narrative aspects of literature, characterizes a tradition of encyclopedic books preceding

[19] James H. Maddox, Jr., *Joyce's Ulysses and the Assault upon Character* (New Brunswick: Rutgers University Press, 1978), p. 9.

Introduction

Ulysses: Burton's *Anatomy of Melancholy*, Rabelais' *Gargantua and Pantagruel*, Sterne's *Tristram Shandy*. Like these books, *Ulysses* is marked throughout by its extravagant use of rhetoric. Many of the stylistic eccentricities in the chapters can be classified as different types of rhetorical performances: the inventory of rhetorical figures in "Aeolus," the rhetorical rearrangements and figures of sound in "Sirens," the catalogue of oratorical styles in "Cyclops" and "Oxen of the Sun," the pathopoeia in "Circe," the commonplaces catalogued in "Eumaeus," and, finally, the "logical" arguments and proofs from rhetoric marshalled in "Ithaca." Although throughout *Ulysses* the characters make speeches and admire a fellow speaker who offers a well-turned phrase, the self-conscious use of rhetoric shifts from the character to the narrative, as the book advertises its own use of language.

This shift in the use of rhetoric exemplifies a general tendency in the text: what happens on a narrative level in later chapters is anticipated on the level of character at the beginning. The often arbitrary associations that characterize the stream-of-consciousness of the characters in the first six chapters anticipate the arbitrary phrases that pop up in the headings of "Aeolus," as the associative "habit of mind" infiltrates the narrative itself. Bloom's repression of the painful fact of Molly's adultery, evidenced in his gesture of scrutinizing his nails whenever her name is mentioned in an insinuating fashion, anticipates the narrative of "Ithaca," which focuses on material objects while we long to know of the human emotions behind them. Mulligan's parody of the Mass in "Telemachus" and Martin Cunningham's mimicry of Tom Kernan in "Hades" are transferred to the narrative of later chapters such as "Cyclops" and "Oxen of the Sun." And, as Hugh Kenner observes in *Joyce's Voices*, the periphrasis that characterizes Bloom's stream-of-consciousness, his inability to name directly the objects he perceives, becomes a narrative ploy in "Eumaeus."[20]

---

[20] Kenner, *Joyce's Voices*, p. 35.

Introduction

These examples show that dialogue and stream-of-consciousness, the techniques used to develop the characters in the early chapters, anticipate the bizarre narrative occurrences later on. *Ulysses* is a text that begins with the implicit assumption of the primacy of character. In the first half of the book, we watch as the characters attempt to interpret their environments and their pasts; then in "Aeolus" and in later chapters, the book begins to interpret itself and inventory its own past. The book ceases to be primarily a psychological novel and becomes an encyclopedia of narrative possibilities.

My focus is on the protean transformation of styles and on the general movement in the book from writing to rhetorical exhibition, from norm to parody, and from the psychology of the characters to what I call the consciousness of the book. By using this term I hope to avoid the connotation of a specific narrator telling a story that is implied by the term "narrative voice." (I do this with the recognition that all descriptions of the narrative are metaphoric attempts to capture its elusive quality.)

In my discussion, I try to address a number of central questions: Is there a continuity other than narrative that mediates the discontinuity the reader experiences? How do elements of narration (tones and techniques) in the early chapters "suffer a sea change" later on in the book? How does Joyce break down the conventions of the novel and reconstitute them in a new kind of text? Finally, what is the ultimate difference between a linear reading of the text and a spatial one in terms of our interpretation of the book and its characters?

Although I concentrate on those chapters which offer the most radical stylistic experiments, such as "Aeolus," "Sirens," "Cyclops," "Oxen of the Sun," "Circe," "Eumaeus," and "Ithaca," I deal to some extent with the narrative of all the chapters in the book. In addition, by way of introduction I include a discussion of Joyce's stylistic experiments in *Dubliners*—specifically, his early use of the technique of free indirect discourse in the creation of narrative voices. Although I also briefly discuss the style of *A Portrait*, the experiments in *Dubliners* receive closer attention because I believe them to be the most important precursors of the creation of stylistic masks in the later chapters of *Ulysses*.

The close relationship between character and style with which *Ulysses* begins—that is, the domination of the writing by the sensibility of the main character—is anticipated in *Dubliners* and *A Portrait*. From the early stories in *Dubliners* on, Joyce experimented with the particular quality of a character by catching his mental idiom, the cadence of his thought, a practice that frequently led to parody. By looking at Joyce's early experiments with this kind of verbal imitation, one can see how he developed the many "voices" that T. S. Eliot observed. It is in *Dubliners* that we can see the emergence of the different kinds of Dublin voices represented in *Ulysses*. And it is in "The Dead" and *A Portrait* that we can see the emergence of the educated, precise voice associated with the artist figure, the voice that establishes the narrative norm in the "Telemachiad" of *Ulysses*. In these early works, then, one can see the origins of both the narrative norm with which *Ulysses* begins and the stylistic masks with which it ends. As Hugh Kenner has often pointed out, Joyce remained a "sound" man throughout his artistic career; from the economical, scrupulous prose of the early stories to the bizarre exaggerations of the second half of *Ulysses*, Joyce retained his interest in presenting the voices that he heard. In his early work, he began with parody of character through the record of one mind thinking; in *Ulysses*, he ended with parodies of language through the presentation of verbal masks.

I

Dublin Voices

Of his purpose in writing *Dubliners*, Joyce told his publisher Grant Richards in 1906:

> My intention was to write a chapter of the moral history of my country and I chose Dublin for the scene because that city seemed to me the centre of paralysis. . . . I have written it for the most part in a style of scrupulous meanness and with the conviction that he is a very bold man who dares to alter in the presentment, still more to deform, whatever he has seen and heard.[1]

The letter, written in response to Richards' desire for Joyce to alter certain "troublesome" words in his stories, suggests that he saw his artistic choices as both aesthetic and moral. In the phrase "scrupulous meanness," Joyce implies both an aesthetic and moral meticulousness. He defends his diction on the grounds that it is already as pared and carefully chosen as possible (so that no word is arbitrary or dispensable) and that it records the "truth" about Dublin. In the last line of the quotation, Joyce directly links the style of his stories with his moral duty to represent his subject faithfully.

In this description of his technique in *Dubliners*, Joyce articulates what is apparent from reading the stories: that "truth" depends not on the mediation of the storyteller but on the precision of the prose. The style of scrupulous mean-

---

[1] 5 May 1906. In *Selected Letters of James Joyce*, ed. Richard Ellmann (New York: The Viking Press, 1975, p. 83. Henceforth the *Selected Letters* will be abbreviated as *SL*.

ness involves restraint, both in terms of narrative stance and prose style. It implies a reduced role for the narrator, who would present rather than exhort. Six years earlier, in his essay on Ibsen's *When We Dead Awaken*, Joyce had praised drama as the highest form of art because it could present, directly and without alteration, what the artist saw and heard. In Ibsen's play, Joyce said, "the situation is not stupidly explained": the play expresses its own ideas as "briefly and concisely as they can be expressed in the dramatic form," with "from first to last hardly a superfluous word or phrase."[2] In *Dubliners*, Joyce attempted to apply this aesthetic of economy and restraint to a prose medium. "Joyce . . . seldom raises his voice as he examines the less overt manifestations of human behavior," Marvin Magalaner and Richard Kain observe in *Joyce: The Man, the Work, the Reputation*,[3] and this restraint, characteristic of *Dubliners*, reveals Joyce's confidence that one does not have to shout to be heard.

Paradoxically, the lack of authorial intrusion seems, at times, to be an announcement of a narrative feat: with his hands tied behind his back, the author seems to say, he will wrestle with and pin down his city and his characters. Richard Ellmann describes this narrative stance in his biography of Joyce:

> Arrogant yet humble too, it claims importance by claiming nothing; it seeks a presentation so sharp that comment by the author would be an interference. It leaves off the veneer of gracious intimacy with the reader, of concern that he should be taken into the author's confidence, and instead makes the reader feel uneasy and culpable if he

---

[2] See "Ibsen's New Drama," in *The Critical Writings of James Joyce*, ed. Ellsworth Mason and Richard Ellmann (New York: The Viking Press, 1959), pp. 5 and 49.

[3] Marvin Magalaner and Richard M. Kain, *Joyce: The Man, the Work, the Reputation* (New York: New York University Press, 1956), p. 58.

misses the intended but always unstated meaning, as if he were being arraigned rather than entertained.[4]

The clarity and brevity of the style of scrupulous meanness also implies this kind of confidence. In *The Motives of Eloquence*, Richard Lanham discusses clarity as a stylistic ideal: "Clarity," he says, "must not show off. But serious prejudice aside, clarity contains enormous show-off zest. Clarity signifies, after all, an immense act of exclusion, of restraint. It is an affair of timing, potentially—like brevity—of wit."[5]

The style of scrupulous meanness, in conjunction with Joyce's theory of epiphany represented fictionally in *Stephen Hero*, expressed a certain basic confidence in the powers of language as well as in the author's abilities. Joyce's view in *Stephen Hero* (expressed through Stephen) that the artist should very carefully record epiphanies or "sudden spiritual manifestation[s], whether in the vulgarity of speech or of gesture or in a memorable phase of the mind itself"[6] suggests a general belief: a confidence in the adequacy of language to capture an image or emotion or to pinion Dublin lives smartly in a phrase. The burden and the faith of notions such as "*le mot juste*" and the "objective correlative" (a later version of this faith) are evident in Joyce's idea of the "supreme artist" who could "disentangle the subtle soul of the image from its mesh of defining circumstances most exactly and «re-embody» it in artistic circumstances chosen as the most exact for it in its new office" (*SH*, p. 78). These formulations express a belief in style as a kind of perfect expression of an emotion, thought, or type of mind. The mode of scrupulous meanness in *Dubliners* implied, then, narrative restraint, precision and economy of prose style, and a faith

[4] Richard Ellmann, *James Joyce* (New York: Oxford University Press, 1959), p. 88.

[5] Richard A. Lanham, *The Motives of Eloquence: Literary Rhetoric in the Renaissance* (New Haven: Yale University Press, 1976), pp. 21-22.

[6] *Stephen Hero*, ed. Theodore Spencer, rev. ed. (New York: New Directions, 1963), p. 211. *Stephen Hero* henceforth will be abbreviated in the text as *SH*.

(also expressed in the theory of epiphany) in the ability of language to capture reality.

In his notebooks, Joyce himself had attempted to record epiphanies of the "vulgarity of speech" of the Dubliners. The direct reporting of speech in these epiphanies provided Joyce with one method of presenting, without deforming, "whatever he had seen and heard." But, as Stanislaus Joyce says in *My Brother's Keeper*, these epiphanies were "brief sketches, hardly ever more than some dozen lines in length, but always very accurately observed and noted, the matter being so slight. This collection served him as a sketchbook serves an artist."[7] For the longer form of the stories, Joyce experimented with a narrative technique that allowed him to place the sound of Dublin voices in a new narrative context: the technique of free indirect discourse used extensively by Flaubert. This technique renders a character's speech or thoughts in the character's own idiom, while "maintaining the third-person reference and the basic tense of narration" but not the introductory phrases (such as "he said that") of indirect discourse.[8] Providing an alternative between direct and indirect reporting and a chance to present the character's *mental* as well as spoken idiom, this technique suited beautifully Joyce's aims of precision, subtlety, and narrative restraint. In free indirect discourse, the characters would betray their own paralysis. If people could be deposited in the narrative, "formulated, sprawling on a pin," why not allow them to impale themselves?

[7] Stanislaus Joyce, *My Brother's Keeper: James Joyce's Early Years*, ed. Richard Ellmann (London: Faber and Faber, 1958), pp. 134-135.

[8] Dorrit Cohn, *Transparent Minds: Narrative Modes for Presenting Consciousness in Fiction* (Princeton: Princeton University Press, 1978), p. 100. Cohn's term for this technique is "narrated monologue," which refers to reported thoughts alone. Other critics, like Stephen Ullmann, use the term "free indirect discourse" to refer to both reported thoughts and speech (Ullmann, *Style in the French Novel* [New York: Barnes & Noble, 1964]). I prefer the more general term, since Joyce and Flaubert report both speech and thoughts, but it is the reporting of thoughts that is most important to the development of the Dublin voices in Joyce's stories.

In *Dubliners*, Joyce extended Flaubert's use of the technique of free indirect discourse to suit his own narrative purposes. Whereas Flaubert's narrator tended to shift from the borrowed mental speech of his characters to his own more literary prose, Joyce strengthened the link between character and narrator. In the following example from "A Mother," Joyce creates a narrator who is less intrusive, more disguised, than Flaubert's:

> Everything went on smoothly. Mrs Kearney brought some lovely blush-pink charmeuse in Brown Thomas's to let into the front of Kathleen's dress. It cost a pretty penny; but there are occasions when a little expense is justifiable. She took a dozen of two-shilling tickets for the final concert and sent them to those friends who could not be trusted to come otherwise. She forgot nothing and, thanks to her, everything that was to be done was done.[9]

Technically, the third sentence is the obvious example of free indirect discourse, since we are suddenly given Mrs Kearney's mental idiom without any narrative introduction. However, the word "lovely," the English expression "to let into the front of Kathleen's dress," and the self-congratulatory "thanks to her" are all obviously extensions of the small, calculating mind of Mrs Kearney (indeed, both Flaubert and Joyce seem to be particularly hard on overbearing mothers). The entire passage, then, represents Joyce's extension of the technique that he found in Flaubert and his creation of a narrator who borrows wholesale his character's idiom. A look at specific stories in which a third-person narrator "borrows" the language of his characters will illustrate how Joyce created a series of narrative voices that functioned as stylistic masks.

In the stories told from the point of view of a Jamesian, "centered" consciousness, Joyce uses free indirect discourse

[9] *Dubliners*, ed. Robert Scholes in consultation with Richard Ellmann (New York: The Viking Press, 1967), pp. 138-139. All subsequent references to the short stories are to this edition and will be cited in the text.

to reveal the quality of ordinary Dublin lives. The bankruptcy of the lives of Little Chandler, the failed artist in "A Little Cloud," and Maria, the spinster in "Clay," is epiphanized in their language and is made clear to the reader, but not, for the most part, to the character. In the following example from "A Little Cloud," Joyce presents the sound of a Dublin mind thinking and suppressing the realization of its own pain:

> He looked coldly into the eyes of the photograph and they answered coldly. Certainly they were pretty and the face itself was pretty. But he found something mean in it. . . . He found something mean in the pretty furniture which he had bought for his house on the hire system. Annie had chosen it herself and it reminded him of her. It too was prim and pretty. (P. 83)

In the repetition of the word "pretty," Joyce appropriates a word from the little domestic world of "bliss" that Little Chandler and his wife inhabit and transforms it into half-conscious accusation. The deliberateness, the tightness of the neat little sentences, reveal the essence of Little Chandler's mind. Through the sterile, obsessive repetition, Joyce captures the frustration of the character's life.

In "Clay," the narrator adopts Maria's language: her tenses, her pronouns, her clichés are all appropriated, and with them her limitations. He borrows the assumptions of her world and seems to expect that we will sympathize with these assumptions. Maria's world is composed of "nice" people, habitual actions, and familiar faces; it is a world in which children are "tired and sleepy," because in the happy bed-time story Maria has made of her life, the mundane and redundant are comforting friends.

The following is an example of the narrative style of the story:

> The kitchen was spick and span: the cook said you could see yourself in the big copper boilers. The fire was nice

and bright and on one of the side-tables were four very
big barmbracks. These barmbracks seemed uncut; but
if you went closer you would see that they had been cut.
(P. 99)

What we are shown here is a representation of a lonely and
repressed adult mind that operates on the level of childlike
simplicity. By donning language appropriate to Maria, the
narrator appears to concur in her observations. And the
second-person pronoun, "you," seeks to draw the reader
into this chummy association. Irony results from the disparity between the "you" in Maria's thoughts and the reader
who recognizes the processes of repression and rationalization that lead Maria to organize her world in this way.

The language of Maria, like that of the other Dubliners,
is a pastiche of unacknowledged quotations, "received ideas"
about life that help her "control" her world.[10] Like the other
characters in *Dubliners*, Maria composes a story about her
life. Just as Flaubert used the technique of free indirect
discourse to reveal the romance-ridden mind of Emma Bovary, Joyce used it to reveal the minds of characters who
tend to see themselves as central characters in various types
of stories. Maria's unconscious image of herself as the good
fairy godmother in a tale for children is only a more plebeian
and naive version of Little Chandler's romantic image of
himself as a Byronic poet, a poet who fantasizes the review
of his poems (*"Mr Chandler has the gift of easy and graceful
verse. . . . A wistful sadness pervades these poems. . . . The
Celtic note"* [p. 74]). Mr Duffy in "A Painful Case," in fact,
represents all the Dubliners who consciously or uncon-
sciously have "an odd autobiographical habit which led him
to compose in his mind from time to time a short sentence
about himself containing a subject in the third person and

---

[10] See Hugh Kenner's *Dublin's Joyce* (1956; reprint ed., Boston: Beacon
Press, 1962) for the best discussion of the clichéd language of Dublin. The
Dubliners, he says, "can speak only in quotations, and despite their conscious-
ness of effort, their thought runs in grooves." (p. 8).

a predicate in the past tense" (p. 108). Like Don Quixote, who literally attempts to chronicle his own exploits, these characters wish to "write" their own stories.[11]

But through the use of free indirect discourse, the narrator does this for them; he borrows their self-images, their fictions, their clichés. He masquerades as a participant in the world of his characters and appears "unreliable" because he seems to accept his characters' limitations. Free indirect discourse allows him to *seem* to accept the self-image a character has created for himself, while pointing to the insufficiency of that image. The characteristic irony of the stories originates in this masquerade. As Dorrit Cohn puts it, narrated monologues (free indirect discourse) "amplify emotional notes, but also throw into ironic relief all false notes struck by a figural mind."[12]

The wish to present the self-deluded minds of ordinary people is not a new one to the writers of short stories or novels. What is important and unusual in *Dubliners*, however, is Joyce's strong interest in the *language* of the characters' thoughts. Stephen Ullmann's emphasis on the fact that free indirect discourse is essentially "mimetic" (it "retains the expressive elements of speech, and tries to imitate the inflexions and intonations of the speaking voice"[13]) and "oblique" (it is "reported speech masquerading as narrative"[14]) is particularly germane to a study of Joyce's use of the technique. Through the use of free indirect discourse, style becomes an indispensable tool of irony; as a mirror of a type of mind thinking, it can quickly shift from imitation into subtle mockery. Thus, the irony of the stories depends upon a form of stylistic parody. And with the technique of free indirect discourse, style becomes mask—the author becomes a mimic, speaking in someone else's voice.

[11] Kenner has discussed this kind of role playing in his book *Joyce's Voices* (Berkeley: University of California Press, 1978).

[12] Cohn, *Transparent Minds*, p. 117.

[13] Ullmann, *Style in the French Novel*, p. 99.

[14] Ibid., p. 117.

Thus it is the obliqueness of the technique that makes free indirect discourse a more important antecedent of the radical stylistic developments in *Ulysses* than the stream-of-consciousness technique, which purports to give a more direct transcription of the mental process without narrative intrusion. The mimicking in the narrative of the second half of *Ulysses* in part grows out of the mimicking begun in *Dubliners*. But in *Ulysses*, the unreliability of the narrator gives way to the unreliability of the narrative—the mimicking no longer parodies a particular type of mind.

It was this tendency to parody, this very distance between the author and the rather pathetic characters he could so easily pinion, that contributed to a growing ambivalence Joyce felt toward his "betrayal" of Dublin's soul. The suspicion that he might be reaching an artistic cul-de-sac in the stories first surfaces in Joyce's letter to Stanislaus on July 19, 1905:

> Is it possible that, after all, men of letters are no more than entertainers? These discouraging reflections arise perhaps from my surroundings. The stories in *Dubliners* seem to be indisputably well done but, after all, perhaps many people could do them as well. I am not rewarded by any feeling of having overcome difficulties. . . . The Dublin papers will object to my stories as to a caricature of Dublin life. Do you think there is any truth in this? At times the spirit directing my pen seems to me so plainly mischievous that I am almost prepared to let the Dublin critics have their way. All these pros and cons I must for the nonce lock up in my bosom. Of course do not think that I consider contemporary Irish writing anything but ill-written, morally obtuse formless caricature.[15]

This letter, written about midway through the composing of the short story collection, was sent to Stanislaus only seven days after another in which Joyce said: "I am uncom-

[15] *SL*, p. 70.

monly well pleased with these stories. There is a neat phrase of five words in *The Boarding-House*: find it."[16] Obviously the July 19 letter was written in a rather harried frame of mind and is not to be regarded as a final pronouncement. Throughout the letters, the alternation is evident between Joyce's glorification of his achievement and his fear that it had all been too easy. But what is obvious is that Joyce began to worry about the facility with which he could use the weapon of his style to pin down the little people of Dublin, and the phrase "well done" in his letters begins to read as "too easily done." In another letter to his brother, written in September 1905, Joyce, in a more flamboyant but still harried mood, wrote:

> Give me for Christ' sake a pen and an ink-bottle and some peace of mind and then, by the crucified Jaysus, if I don't sharpen that little pen and dip it into fermented ink and write tiny little sentences about the people who betrayed me send me to hell.[17]

The "tiny little sentences" and the "neat phrases" endemic to the style of scrupulous meanness became linked in Joyce's mind with the accusation that his portraits were caricatures that displayed his condescension. Interestingly, the word "betrayal," used frequently by Joyce to describe his purpose in writing *Dubliners* ("I call the series *Dubliners* to betray the soul of that hemiplegia or paralysis which many consider a city"[18]), now describes his treatment by others.

By September 1906, when all the stories but "The Dead" had been composed, Joyce again wrote to his brother:

> Sometimes thinking of Ireland it seems to me that I have been unnecessarily harsh. I have reproduced (in *Dubliners* at least) none of the attraction of the city for I have never felt at my ease in any city since I left it except in Paris.

[16] *SL*, 12 July 1905, p. 63.
[17] *SL*, ca. 24 September 1905, p. 76.
[18] *SL*, early July 1904, p. 22.

I have not reproduced its ingenuous insularity and its hospitality. The latter "virtue" so far as I can see does not exist elsewhere in Europe.[19]

Ellmann suggests in his biography that in "The Dead," written in 1907, Joyce tried to redress the wrong he had done by presenting the hospitality of Dublin.[20] The greater sympathy in "The Dead," however, can be seen as part of a general movement from what Joyce perceived as a too-easy linguistic parody to a more flexible prose henceforth associated with Joyce's educated, "artistic" male characters. Gabriel Conroy in "The Dead" represents the last in a line of male figures in *Dubliners* with artistic interests or pre-tensions—from Mr Duffy, reading Wordsworth and Haupt-mann, to Little Chandler, the "melancholy" poet—a line that culminates in the figure of Stephen Dedalus. As the main character in the transitional story between *Dubliners* and *A Portrait*, Gabriel represents Joyce's increasing inter-est in a character whose mind is a more sensitive instrument than that of the other Dubliners he had chosen as subjects.

In a very interesting study of *Dubliners* and other short stories, Frank O'Connor says that in "The Dead" Joyce "had begun to lose sight of the submerged population that was his original subject."[21] By "submerged population," O'Connor means the ordinary people of Dublin who are victims of the society, whose identities are totally "deter-mined by their circumstances."[22] Like the other Dubliners, Gabriel Conroy is molded by his environment, but he is the first one who seems to be capable of understanding his circumstances and trying to transcend them. As a middle-aged, unhappy representative of that society, he has none of Stephen Dedalus's desire to try to fly by the nets his

[19] *SL*, 25 September 1906, pp. 109-110.

[20] Ellmann, *James Joyce*, p. 239.

[21] Frank O'Connor, *The Lonely Voice: A Study of the Short Story* (Cleveland: The World Publishing Company, 1962), p. 125.

[22] Ibid.

country has set for him, but in his ability to comprehend the emptiness of his own life, he at least anticipates Stephen.

The movement away from the limitations of the "sub-merged population" is reflected in a concomitant shift of emphasis from one kind of epiphany to another, from the "vulgarity of speech or of gesture" to a "memorable phase of the mind itself." The first kind of epiphany generally exposes the foibles and limitations of the naive character to the reader alone; the second kind focuses on a revelation to the characters as well as the reader.[23] In "The Dead," Joyce presents both kinds of epiphanies, culminating with the lyrical epiphany in the final paragraphs. Gabriel's self-con-sciousness, priggishness, and conventionality, which, for most of the story, he fails to acknowledge, are revealed in much the same way as the foibles of the other characters in *Dubliners*, in the "vulgarity of speech or of gesture." Gabriel rudely offers Lily a coin, utterly failing to understand her pride, and in his after-dinner speech he reveals his conven-tionality and sentimentality. But the focus of the story nar-rows to Gabriel's sudden realization of his self-delusion. In Gabriel's first epiphany near the end of the story, he sees himself "as a ludicrous figure, acting as a pennyboy for his aunts" (p. 220); this exaggerated view is the converse of the romantic elation that he has been experiencing. At the end of the story, however, Gabriel progresses from this mel-odramatic self-image to a "memorable phase of the mind" that reveals to him his vulnerability and a sense of his own mortality. The whole story builds to this lyrical moment,

---

[23] In his book *Joyce's Dubliners: Substance, Vision, and Art* (Durham, N.C.: Duke University Press, 1969), Warren Beck finds two kinds of epiphanies in *Dubliners* and calls them "naturalistic-objective" and "subjective-psycho-logical," distinguishing, as I do, between a revelation to the reader alone and a revelation to both the character and the reader (pp. 22-24). I prefer to use Stephen Dedalus's terms in *Stephen Hero* because Joyce chose them, because they refer to the *subject* of the epiphany, and because the terms "subjective-psychological" and "naturalistic-objective" are unwieldy.

a moment that anticipates the epiphanies in *A Portrait of the Artist as a Young Man.*

In addition to the epiphanies, the third-person narration in "The Dead" reflects the focus on a more sensitive type of consciousness; the kind of linguistic parody found in the other stories is abandoned after the first few pages. The story itself records the transition from one kind of prose and narrative voice to another. "The Dead" begins with the kind of social parody that has been found in the previous stories— a parody of the breathless and naive idiom of Lily, "the caretaker's daughter." In the diction and the rhythm of the prose in the second paragraph, for example, we see that, like Maria in "Clay," Lily finds comfort in generalization and habit; hers is a mind that is eager to find similarities and is almost incapable of discrimination.[24] In Lily's world, people "scamper" like little animals (p. 175). Like the world depicted in "Clay" and "A Little Cloud" in which people "blush and smile," it is a world of repressed emotions represented in prose that sometimes reduces its characters to little puppets.

But unlike Maria, Lily inhabits someone else's story, and that other character, Gabriel Conroy, is forced to face the inadequacy of the "fictions" that Dublin society encourages its people to create. The fond parody representing Lily's consciousness gives way to a more sober, formal prose once Gabriel enters. The third-person narration and Gabriel's perceptions merge, and, through free indirect discourse, the narration passes unobtrusively from the external action to the character's thoughts:

> He waited outside the drawing-room door until the waltz should finish, listening to the skirts that swept against it

[24] "It was always a great affair, the Misses Morkan's annual dance. Everybody who knew them came to it, members of the family, old friends of the family, the members of Julia's choir, any of Kate's pupils that were grown up enough and even some of Mary Jane's pupils too. Never once had it fallen flat. For years and years it had gone off in splendid style as long as anyone could remember" (pp. 175-176).

28

and to the shuffling feet. He was still discomposed by the girl's bitter and sudden retort. It had cast a gloom over him which he tried to dispel by arranging his cuffs and the bows of his tie. Then he took from his waistcoat pocket a little paper and glanced at the headings he had made for his speech. He was undecided about the lines from Robert Browning for he feared they would be above the heads of his hearers. Some quotation that they could recognise from Shakespeare or from the Melodies would be better. (P. 179)

The language has a studied, literate quality to it: "discomposed," "dispel," and the conjunction "for" display the formality and precision of a writer's prose. Gabriel's pretentiousness is made evident in the passage, but the narrative voice associated with Gabriel does not, for the most part, condescend to him. A more careful balance between sympathy and irony tends to replace the parody of the earlier stories. Although the bankruptcy of his life is exposed during the story, Gabriel manages to escape being "formulated" in a tiny phrase like most of his predecessors. The technique of free indirect discourse is now applied not to spinsters, would-be poets, or overbearing mothers—all easy targets of ridicule—but to a sensibiiity more educated, more complex, more like that of Joyce himself, a person whose exposure posed more risks and more rewards.

 This technical development seems to represent a larger narrative decision on Joyce's part concerning his initial enterprise of presenting "what he had seen and heard." Presentation always involves the selection of particular idioms; the choice of idioms itself reflects a bias and implies a scale of values. Feeling that his stories were sometimes dangerously close to caricature, Joyce could have arrived at two different conclusions: that "ordinary" people *could* be complex and significant enough to be written about without condescension and that something in his own presentation of them had led him to misrepresent them; or that the "soul" of these ordinary people *had* been captured in the stories and that it was now time to portray someone intrinsically more special—the artist. In focusing first on Gabriel Conroy and then on Stephen Dedalus, Joyce seems to have accepted, for the time being, the second conclusion. Not until Leopold Bloom took over the center stage from Stephen in *Ulysses* did Joyce again focus on a more "ordinary" citizen of Dublin, this time showing that the citizen could be just as fascinating as the artist.

The narrative voice in "The Dead" is the voice that Joyce attempted to perfect as a medium for capturing the sensibility of the serious male figure he wished to explore. This formal, educated voice, which is bequeathed from Gabriel Conroy to Stephen Dedalus in *A Portrait* and which provides (with slight modification) the basic narrative voice of *A Portrait* and the "Telemachiad" of *Ulysses*, is the early style that is most recognizably James Joyce's. The following sentence is a typical example of this style:

> The high colour of his cheeks pushed upwards even to his forehead where it scattered itself in a few formless patches of pale red; and on his hairless face there scintillated restlessly the polished lenses and the bright gilt rims of the glasses which screened his delicate and restless eyes. (P. 178)

The balanced rhythms, the semicolon separating two long clauses, the inversion of subject and verb and the placement of the adverb between them ("there scintillated restlessly the polished lenses") are hallmarks of Joyce's early style. In an essay entitled "A Study of James Joyce's *Ulysses*," Philip Toynbee describes the concept of the "authentic voice": "He [the author] constantly and frankly declares himself, says in effect to the reader, 'This is the style I have evolved at this stage. This is my authentic voice. I have chosen this word, this phrase, because they seem to me to be the most accurate and the most satisfying.' "[25] In Joyce's case, the narrative voice of "The Dead" was this kind of voice. It epitomized Joyce's belief in style as the perfectly adequate translator of life into art, but it relinquished some of the anger of the earlier narrative voices. Here Joyce applied the technique of free indirect discourse to a mind that demanded more sympathetic identification.

The major departure from the restraint and precision of this voice in "The Dead" is the last paragraph of the story. The lyrical passage at the end of the story records Gabriel's epiphany, that "memorable phase of the mind itself." Since the alliterative, aesthetic style, reminiscent of Walter Pater is in striking contrast to the more precise language in the rest of the story, critics have tended to see this passage as ironic. I think that this reading erroneously imposes Joyce's later viewpoint on the story. During the writing of *Ulysses*, the idea of a lyrical epiphany, a "sudden spiritual manifestation," does become ironic; the "languid floating flower" of the passage that ends the "Lotus-Eaters" chapter, for example, is a comic version of the kind of epiphany that ends "The Dead." In addition, lyrical flights of this kind are mocked and parodied in *Ulysses*, first in the form of one character mimicking another (see the "Aeolus" chapter) and then in the third-person narration itself. But the lyricism of the final passage of "The Dead" is meant to record Gabriel's moment of epiphany, and, at the time it was written, it was an "authentic" voice in which to manifest this "memorable phase of the mind."

In fact, Joyce's work is full of instances of the repetition of tones, first used seriously, then rewritten in a later work as parody. For example, as Fritz Senn has observed, the evocative cadences of the epiphany on the beach in *A Portrait*

[25] Philip Toynbee, "A Study of James Joyce's *Ulysses*," in *James Joyce: Two Decades of Criticism*, ed. Seon Givens (New York: Vanguard Press, 1948), pp. 251-252.

31

are repeated parodically in "Nausicaa."[26] The particular lyrical tone found at the end of "The Dead" has caused special problems for critical interpretation, precisely because Joyce used it repeatedly with differing attitudes. Indeed, Joyce's relationship to "purple prose" is not a constant one. At times he seems to emulate Walter Pater, as in the lyrical epiphany at the end of Chapter Four of *A Portrait*; at times, however, he writes against Pater, as in the scrupulous style of most of *Dubliners* and in "Sirens," where Joyce plays with and parodies the idea of language aspiring to the condition of music. When he wrote "The Dead," however, both the denotative, more precise style and the evocative, alliterative style were "authentic" voices for Joyce, that is, voices in which he wanted to excel.

In the course of writing *Dubliners*, then, Joyce experimented with the relationship between the speech idioms of his characters and the narrative voice of the stories. By means of the technique of free indirect discourse, he established a convention that was central to his work from then on: the adaptability of the third-person narration to the sensibility of the character. Joyce's experiments with free indirect discourse in *Dubliners* issued in two major *kinds* of voices that are repeated in different parts of *Ulysses*.

The technique of free indirect discourse applied to the mind of the "artist" figure like Gabriel Conroy issues in a formal, educated, sometimes poetic prose—it shows style "striving toward one particular form of perfection."[27] Even when the sentiments it reports are treated ironically, the beauty of the prose can remain intact. It is this voice that will develop into the initial style of *Ulysses*.

The technique of free indirect discourse applied to the minds of the "submerged population" of Dublin issues in essentially parodic voices. Because the prose of these voices

---

[26] See Fritz Senn, "Nausicaa," in *James Joyce's Ulysses: Critical Essays*, ed. Clive Hart and David Hayman (Berkeley: University of California Press, 1974), pp. 285-286.

[27] See Toynbee, "A Study of James Joyce's *Ulysses*," p. 252.

is clearly not a writer's prose, the narrative mimicry seems more overt. In quoting the speech idioms of these Dubliners, the prose is doubly "borrowed": it is obviously borrowed from the character whom it describes because it is so different from the prose one would expect from a writer; it is similarly borrowed from the society to which the character belongs because it is so clichéd and stereotypic. It is this parodic aspect of free indirect discourse that is most important to an understanding of the later chapters of *Ulysses*, in which style as mask replaces style as authentic voice and the narrator's role as mimic becomes paramount. In *Dubliners*, these voices were still consistent with a belief that language could capture reality: each voice of Dublin revealed the precise quality of the life story it told. It is not until *Ulysses* that parody is no longer attached to a specific character and begins to undermine the notion of style as an "absolute manner of seeing things."

In 1906, a year before he wrote "The Dead," Joyce had abandoned the writing of *Stephen Hero*, an autobiographical novel that he later referred to as "a schoolboy's production."[28] In *Stephen Hero*, it does seem as if Joyce had not yet developed the signature style that dominates "The Dead," *A Portrait*, and the "Telemachiad" of *Ulysses*. The following sentences are typical of the style of *Stephen Hero*: "It must be said simply and at once that at this time Stephen suffered the most enduring influence of his life" (*SH*, p. 40); "He was aware that though he was nominally in amity with the order of society into which he had been born, he would not be able to continue so" (*SH*, p. 179). Although these sentences display the formality of the signature style, they lack its precision and restraint. One only has to compare these sentences with the prose in *Dubliners*, also written for the most part between 1904 and 1906, to fully appreciate the restraint in the narration of the stories. In *Stephen Hero*,

[28] Joyce's statement was quoted by his secretary in 1938, in a letter to Theodore Spencer, the editor of *Stephen Hero*. It is mentioned in Spencer's introduction to *Stephen Hero*, p. 8.

it seems that Joyce's expressive powers were devoted to the autobiographical portrayal of character rather than to the establishment of an individual, authentic style. After completing "The Dead" in 1907, Joyce rewrote *Stephen Hero* as *A Portrait*, a work in which he used style to objectify the mind of his character in a way that expanded his experiments in "The Dead" and anticipated the "Telemachiad."

In *A Portrait*, the style of the writing develops along with the character of Stephen Dedalus; it intentionally mirrors his growth in its increasing maturity. The simple vocabulary and syntax of the early chapters of *A Portrait* ("That was not a nice expression. His mother had told him not to speak with the rough boys in the college. . . ."[29]) represent the rhythms of the child rather than the rhythms of a child-adult like Maria in "Clay." After this initial imitation of Stephen's childhood rhythms, we find the two strands of narration in *A Portrait* that Joyce used in "The Dead": the formal, literate, denotative prose and the looser, more evocative lyricism, both of which register the sensitive mind of Stephen Dedalus.

In "Style and Auctorial Presence in 'A Portrait of the Artist as a Young Man,' " Nancy Wilds says that these voices are sometimes ironic, sometimes not.[30] The formality of the prose can be exaggerated into the priggishness of the young scholar; the lyricism can become the decadent prose of the prematurely weary young artist. Because different values are ascribed to a voice at different points in the narrative, critics have had difficulty in determining Joyce's point of view toward Stephen.[31] If the insufficiency of

[29] *A Portrait of the Artist as a Young Man*, text corrected by Chester G. Anderson and ed. Richard Ellmann (New York: The Viking Press, 1964), p. 9. All subsequent references to *A Portrait* are to this edition and will be included in the text.

[30] Nancy Wilds, "Style and Auctorial Presence in 'A Portrait of the Artist as a Young Man'," *Style* 7 (Winter 1973): 53.

[31] See Wayne C. Booth's discussion of *A Portrait* in *The Rhetoric of Fiction* (Chicago: The University of Chicago Press, 1961), pp. 323-336.

Maria's or Little Chandler's self-image is revealed in the style of narration, the insufficiency of Stephen's self-image is less clearly asserted. Does the stilted, rhetorical quality of the prose of the following sentence point to Stephen's tendency toward self-dramatization or is it merely Joyce's way of characterizing the artist: "His sensitive nature was still smarting under the lashes of an undivined and squalid way of life" (p. 78)? Joyce's increasing interest in the character of the artist and his decreasing interest in the ordinary "submerged population" of Dublin coincided with a heightened ambiguity of point of view. A complex irony is the result.

But point of view is less important to our discussion here than the creation of a kind of stylistic sympathy between narrator and character—that is, the creation of the narrative voice out of the linguistic resources of character. The use of free indirect discourse permits the unobtrusive passage from the inside to the outside of the character's mind. The following line of third-person narration affords us a glimpse of Stephen in language appropriate to him: "He stood still in deference to their calls and parried their banter with easy words" (p. 168). This is Stephen as he sees himself in his better moments—keeping his attackers at bay.[32] The educated, precise, dramatic diction ("deference," "parried," "banter") is exactly what Stephen would use as an aspiring artist, and the narrator's prose is dominated by it. Arnold Goldman points out the difficulty of distinguishing the narrator from the character when free indirect discourse is used: "When the voice of the narrator is a mimic of his characters— a systematization of a possibility always latent in indirect discourse—it is . . . extremely difficult to make definitive

---

[32] This defensive self-image reappears in Stephen's stream-of-consciousness in the "Proteus" chapter of *Ulysses*: "I just simply stood pale, silent, bayed about." See *Ulysses*, rev. ed. (New York: Modern Library-Random House, 1961), p. 45. All subsequent quotations from *Ulysses* refer to this edition and will be cited in the text. According to Richard Ellmann, this image was Joyce's favorite self-portrayal (see *James Joyce*, p. 150n).

descriptions. Any particular instance not part of actual dialogue may be Stephen thinking, Joyce describing Stephen
thinking, Joyce describing how Stephen might have thought,
or some indeterminate state between these."[33] (Goldman
here is speaking of the early chapters of *Ulysses*, but what
he says applies to *A Portrait* as well.) And the stylistic link
between character and narrator is strengthened in a portrait
of the artist, even a developing one.

The point is that the narrative of *A Portrait* is so colored
by Stephen's sensibility (since it "borrows" the diction and
rhythm of his character, both in describing him and in describing the world around him) that we associate this
rhythm and diction with Joyce's early narrative style. The
portrait of the artist is also the portrait of the artist's style;
as Joyce presents Stephen's artistic development, he also
tries to perfect his own narrative style. In Chapters Four
and Five of *A Portrait*, we find the kind of sentences that
are especially characteristic of Joyce: "The priest let the
blindcord fall to one side and, uniting his hands, leaned his
chin gravely upon them, communing with himself" (p. 157);
and "A lean student with olive skin and lank black hair
thrust his face between the two, glancing from one to the
other at each phrase and seeming to try to catch each flying
phrase in his open moist mouth" (p. 196). The care in the
choice of adjectives ("lank black hair," "open moist mouth"),
the heavy use of present and past participial phrases, the
placement of the modifying adverb after, rather than before,
the transitive verb ("leaned his chin gravely upon them"),
the compound word ("blindcord"), the phonetic song
played by the changing consonants, all indicate how "scrupulous" and well written the narration is. These characteristics of style, associated with the figure of the artist, are
developed further in the early chapters of *Ulysses* and provide the book's initial style.

[33] Arnold Goldman, *The Joyce Paradox: Form and Freedom in His Fiction*
(London: Routledge & Kegan Paul, 1966), p. 79.

Dublin Voices

Joyce's stylistic signature evolved from the precision and restraint implied in the narrative mode of scrupulous meanness and the linguistic borrowing inherent in the technique of free indirect discourse. I have considered the development of Joyce's signature style in the fiction preceding *Ulysses*. In the next chapter, we will see how this style provides the narrative norm of the early chapters of *Ulysses*, a norm that is abandoned during the course of the book.

II

The Narrative Norm

The first three chapters of *Ulysses* pay homage to both the personal tradition Joyce had created in his previous works of fiction and to the traditional novel. In its dominant narrative voice and interest in the character of the artist, the "Telemachiad" resembles *A Portrait* in particular, and even the reader of *Ulysses* who fails to recognize this continuity will experience a sense of security from the presence of this narrative voice. The staples of the novel—third-person narration, dialogue, and dramatization of a scene—also promise narrative security to the reader who begins *Ulysses*: they act as signposts promising him familiar terrain on the subsequent pages. No matter what we may know about the structural apparatus and levels of allegory in the work after reading Joyce's notesheets, letters, and tips to Stuart Gilbert, what we experience when beginning *Ulysses* is a novel that promises a story, a narrator, and a plot. "Stately, plump Buck Mulligan came from the stairhead" (pp. 2-3) is a plausible beginning for any novel. *Ulysses* begins like a narrative with confidence in the adequacy of the novel form.

It is important to underscore the initial narrative promises to the reader made in the novel not only because they will be broken later on but also because they provide an interesting contrast to the change in Joyce's basic conceptions of plot and significance in fiction, a change that must have antedated, at least in part, the beginning of the novel. *Ulysses* offers, in a sense, a "rewriting" of *Dubliners*: it presents another portrait of Dublin designed to reveal the soul of the city and its citizens. But in arriving at the basic conception of *Ulysses*—the condensing of the wanderings of Odysseus to one day in the life of certain Dublin citizens—Joyce radically altered his conception of what a portrait of Dublin should be.

In the initial conception of *Ulysses*, Joyce departed from the aesthetic of economy and scrupulous choice that had directed the writing of *Dubliners* in favor of an aesthetic of comprehensiveness and minute representation. This aesthetic is implied in Joyce's statement to Budgen about his desire to give so complete a picture of Dublin in *Ulysses* that if the city were to disappear it could be reconstructed from the book.[1] Although the "story" of *Ulysses* takes place during one day only, this day is infinitely expansible by being infinitely divisible—the rendering of the complete "details" of life almost obscure the sense of story. Unlike *Dubliners*, which promises to end the narrative as soon as the "soul" of a character is revealed, *Ulysses* offers no clear principle of completeness. The frustration critics felt at what they thought of as Joyce's infidelity to the minimal requirements of a story is reflected in Edmund Wilson's comment in *Axel's Castle*: "It is almost as if he had elaborated [the story] so much and worked over it so long that he had forgotten . . . the drama which he had originally intended to stage."[2]

Ulysses also offers no clear principle of emphasis or proportion. In the stories of *Dubliners*, the right "trivial" incident in the life of a character epiphanizes the meaning of the life; in *Ulysses*, no one particular incident in a life is considered to be of supreme importance. Because the characters carry within them the same problems, desires, and past, no matter when we see them, no day is essentially different from any other. If *Dubliners* focuses on a particularly significant day in the lives of its characters, *Ulysses*

---

[1] Frank Budgen, *James Joyce and the Making of Ulysses* (1934; reprint ed., Bloomington: Indiana University Press, 1960), pp. 67-68.

[2] Edmund Wilson, *Axel's Castle: A Study in the Imaginative Literature of 1870-1930* (New York: Charles Scribner's Sons, 1959), p. 217.

focuses on any day in Dublin's diary, and the day happens to be June 16, 1904. It is as if an entry in the diary of Dublin, rather than in a personal diary such as the one that ends *A Portrait*, was blown up in a great, Brobdingnagian gesture; in the world of *Ulysses*, as in Brobdingnag, a molehill can indeed become a mountain. The slight rise in the plot that the theory of epiphany suggests is almost completely eliminated in the narrative of *Ulysses*. What is important here is not the transition between a "short story" and the long story of development told in a traditional novel but the transition from fiction interested in plot to fiction in which plot becomes synonymous with digression.

The stream-of-consciousness technique in the "Telemachiad" does alert the reader to some of these changes in overall conception. In using this technique increasingly until it almost dominates the narrative in Chapter Three ("Proteus"), Joyce offered his third-person narrator less and less to do. The retrospective narrative voice of a conventional novel is replaced almost entirely, so that "plot" changes from a form of narrative memory to a rendering of "the very process in which meaning is apprehended in life."[3]

But in the first three chapters of the novel (even in "Proteus"), the third-person narrator exists and serves some important narrative functions. The dominant narrative voice in the "Telemachiad" provides the narrative norm for the novel (and continues in subsequent chapters), and it is the voice that, for a long time, was ignored in critical discussions of *Ulysses*. Although some critics have described the quality of this voice,[4] many recent critics have tended to pass over

[3] S. L. Goldberg, *The Classical Temper: A Study of James Joyce's Ulysses* (London: Chatto and Windus, 1961), p. 92.

[4] See David Hayman's *Ulysses: The Mechanics of Meaning* (Englewood Cliffs, N.J.: Prentice-Hall, Inc., 1970), especially pp. 75-79, and Anthony Burgess's *Joysprick: An Introduction to the Language of James Joyce* (London: André Deutsch, 1973) for two of the earliest and best discussions of this narrative norm. Recently, discussions of the narrative norm have become more common. See, for example, Hugh Kenner's *Joyce's Voices* (Berkeley: University of California Press, 1978), and Marilyn French's *The Book as World: James Joyce's Ulysses* (Cambridge, Mass.: Harvard University Press, 1976).

this narrative norm on the way to discussions of narrative distortions that occur primarily in the latter half of the book.[5] But the primary reason for this omission is the importance that decades of critics have placed on the stream-of-consciousness technique in the early chapters: in focusing on the "innovativeness" of this technique, they have tended to underestimate the importance of the narrative norm.

The narrative conventions established in the early chapters of *Ulysses* include the presence of an identifiable and relatively consistent style of narration that persists in the first eleven chapters of the book and the tendency of the narrative to borrow the pace and diction of the characters' language. In other words, the conventions include *both* the continued presence of a particular style *and* the adaptability of style to character. Critics who focus on the stream-of-consciousness emphasize the importance of the character's mind and treat the third-person narration as an adjunct of character.[6] This is only partly correct, since it fails to acknowledge the recognizable, idiosyncratic narrative voice that does exist.

For example, the following sentences, the first from "Telemachus," the second from "Proteus," display the characteristic Joycean qualities seen in *A Portrait* and now heightened in *Ulysses*: "Two shafts of soft daylight fell across the flagged floor from the high barbicans: and at the meeting of their rays a cloud of coalsmoke and fumes of fried grease floated, turning" (p. 11); and "The cry brought him skulking back to his master and a blunt bootless kick sent him unscathed across a spit of sand, crouched in flight" (p. 46). The denotative style in *A Portrait* is evident here, with

[5] See, for example, Wolfgang Iser, *The Implied Reader: Patterns of Communication in Prose Fiction from Bunyan to Beckett* (Baltimore: The Johns Hopkins University Press, 1974), pp. 179-233, and Ben D. Kimpel, "The Voices of *Ulysses*," *Style* 9 (Summer 1975): 283-319.

[6] See, for example, Erwin R. Steinberg's *The Stream of Consciousness and Beyond in Ulysses* (Pittsburgh: University of Pittsburgh Press, 1973) for the most exensive treatment of Joyce's use of the stream-of-consciousness technique.

greater syntactic dislocation and more unusual diction. The extreme concern with the sounds of words—that is, the alliteration ("flagged floor," "blunt bootless," "spit of sand") and what Anthony Burgess has called the "clotted" effect of the double and triple consonants[7]—and the strange placement of the modifying adverb ("fried grease floated, turning") produce a sentence that, as Burgess says, reveals "a distinctive approach to what might be termed literary engineering."[8] This is prose that is competently, indeed masterfully crafted, precisely and poetically written.

Especially in the "Telemachiad," this literate, formal, poetic language is associated with the character of Stephen Dedalus. In the first three chapters, we perceive the world largely through the eyes of an aspiring artist, and, as in *A Portrait*, the linguistic "sympathy" between character and narrative voice blurs the distinctions between them. "Woodshadows floated silently by through the morning peace from the stairhead seaward where he gazed" (p. 9) is a narrative statement that "borrows" Stephen's lyricism. Throughout the chapter, the narration will often present Stephen's poetic and melancholy perceptions of things in language appropriate to his sensibility.

But despite the close connection between the style and the mind of Stephen in the "Telemachiad," the style exists independently in subsequent chapters, as is evident from the following examples:

> The caretaker hung his thumbs in the loops of his gold watch chain and spoke in a discreet tone to their vacant smiles. ("Hades," p. 107)

> It passed stately up the staircase steered by an umbrella, a solemn beardframed face. ("Aeolus," p. 117)

> The young woman with slow care detached from her light skirt a clinging twig. ("Wandering Rocks," p. 231)

[7] Burgess, *Joysprick*, p. 68.
[8] Ibid., p. 74.

Miss Douce's brave eyes, unregarded, turned from the crossblind, smitten by sunlight. ("Sirens," p. 268)

In the first eleven chapters of *Ulysses*, this narrative style establishes the empirical world of the novel; it provides stability and continuity. The persistence of this type of narrative sentence provides a sign of the original narrative authority amidst the increasingly bizarre narrative developments of the later chapters, until it disappears in "Cyclops." (It reappears briefly in "Nausicaa," for reasons I will discuss later.) It is a style that orients the reader and offers him a certain security by establishing the sense of the solidity of external reality.

It seems to me that this type of narrative sentence, along with the other staples of the narrative mode of the early chapters—interior monologue, free indirect discourse, and dialogue—functions as the "rock of Ithaca," "the initial style" to which Joyce alluded in a letter to Harriet Weaver in 1919: "I understand that you may begin to regard the various styles of the episodes with dismay and prefer the initial style much as the wanderer did who longed for the rock of Ithaca."[9] This is the nonparodic style that establishes the decorum of the novel. When it disappears later on in the text, we realize that it too was a choice among many possibilities, a mode of presentation. But in its seeming fidelity to the details of both the thoughts and actions of the characters it provides us with a sense of the real world of the novel. With all its precision and fastidiousness, it functions for us as a narrative norm.[10]

---

[9] Letter, 6 August 1919, *Letters of James Joyce*, Vol. 1, ed. Stuart Gilbert (New York: The Viking Press, 1957), p. 129. However, when I refer to the "initial style" henceforth, I mean specifically the prose style of the third-person narration.

[10] Hugh Kenner's ingenuity and prolificacy illustrate the possibilities for characterizing the early narrative style of *Ulysses*. In *The Stoic Comedians: Flaubert, Joyce, and Beckett* (Berkeley: University of California Press, 1962), the following narrative sentence is cited as an example of Joyce's characteristic manipulation of language and his "resolute artistry": "Two shafts of soft day-

However, while the decorum of the novel is established, the presence of another narrative strand in the first chapter slyly questions the assumptions about language upon which the normative style is based. The effect of this narrative strand is subtle, nothing like the radical disruptions of narrative stability in the later chapters. And yet this narrative fluctuation in the first chapter of the book serves as a warning to the reader of the strange narrative distortions to come. The following passage illustrates the intertwining of the narrative strands in the first chapter:

> He [Mulligan] shaved evenly and with care, in silence, seriously.
>
> Stephen, an elbow rested on the jagged granite, leaned his palm against his brow and gazed at the fraying edge of his shiny black coat-sleeve. Pain, that was not yet the pain of love, fretted his heart. (P. 5)

The second sentence is an example of the denotative narrative norm. The past participle "rested," surprising the reader prepared to encounter the present participle "resting," is a characteristic kind of dislocation. The third sentence, "Pain, that was not yet the pain of love, fretted his heart," is a clear example of free indirect discourse. But the first sentence is puzzling—the number of adverbs and adverbial phrases surprises us. There is a naive quality to this writing that separates parts of speech as if they were about to be diagrammed.

In fact, the first chapter of *Ulysses* provides numerous

---

light fell across the flagged floor from the high barbicans: and at the meeting of their rays a cloud of coalsmoke and fumes of fried grease floated, turning" (pp. 30-31). In *Joyce's Voices*, the same marked precision is said to exemplify the "fussiness of setting and decor" of "Edwardian novelese" (pp. 68-69). Both descriptions are intriguing, the second moving us, as it does, further away from a view of the early style as normative and nonparodic. The style becomes just another example of a particular kind of rhetoric, despite its temporal primacy in the text. Although the sentence does exhibit stylistic idiosyncrasies, I favor Kenner's first description of it as an example of Joyce's characteristic style, more normative at this point than parodic.

examples of this naive narrative quality. This strand of the narration reveals itself in the repeated use of certain formulaic narrative constructions of which no student of creative writing, however inexperienced, would be proud. The proliferation of the following phrases in the early pages of the novel suggests that something strange is taking place in the narrative: "he said sternly," "he cried briskly," "he said gaily" (p. 3); and "He laid the brush aside and, laughing with delight, cried," "Stephen said quietly," "he said frankly," "Stephen said with energy and growing fear," "he cried thickly" (p. 4). What kind of narrative world is created by these descriptions and what purpose could Joyce have had in using this type of prose in the beginning of the novel?

Joyce called the technique of this chapter "narrative young," and this description, while it probably refers to Stephen to some extent, also applies to the quality of narration: it is appropriate to the self-conscious, naive literary style exemplified above. Unlike the naiveté of the narrator in stories like "Clay" in *Dubliners*, stories in which through free indirect discourse the narrator ostensibly accepts his protagonist's assessment of the world, the naiveté of the narrative in "Telemachus" is literary as well as psychological. We notice an innocence concerning the very act of telling a story, an innocence that is a quality of the narrative itself rather than a property of a particular character.

What we are provided with in the early pages of *Ulysses*, disturbing the basically serious and authoritative narrative voice that creates a world we can believe in, is a different narrative strand that parodies the process of creation. Prose like "he cried thickly" and "he said contentedly" is the unsophisticated prose of fourth-rate fiction; a novel that begins this way parodies its own ability to tell a story. Even in the first chapter of the novel, Joyce begins to turn novelistic convention into novelistic cliché, and it is here that the reader glimpses language beginning to quote itself, its characteristic activity in the latter half of the book. While making use of the conventional tools of the novel, Joyce uses one strand of the narrative to upset the stability created by these conventions and to point to their inadequacy. As the normative style asserts its ability to capture reality in language, this narrative voice advertises its own incompetence. The world in which Buck Mulligan wears a "tolerant smile" and laughs "with delight" or in which Stephen says something "with energy and growing fear" is about as far from Henry James's world of "delicate adjustments" and "exquisite chemistry"[11] as a novelist can get. The sentences of this naive narrative point to the falsification and oversimplification that language wreaks on emotions by organizing them in discrete grammatical parts.

This narrative strand in Chapter One provides the first example of narrative performance and stylistic bravado in *Ulysses*, different from that in later chapters like "Cyclops" and "Ithaca," but stylistic exhibition nonetheless. There is a comic excess of labor in evidence in the narration: the narrator seems to wrestle with the discrete parts of speech available to him only to pin down the most commonplace of descriptions. The subtle nuances captured in sentences of the "initial style" elude the narrator's grasp. The excess of labor here is the antithesis of the coolness of scrupulous meanness in *Dubliners*—the production of meaning seems to be a Herculean task.[12] But there is an air of safety that surrounds the "risks" the narrator seems to take. He is like a clown walking a tightrope only one foot above the ground. What is suppressed here is not so much a narrator as a grin.

It is possible to explain this adverbial mania in "Telemachus" in relation to the characters described. Hugh Ken-

---

[11] See James's Preface to *The Tragic Muse*, reprinted in *The Art of The Novel: Critical Prefaces* by Henry James (New York: Charles Scribner's Sons, 1962), p. 87: "To put all that is possible of one's idea into a form and compass that will contain and express it only by delicate adjustments and an exquisite chemistry . . . every artist will remember how often that sort of necessity has carried with it its particular inspiration."

[12] This sense of the excess of labor in the writing appears again in subsequent chapters like "Sirens," "Eumaeus," and "Ithaca," even though different styles are used in each case.

ner, for example, has discussed the presence of these adverbs in regard to the role playing of Stephen and Buck Mulligan.[13] While the thematic connection between the adverbial style and the role playing of the characters makes sense, it limits the significance of the strange verbal tic by giving it so exclusively a character-based explanation. The adverbial style tells us something about the kinds of utterances we find in certain types of narratives, as well as something about the characters in this one. The presence of the naive literary style suggests that the text as well as the character is trying on a costume. In Chapter One, we get a brief glimpse of the kind of narrative mimicry that dominates the later chapters of the book—the mimicry of a type of text rather than a particular character. What I find most interesting about the naive narrative strand in Chapter One is the beginning of an interest in language apart from character, language that calls attention to its own clichéd nature without providing the vehicle for the ironic exposure of a character. Instead of parodying the linguistic idiosyncrasies of a type of character, the narrator dons a stylistic mask of innocence to parody the very enterprise of telling a story. Parody is cut loose from the concerns of character and becomes an aspect of narrative.

Thus, Steinberg and other critics interested in the early chapters of *Ulysses* seem to me to have erred in assuming that if the narrator is not an *unreliable character* in the story (like the lawyer in Melville's "Bartleby, the Scrivener," for example, or the narrator in Ford's *The Good Soldier*), then the narrative can be trusted. Frank Kermode writes in an essay entitled "Novels: Recognition and Deception" that "we have bothered too much about the authority of the narrator and too little about that of the narrative,"[14] and this distinction between the authority of the narrator and the

---

[13] See Kenner, *Joyce's Voices*, pp. 69-70.

[14] Frank Kermode, "Novels: Recognition and Deception," *Critical Inquiry* 1 (Sept. 1974): 117. Kermode's comment, made in reference to Ford's *The Good Soldier*, seems to me to apply much more appropriately to *Ulysses*.

narrative is an extremely important one for the reading of *Ulysses*.

The tone of the opening chapter of *Ulysses*, then, seems to oscillate: in certain parts of the narrative *Ulysses* announces itself as a comedy, but for the most part it is dominated by the rather bitter and serious Stephen Dedalus. The copresence of the naive aspect of the narrative and the well-written, precise narrative norm makes it difficult for the reader to form a clear perception of a unified narrator.

And yet, this one narrative strand found in the first chapter of the novel is quickly overshadowed by the narrative norm and the stream-of-consciousness technique in the rest of the "Telemachiad." The mimicry of a type of text rather than a character will resurface in later chapters—most obviously in "Cyclops" and "Oxen of the Sun." But after Chapter One, this naive parodic style vanishes. Despite Joyce's developing interest in representing the inadequacies of language, despite the warning about the enterprise of novel writing in the first chapter, it is character, not narration, that is the most important subject of the first six chapters of the novel. Simultaneous with Joyce's perceptions of the limitations of both the conventional novel and his own previous fiction was an interest in further developing a method with which to present the workings of consciousness. The "Proteus" chapter is, as critics have suggested, the culmination of the "Telemachiad," not only chronologically, but stylistically as well; here the stream-of-consciousness technique reaches its peak in transcribing an educated, artistic mind. The use of stream-of-consciousness was experimental for Joyce when he wrote the "Telemachiad"—it carried further the "direct" representation of the mind of the artist begun in *A Portrait*. It is the drama of the character's mind, rather than the drama of novel writing, that is still paramount. As S. L. Goldberg has pointed out, the paragraph is still a dramatic unit of consciousness, the "artistic medium of a particular *act* of understanding."[15]

[15] S. L. Goldberg, *Joyce* (Edinburgh, 1962; reprint ed., New York: Capricorn Books, 1972), p. 90.

The Narrative Norm

In the next three chapters of *Ulysses*, devoted to Leopold Bloom, this interest in character is still paramount. In these chapters, the reader finds the same texture of narration as in the "Telemachiad": a combination of third-person narration, dialogue, free indirect discourse, and the stream-of-consciousness of the character. The denotative norm of the "Telemachiad" persists in these chapters: "By lorries along Sir John Rogerson's Quay Mr Bloom walked soberly, past Windmill Lane, Leask's the linseed crusher's, the postal telegraph office" (p. 71, "Lotus-Eaters"); "The metal wheels ground the gravel with a sharp grating cry and the pack of blunt boots followed the barrow along a lane of sepulchres" (p. 104, "Hades"). The denotative norm continues to establish our sense of external reality and our sense of a narrative presence by assuring us that despite the introduction of a new character who sees the world differently from Stephen Dedalus, the world is the same. This second triad of chapters continues to build up our sense of what the world of Dublin and the world of the novel are like. The symmetry of this second triad with the "Telemachiad" and the persistence of the same basic rules of narration encourage us to group the first six chapters together as providing the norm of the book.

As in the "Telemachiad," one finds in these chapters a sympathy between narrator and character that again involves the borrowing of linguistic habits. To turn the page from the heraldic image of Stephen Dedalus "rere regardant" and to encounter Leopold Bloom eating "with relish the inner organs of beasts and fowls" is to sense a difference in mood that depends in part on a change in style. The language associated with Bloom (both his stream-of-consciousness and some third-person narration) is more simple syntactically, more colloquial, and more redundant than Stephen's. (See, for example, the prose of the opening of the chapter.)

What is most interesting about the "sympathy" between narrator and character in Bloom's chapters, however, is its occasional comic manipulation. Although the exchange between character and narrator in these chapters follows the

49

rules set in the "Telemachiad," at times this exchange seems to pick up speed. In the following passage from "Hades," for example, Bloom and the narrator carry on a rapid and weird exchange of images:

> The whitesmocked priest came after him tidying his stole with one hand, balancing with the other a little book against his toad's belly. Who'll read the book? I, said the rook.
>
> They halted by the bier and the priest began to read out of his book with a fluent croak. (P. 103)

The narrator describes the priest's belly as "his toad's belly"; then it is Bloom presumably who thinks "Who'll read the book? I, said the rook." Again, the third-person narration resumes in what seems like the initial style, except for the presence of the word "croak." Soon after this passage, Bloom looks at the priest and thinks "Eyes of a toad too," and the word "too" must refer to the "toad's belly" mentioned in the narrator's statement. There is a strange kind of play between narrator and character, almost a parodic form of sympathy between the two. This is a kind of "sympathy" that reduces the distance between the telling of the story and the story itself, a distance that will be manipulated in increasingly bizarre ways as the book progresses. This passage in "Hades" looks forward to the exchanges between narrator and speaker in "Scylla and Charybdis":

> —Yes, Mr Best said youngly, I feel Hamlet quite young. (P. 194)

> —Bosh! Stephen said rudely. A man of genius makes no mistakes. His errors are volitional and are the portals of discovery.
>
> Portals of discovery opened to let in the quaker librarian, softcreakfooted, bald, eared and assiduous. (P. 190)

Recently, Hugh Kenner has pointed out another anomaly of the second triad of chapters that emphasizes the artifice of the text. In his article, "The Rhetoric of Silence," Kenner cites several omissions in the text, some of which are highly significant to the plot. Chief among these gaps is a missing scene between Molly and Bloom, in which she tells him when Boylan is coming to Eccles Street ("At four"), and Bloom tells her he will attend the Gaiety Theatre (the cue she needs to assure her Bloom will not be home at four). Based upon Bloom's later recollection of Molly's words ("At four, she said" [p. 260]), and Molly's recollection of Bloom's statement that he would be dining out ("he said Im dining out and going to the Gaiety" [p. 740]), Kenner deduces that the painful scene between the two is omitted or repressed in the narrative. Since we cannot locate this conversation among the exchanges between Molly and Bloom that are recorded, Kenner concludes that they must have occurred offstage, like Molly's adultery or Bloom's visit to the insurance office on behalf of Paddy Dignam's widow.[16] Although this particular gap in the conversation can be recognized only retrospectively, when the missing lines are recollected, this playfulness in the selection of dramatized details puts into question our initial assumption that the narrative is recording all significant action. But, as Kenner says, we can reconstruct the scene in our minds, based on our knowledge of the characters and our sense of the empirical world that Joyce goes to such lengths to depict.[17] As Stephen discovers in "Proteus," the world is "there all the time without you . . . world without end" (p. 37). Narrative selection rather than empirical reality is questioned; the concept of omission presupposes that something in particular is being omitted.

In the second triad of chapters, we move closer to the comic play to come. In fact, I would argue that the mind of Leopold Bloom and the more comic and parodic tone of his chapters predict the direction of the rest of the narrative.

[16] Hugh Kenner, "The Rhetoric of Silence," *James Joyce Quarterly* 14 (Summer 1977): 382-394.

[17] Ibid., p. 383.

It is Bloom's rather than Stephen's sensibility that dominates the *kind* of book *Ulysses* will become. The opening of the book to the subliterary as well as the literary and the movement from statement to cliché are predicted by the movement from Stephen Dedalus to Leopold Bloom. In some ways, the general tone and feeling of the book and some of the narrative strategies of the later chapters are also predicted in the book's first half.

By the end of "Hades," we have been introduced to the two main characters in a thorough way. In the stream-of-consciousness of each character, in each private memory emerges a particular way of making sense of the world and the self. In "reading" the world, the characters rely on different tools of interpretation: Bloom on clichés and bits of popular information, Stephen on abstruse allusion and esoteric philosophy. Both characters, however, are concerned with making sense of their pasts, not by an act of retrospection, as can be found in the novels of James or Proust, but in random associations that surface while they live their lives. "It is the 'stream of consciousness' which serves to clarify or render intelligible both the element of duration in time and the aspect of an enduring self. The technique is designed to give some kind of visible, sensible impression of how it is meaningful and intelligible to think of the self as a continuing unit despite the most perplexing and chaotic manifold of immediate experience."[18] Amidst the sense of the "immediate experience" of life that we get in the first six chapters of *Ulysses* is the faith in character not as a "construct" seen from the outside but, nevertheless, as a "self" that is constant.

Thus, in the early chapters of *Ulysses* the characters carry the main burden of interpreting the world. "Proteus" is the culmination of Stephen's attempt to interpret his surround-

[18] Hans Meyerhoff, *Time in Literature* (Berkeley: University of California Press, 1955), p. 37.

ings. In fact, his portentous announcement, "Signatures of all things I am here to read," is one of the most explicit declarations of character as interpreter in literature. As Fredric Jameson has said of psychological novels in general (and this applies to the early chapters of *Ulysses*), the character "from within the book, reflecting on the meaning of his experiences, does the actual work of exegesis for us before our own eyes."[19] In subsequent chapters, the reader and the writer participate more strenuously in the hermeneutic process. But in the beginning of the book, the major "burden" of interpretation is placed on the characters.

By providing a norm in its first six chapters that later would be subverted, the novel encompasses its author's changing interests; it can thus be said that the book, as well as Joyce, the author, changes its mind. When he wrote the first six chapters, Joyce did not yet fully realize the direction the second half of the novel would take. But his decision to leave the first chapters substantially intact was made after writing the entire novel. The opening section of the book was left as a kind of testimony to an older order, a norm for the reader at the same time as it is an anachronism in terms of the book as a whole. Consequently, the opening of the novel does not prepare the reader for what follows. A novel usually offers its reader built-in strategies for interpreting the world it presents. The concept of development in most novels insures that the early parts of the work in some way prepare the reader for what is to come (Henry James's *Prefaces* devote considerable space to this idea of preparation). But the first six chapters of *Ulysses* lead the reader to have certain unfulfilled expectations, that is, they make a certain contract that is subverted (for instance, that the normative voice will be sustained throughout the novel, that character will be the major concern). Although Joyce, unlike Kierkegaard, never openly confessed to this kind of "decep-

[19] Fredric Jameson, "Metacommentary," *PMLA* 86 (Jan. 1971): 13.

tion,"[20] *Ulysses* begins by deliberately establishing narrative rules that are bent and finally broken later on.

In *Ulysses*, Joyce leaves the "tracks" of his artistic journey. Throughout his career Joyce transformed and developed his materials, but in the process he tended to outgrow a specific form and move on to another. Before writing *Ulysses* he had abandoned poetry for the short story and the short story for the extended narrative record of the growth of the artist's mind in *A Portrait*. Then, as S. L. Goldberg has observed, discovering that the record of the growth of the artist's mind was severely limited by the artist's awareness,[21] he began *Ulysses*. Realizing that Stephen had "a shape that [couldn't] be changed,"[22] he became more interested in Leopold Bloom. And, finally, finding obsolete the idea of a narrative norm that tells a story, with "Aeolus" as a clue and with "Wandering Rocks" and "Sirens" as the new formal beginning, he went beyond the novel to something else. In each case, the changes in form and style reflect the shedding of an artistic belief no longer sufficient to his vision.

[20] See Søren Kierkegaard, *The Point of View for My Work as an Author: A Report to History and Related Writings*, trans. Walter Lowrie; ed. Benjamin Nelson (New York: Harper & Brothers, 1962). The work announces that for the purpose of arriving at "truth." Kierkegaard had lulled his unsuspecting readers into a sense of narrative security in his aesthetic writings, only to subvert this security later in the religious writings.

[21] See Goldberg, *Joyce*, p. 63.

[22] Quoted in Budgen, *James Joyce and the Making of Ulysses*, p. 105.

III

"Aeolus": Interruption and Inventory

In "Aeolus," the reader encounters a kind of double writing—the narration of the story continues, but it is now punctuated with boldfaced phrases that seem to come out of nowhere. These phrases function, for the most part, like subheads or subtitles in a newspaper, which label and classify the various sections of the narration (for example, "THE WEARER OF THE CROWN," "ERIN, GREEN GEM OF THE SILVER SEA," "THE CROZIER AND THE PEN"). The headings, however, are more disconcerting than helpful to the reader, for the spirit that motivates their creation seems arbitrary and capricious. They italicize the most trivial of events and seem singularly inappropriate in tone and content to the "features" that follow. For example, the casual departure of Bloom is italicized as "EXIT BLOOM," and the description of the Dublin tramway system is labelled "IN THE HEART OF THE HIBERNIAN METROPOLIS." The headings seem to participate in a game of emphasis and classification. In a book that has refused to provide chapter titles, this sudden spasm of ordering and italicizing is bizarre narrative behavior.[1]

In confronting these seemingly arbitrary interruptions in the text, the reader has a number of choices. Because the

---

[1] The most cautious way to describe the headings would be to say that they display peculiarities of typography and layout that make them stand out from the rest of the text, since boldface is used in most but not all editions of *Ulysses*. (The Limited Editions Club of 1935, for example, issued an edition that varied the typography of the headings.)

narration of the story continues beneath the headings, he can try to ignore the intrusions and proceed, however limpingly, through the chapter to "Lestrygonians." For as bizarre as the headings may be, the texture of the narration beneath them is largely that of the first six chapters: a combination of dialogue, interior monologue, and third-person narration. The narrative norm continues in "Aeolus," providing stability and continuity in sentences like "He extended elocutionary arms from frayed stained shirtcuffs, pausing" (p. 131).

In a rather conventional way, the narrative beneath the headings (the "micro-narrative")[2] develops the plot and characters of the early chapters. In any novel, one would expect that the two main characters introduced separately at the beginning of the novel would come together as the plot develops. The formal symmetry of the triads of chapters with which *Ulysses* begins creates particularly strong expectations of the convergence of plot lines and characters in the seventh chapter, and these expectations are fulfilled in "Aeolus," as Stephen Dedalus's and Leopold Bloom's paths cross. (In typical Joycean fashion, the formal symmetry of the text contrasts with the casualness with which the characters regard each other.) "Aeolus," then, can be said to provide the beginning of the middle of the novel we have been reading.

However, in order to read the seventh chapter as the first six, the reader must perform a different operation on the text, an act, in this case, of suppression. He must pretend that stitching together the micro-narrative is the same as reading an uninterrupted version of the story. In fact, to read the chapter in this way is to read it almost as it appeared in *The Little Review* in 1918, for in its first published form,

[2] In "Indeterminacy and the Reader's Response in Prose Fiction" (*Aspects of Narrative: Selected Papers from the English Institute*, ed. J. Hillis Miller [New York: Columbia University Press, 1971], pp. 1-45), Wolfgang Iser divides the "Aeolus" chapter into its micro- and macro-structure, and my own terminology is an extension of his.

the chapter did not contain the headings. Joyce inserted the headings in 1921 while writing the later chapters of the book, a change he referred to as the "recasting" of "Aeolus."[3] Although Joyce altered and supplemented all of the chapters, "Aeolus" is the only one to undergo such a major structural change. One has only to read the chapter as it was printed in 1918 to realize how much the reading experience is altered by the headings. As it appears in *The Little Review*, the chapter seems like a direct sequel to the first six; as it appears in the 1922 version of the book, it offers a departure from the "novel" of the first six chapters and an adumbration of the experimentation in the subsequent chapters.[4] It seems that Joyce deliberately altered the chapter to make it predict the antics of the later chapters and to give the reader early notice that the form of the novel was becoming obsolete. The devices of interruption and double writing in "Aeolus" anticipate the "Cyclops" chapter, the game of classification played in "Aeolus" anticipates the catechism of "Ithaca," and, finally, the language of the headings—that clichéd voice of the press—anticipates the language of "Eumaeus."

Although the headings did not exist in the original published version of the chapter, they are congruent with the symbolic schema that Joyce sent to Carlo Linati in 1920. According to this schema, rhetoric is the art of the chapter, the organ is the lungs, and the technique is listed as including tropes and deliberative, forensic, and public oratory.[5] The headings, full of rhetorical tropes, function as the

[3] See a facsimile of the corrected placards of the chapter in the volume entitled *Ulysses: "Aeolus," "Lestrygonians," "Scylla and Charybdis," & "Wandering Rocks." A Facsimile of Placards for Episodes 7-10*, pp. 13-20, in *The James Joyce Archives*, ed. Michael Groden (New York: Garland Publishing, Inc., 1978). See also Joyce's letter to Harriet Weaver, 7 Oct. 1921, in *Letters of James Joyce*, Vol. 1, ed. Stuart Gilbert (New York: The Viking Press, 1957), p. 172.

[4] See *The Little Review*, Oct. 1918.

[5] Reprinted in Richard Ellmann, *Ulysses on the Liffey* (New York: Oxford University Press, 1972), Appendix.

sign of the press, the modern descendant of the Ciceronian orator. But to view the headings in relation to Joyce's intentions articulated in his symbolic schema does not lessen the strangeness of encountering them on the page.[6] For although the headings conform to a logic of symbolism, they violate the logic of the narrative. According to the conventions of the realistic novel, there is nothing at all "logical" about the use of headings to help narrate the events in a newspaper office. There is, in fact, some whimsical pun of form and content enacted in the chapter, a mimicking or imitation that is a linguistic form of play.

In "Aeolus," the book begins to advertise its own artifice, and in doing so, it calls attention to the processes of reading and writing. For the headings not only provide a puzzle to the reader but they are also a sign of a new kind of writing in the book—a writing that undermines the norms established in the first six chapters. Jean Ricardou has said that the novel has metamorphosed from "the writing of a history" to "the history of a writing."[7] I would say that the "Aeolus" chapter includes both the writing of a history and the history of a writing. Joyce's distinction, and the distinction of the "Aeolus" chapter in particular, is that the concerns of the earlier chapters are not abandoned; Joyce's characteristic gesture is not to obliterate but to incorporate. On the one

---

[6] See the following critics for a "symbolic" reading of the headings: William York Tindall in *A Reader's Guide to James Joyce* (New York: Farrar, Straus & Giroux, 1959) and in *James Joyce: His Way of Interpreting the Modern World* (New York: Charles Scribner's Sons, 1950); A. Walton Litz in *The Art of James Joyce: Method and Design in Ulysses and Finnegans Wake* (New York: Oxford University Press, 1964); and Stuart Gilbert in *James Joyce's Ulysses: A Study*, rev. ed. (New York: Vintage Books-Random House, 1952). Litz significantly amends his reading of *Ulysses* in two subsequent articles: "The Genre of *Ulysses*," in *The Theory of the Novel: New Essays*, ed. John Halperin (New York: Oxford University Press, 1974), pp. 109-120, and "Ithaca," in *James Joyce's Ulysses: Critical Essays*, ed. Clive Hart and David Hayman (Berkeley: University of California Press, 1974), pp. 385-405.

[7] Quoted in Richard A. Lanham, *The Motives of Eloquence: Literary Rhetoric in the Renaissance* (New Haven: Yale University Press, 1976), p. 222.

hand, the writing of a history continues: events occur, speeches are made, characters interact. On the other hand, questions are raised about writing and reading novels. A hermeneutic shift occurs: whereas the stream-of-consciousness technique of the early chapters is designed to reveal the process of the characters trying to interpret their worlds, in "Aeolus," the narrative strategy illuminates the process of interpretation on the part of the reader and writer.[8] The writing and the reading of the book become self-conscious in a particular way: with the intrusion of the headings, the book begins to "interpret" itself. The book turns back on itself to comment on and parody its own assumptions, explicitly in the way the headings "comment" on or rewrite the micro-narrative and implicitly in the way the chapter exceeds and incorporates the novel we have read in the early chapters. Although the plot continues, the novel begins a radical questioning of the authority of its writing.

In the rest of this chapter I will examine the implications, for both the writing and reading of *Ulysses*, of Joyce's disruptions of his initial style in "Aeolus." Although my primary concern is with the implications of the headings, I will also discuss the significance of the inventory of rhetorical figures in the chapter, for the second major change Joyce made between the version of the chapter printed in *The Little Review* and its final form was the addition of thirty rhetorical figures.[9] The rhetorical inventory that resulted, in addition to the headings, contributes to the flaunted artifice of the chapter. Both the headings and the rhetorical figures undermine the norms established in the first six

---

[8] See Wolfgang Iser for an interesting discussion of the hermeneutic "gaps" that occur in "Aeolus" and the problems they cause for the reader (in "Indeterminacy" and in his book *The Implied Reader: Patterns of Communication in Prose Fiction from Bunyan to Beckett* [Baltimore: The Johns Hopkins University Press, 1974], pp. 212-214) Iser locates the "meaning" of the chapter in the disruption of the reader's expectations: according to him the chapter is *about* our attempts to make sense of the hermeneutic gaps in the text.

[9] See Litz, *The Art of James Joyce*, pp. 49-50.

chapters, and, hence, the reader's expectations. An analysis of both devices will help to elucidate some of the theoretical assumptions behind the stylistic games in the chapter.

The circumscription of the initial style of narration by the headings signals the contingency of its power. The headings, visually, temporally, and stylistically discontinuous from the original narration, puncture the myth of its absolute authority. In boldfaced print and capital letters, they announce the presence of a power outside that of the initial third-person narration which has claimed authority for the establishment of the empirical world of the novel.[10] Instead of continuous narration in "Aeolus," we find competing discourses.

As many recent critics (Roland Barthes in particular) have observed, the continuity of prose on a page represents the language of temporal duration and functions as the sign of the traditional novel.[11] The continuous prose of a novel allows us to see the language of the novel as the continuous "discourse of an explicit or implicit narrator who tells us about events in a world."[12] The discontinuity created by the headings thus has important implications for the reading of the novel: it destroys the illusion of a stable narrative voice. It also destroys the "myth of development" reflected in continuous prose. As Barthes says in "Littérature et discontinu":

> [L]a surface de la page . . . est dépositaire d'une valeur essentielle, qui est le *continu* du discours littéraire. . . . Le Livre (traditionnel) est un objet qui *enchaîne*, *développe*, *file* et *coule*, bref a la plus profonde horreur du vide. . . .

---

[10] The force with which the reader is meant to feel the contingent power of a narrative agency he has considered absolute can be compared to the effect of the sudden disappearance of the "History of Don Quixote de la Mancha" in Part I, Chapter Eight, of Cervantes' *Don Quixote*.

[11] See Barthes, "Littérature et discontinu," in *Essais critiques* (Paris: Seuil, 1964), pp. 175-187.

[12] Jonathan Culler, *Structuralist Poetics: Structuralism, Linguistics, and the Study of Literature* (Ithaca, N.Y.: Cornell University Press, 1975), p. 195.

Car ce qui se cache derrière [la] condamnation du discontinu, c'est évidemment le mythe de la Vie même. . . .
[T]oute Littérature . . . doit être un récit, une fluence
de paroles au service d'un événement ou d'une idée qui
«va son chemin» vers son dénouement ou sa conclusion.[13]

The visual disturbance to the narrative continuity in "Aeolus" calls into question the notions of origin (narrator) and
development (plot) upon which the novel is based. The
constructs of narrator and plot are revealed to be "myths"
of novel writing and novel reading.

But the creation of the norms of the novel we have been
reading depends not only upon the continuity of prose on
the page but also upon the consistency of style of the third-
person narration. The disturbance created by the headings
is stylistic and tonal as well as visual. The precise, denotative
style of narration has functioned as both the "signature" of
the narrator and the sign of the representation of reality in
the novel. The intrusion of the headings introduces a kind
of language into the novel that inhibits the dual movement
upon which the writing and reading of the traditional novel
and the early chapters of *Ulysses* are based: the movement
back to a creating consciousness—an "origin"—and the
movement back to life—the "original." The inscriptive quality of the writing undermines the expressive and the mimetic
functions of language: the boldfaced type destroys both the
illusion of a narrator and the transparency and innocence

---

[13] Barthes, "Littérature et discontinu," p. 177. Richard Howard translates
this passage as follows:

    The surface of the page . . . is the depository of an essential value, which
is the continuity of literary discourse. . . . The (traditional) Book is an object
which *connects, develops, runs,* and *flows,* in short, has the profoundest horror
vacui. . . . For what is hidden behind [the] condemnation of discontinuity
is obviously the myth of life itself. . . . [A]ll literature . . . should be a
narrative, a flow of words in the service of an event or an idea which "makes
it way" toward its denouement or its conclusion.

See Roland Barthes, "Literature and Discontinuity," in *Critical Essays*, trans.
Richard Howard (Evanston, Ill.: Northwestern University Press, 1972), pp.
173-174.

of language as an instrument of representation. The newspaper headings operate in conjunction with the inventory of rhetorical figures in the chapter to this effect; specifically, they undermine the novelistic constructs of narrator and plot, a dual-pronged attack that escalates as the book progresses.

The most prominent interpretive problem created by the headings is the blocking of the movement back to an originating consciousness. The primary fact of the headings is that they seem to rise unbidden in the novel: they intrude upon the security of the novel from an unknown source. If the introduction of the headings into the text signaled only the appearance of a new narrative persona, the text could be compared with many other novels concerned with point of view, such as those of Henry James or William Faulkner. What is different about the headings in "Aeolus" is that they destroy the notion of a coherent narrating "self." The attempt to read the headings as the utterance of a new narrative persona, in fact, has led to some rather comical conjecture. Richard Ellmann says (presumably with tongue in cheek): "Their authorship is unclear. Is it perhaps the muse of the fourth estate—if the fourth estate has a muse—who becomes slowly infected with a lung disease?"[14] Rather, I think we can say that the headings represent a discourse generated in the text that advertises the fact that it is "written," anonymous, and public—that is, cut off from any single originating consciousness.

The "written" or printed nature of the book is introduced most forcibly through the headings. Although the initial style of narration is a "written" style that calls attention to the arrangement of words on a page, it can still be naturalized in a communicative circuit. Even the naively written style in "Telemachus" emphasizes the energy required by a writer to capture reality in language. But the introduction of the idea of the mechanical reproduction of language adds

[14] See Ellmann, *Ulysses on the Liffey*, p. 73.

a different dimension to the writing. The headings surface as marks on a page, as if they were produced mechanically. Writing seems to be divorced from the writer.

Jacques Derrida's theory of the ontological status of writing is especially relevant here. He says: "To write is to produce a mark that will constitute a sort of machine which is productive in turn, and which my future disappearance will not, in principle, hinder in its functioning. . . . writing [is] an iterative structure, cut off from all absolute responsibility, from *consciousness* as the ultimate authority, orphaned and separated at birth from the assistance of its father."[15] It is precisely this process of estrangement from consciousness as ultimate authority that is felt in "Aeolus." What Derrida's programmatic statement about writing ignores is the way in which certain texts seem more written than others and certain parts of a text more written than other parts. All of *Ulysses* is, of course, "written," but it is in "Aeolus" that the force of the process of alienation Derrida describes is first felt. The artist "paring his fingernails" is no longer an adequate image for the process of artistic creation. The book now seems cut off from the notion of human origin; the metaphors of filiation, which Edward Said has so persuasively argued provide the essential image of creation in the traditional novel, no longer apply to the writing of *Ulysses*.[16]

In "Aeolus," Joyce plays with the distance between printed language and consciousness as ultimate authority. This concept requires careful stating. Both manipulation and absence are implied by the headings: they are narrative

[15] Jacques Derrida, "Signature Event Context," trans. Samuel Weber and Jeffrey Mehlman, *Glyph* 1 (Baltimore: The Johns Hopkins University Press, 1977): 180-181.

[16] Edward Said, *Beginnings: Intention and Method* (New York: Basic Books, Inc., 1975). See Chapter Three. Whereas the "mutilation" of the text in Chapter Nine of *Don Quixote* leads, as Said points out, to a new series of fathers and stepfathers (p. 93), the mutilation of the text in "Aeolus" obviates this process of generation.

intrusions of some sort that have the effect of making us feel cut off from the original narrative consciousness that we have come to trust. David Hayman says that the headings introduce the presence of an "arranger," a kind of master puppeteer, different from either the author or the original narrator, who begins to make his power felt in "Aeolus" and wields it more and more intrusively in subsequent chapters.[17] Although Hayman's term is excellent for capturing the sense of intrusion in the headings, it posits the existence of a narrative consciousness. As I have said, the effect of the headings depends upon our *not* being able to naturalize them in this way. The boldfaced print does act like a buttonholing gesture in the text, but it represents writing's way of claiming its authority when the power of the speaking voice has disappeared. Indeed, Joyce plays with the distance between the written marks on a page and a speaking voice in certain headings that could not possibly be produced by a human voice, such as the series of question marks (p. 132) and the abbreviations ("DAMES DONATE DUBLIN'S CITS SPEEDPILLS VELOCITOUS AEROLITHS, BELIEF" [p. 148]). Although the level of diction becomes less formal and more colloquial as the chapter progresses, Joyce reminds us that this is *printed* language representing vocal tone.

The headings function as the sign of language divorced from a single consciousness, however, not only because they are so obviously written and printed but also because they represent anonymous, collective discourse. For the language of the headings is the borrowed language of that agency of collective authorship, the press. In the term "the press" itself, the plural agents of communication are equated with the mechanical means of reproduction. The process of authoring, then, loses its privileged status twice over; it is

---

[17] David Hayman, *Ulysses: The Mechanics of Meaning* (Englewood Cliffs, N.J.: Prentice-Hall, Inc., 1970).

appropriated by both mechanical reproduction and the collective enterprise of production.

In "Aeolus," the borrowing of language implicit in the use of the technique of free indirect discourse is transformed into the borrowing of a language that exists independently of any one mind. The language of the headings belongs to no particular character. This change represents an important step in the evolution of the technique of free indirect discourse. In the "Telemachiad," the narrator "borrows" the language and education of Stephen Dedalus, producing a kind of sympathy of minds, an "intersubjectivity" between narrator and character. Used in this way, the technique allows both reader and writer to interpret the sudden appearance of a certain type of language as the language of a particular consciousness. As we have seen, this use of free indirect discourse follows the technique established by Flaubert. In the chapters in which Leopold Bloom is introduced, this sympathy or intersubjectivity between narrator and character continues. The narrator now borrows the prose of his new character (sometimes with comic effects). In both of these examples, the technique of free indirect discourse enables the narrator to move freely and unobtrusively into and out of the mind of his characters, without interrupting his own narrative to offer a direct quotation.

But in "Aeolus," the headings are so obviously separated from the narrative that the act of displacement of the narrative, made unobtrusive by free indirect discourse, is consequently advertised. Instead of the sly indirection of the linguistic "borrowing" in the technique of free indirect discourse, the reader finds in "Aeolus" a palpable disruption of the narrative. The activity of quotation is an encroachment on the writing of the narrative. In *Beginnings* Said asserts that any quotation involves encroachment, to a greater or lesser extent.[18] A comparison between the free

[18] "For although quotation can take many forms, in every one the quoted passage symbolizes other writing as encroachment, as a disturbing force moving potentially to take over what is presently being written. . . . [A]lways,

indirect discourse in the early chapters of *Ulysses* and the appearance of the headings in "Aeolus" reveals an important difference in the degree to which the encroachment is felt in the text. We have proceeded from the sympathy implied in the written act of "quoting" the language of Stephen Dedalus and Leopold Bloom to the contamination of the narrative by other writing in "Aeolus."

This "other writing" is comprised of both allusions to specific written texts (for example, to Virgil, Cicero, or Poe) and to the portable phrases of Dublin life ("SHORT BUT TO THE POINT," "RHYMES AND REASONS," "FAIR JUNE DAY"). In all of these examples, quoted language surfaces in the text not as the thought or speech of a particular character (as the Shakespearean allusion "nipping and eager airs" in the third-person narration of "Proteus" [p. 38] can be read as a phrase borrowed from Stephen's educated mind) but as the fragments of other texts intruding upon the narrative. The clichés in the headings, rather than the literary allusions, do most to disrupt the stylistic norm, which is itself a literate and literary prose. (In fact, the literary allusions in the headings suffer a popularization; for example, "SOPHIST WALLOPS HAUGHTY HELEN SQUARE ON PROBOSCIS. SPARTANS GNASH MOLARS. ITHACANS VOW PEN IS CHAMP" [p. 148].)

The language of the headings is a language of common denominator, the received and receivable ideas of society, and in this sense, it is very different from the language of the initial style. This is the language of "the allembracing give us this day our daily press" (p. 647), which, as this quotation from "Eumaeus" suggests, provides the suste-

---

even when in the form of a passing allusion, [quotation] is a reminder that other writing serves to displace present writing, to a greater or lesser extent, from its absolute, central, proper place" (*Beginnings*, p. 22). Although this statement obviously applies to the use of quotations from a given written text, it also applies, I think, to the mass importation of headings from newspapers, which exhibits just as surely the kind of borrowing and displacement that Said describes.

nance and sacredness of modern life. In the language of the headings, the fine tuning and sotto voce of the initial style are usurped by the idols of the marketplace loudly proclaimed. (Indeed, the assertiveness of the headings must be read against the banality of their message.) The language of the novel is invaded by a language not its own, as if the pen received automatic writing and the voice could produce only an echo of other voices. Writing thus becomes an act of rewriting, the recycling of phrases that retain the memory of their prior use. The language of the text no longer points to an originating consciousness but to the text of received ideas. The displacement of the novel we have been reading is enacted in this way in "Aeolus," and it is this chapter that points the way to the total displacement of the initial style later on. For example, the infiltration of the text by other literary texts is investigated in "Oxen of the Sun." It is, however, the infiltration by received ideas that Joyce seems to find most interesting, that is, the replacement of a literary style with cliché. This process of invasion culminates in "Eumaeus," as clichéd writing submerges all other writing. Since "Lestrygonians," "Scylla and Charybdis," and "Nausicaa" are chapters in which discourse is largely still traceable to a human and identifiable origin, they represent a return to the parameters established in the early chapters.

This interest in the public resources of language rather than the particular speech acts of a persona is reflected in the inventory of rhetorical tropes found in "Aeolus" as well as in the set of received ideas. Just as the received ideas replace style as an expression of personality with style as public memory, so too does the compendium of rhetorical figures shift attention from the particular aesthetic choices of a persona to the total system of rhetorical possibilities available in English. For the addition of thirty rhetorical figures turned the chapter into an inventory of rhetorical possibilities, a kind of rhetorical handbook.

As Stephen Ullmann says in *Style in the French Novel,* it is choice that is the basis of the expressive theory of style.

A style, Ullmann says, is created out of a writer's consistent stylistic idiosyncrasies.[19] The initial style is itself based on such choices: the particular stylistic dislocations and the particular lexicon create the personal signature of the narrator. But in "Aeolus," each rhetorical figure refers us to the entire set of figures in the chapter, and this movement subverts the notion of stylistic choice. The sense of impersonality in the chapter thus stems from not only the printed, anonymous headings but also the presence of the whole panoply of rhetorical figures. The writing is like an exercise in manipulating parts of the rhetorical system—in wielding verbal machinery according to certain established rules. The expressive function of language is undermined by an interest in the resources of the linguistic system. The inclusion of the inventory of rhetorical tropes in the chapter marks a shift in the novel's interest in *la parole*, the actualized speech choices of a particular speaker, to the resources of *la langue*, the possibilities that lie beneath any particular choices made.

Of course, the use of rhetorical figures is not confined to "Aeolus" alone. The initial style is itself a rhetorical one, and thus many of the figures used in "Aeolus" are perfectly consistent with the figures in the earlier chapters.[20] For example, the narrative statement, "They watched the knees, legs, boots vanish" (p. 118), may illustrate the scheme of asyndeton, but the sentence could easily be found in the initial style of the first six chapters and thus reveals nothing new about the language of "Aeolus." In addition, a great number of tropes in the chapter are located in the dialogue of Irishmen well acquainted with the art of rhetoric, as the subject of the dialogue reveals, and thus can be naturalized in this way. But the use of rhetoric in "Aeolus" is different

[19] Stephen Ullmann, *Style in the French Novel* (New York: Barnes & Noble, 1964), pp. 6-9.

[20] For a catalogue of the figures used in "Aeolus," see Gilbert's *James Joyce's Ulysses* (pp. 194-198), and Don Gifford and Robert J. Seidman's *Notes for Joyce: An Annotation of James Joyce's Ulysses* (New York: E. P. Dutton Co., Inc., 1974), pp. 519-525.

from its use in the chapters that precede it in both the cumulative effect created by so many rhetorical figures that obtrude in the writing and in the presence of certain figures, like the chiasmus and the neologism, in which the surface of the language disrupts its semantic function (a rhetorical practice that culminates in "Sirens"). The rhetorical schemes in "Aeolus" divert attention from the "reality" they transcribe to the verbal surface of the prose. A look at specific rhetorical figures will illustrate the opacity and "play" of language in the chapter.

The first example of a rhetorical figure in which the semantic function of language is undermined is the chiasmus: "Grossbooted draymen rolled barrels dullthudding out of Prince's stores and bumped them up on the brewery float. On the brewery float bumped dullthudding barrels rolled by grossbooted draymen out of Prince's stores" (p. 116). Interestingly, Joyce added the figure of chiasmus late in the life of the chapter, at the same time as he added the headlines. In *The Little Review*, the segment exemplified the rhetorical figure of repetition rather than chiasmus: "Grossbooted draymen rolled barrels dullhudding out of Prince's stores and bumped them up on the brewery float. Grossbooted draymen rolled barrels dullthudding out of Prince's stores and bumped them up on the brewery float."[21] Even in this version, the repetition of the same sentence marks a stylistic departure from the normal use of language we would expect in any novel (and have come to expect in this one), for it serves no functional purpose in the narration. Linguistic space expands with no corresponding expansion of our consciousness of "event." The repetition is a gratuitous act of writing.

By changing the figure to that of chiasmus, however, Joyce made the written quality of the language even more obtrusive. For chiasmus shifts our attention from the meaning of a sentence to its spatial arrangement on the page.

[21] See *The Little Review*, Oct. 1918.

The figure makes us aware of the difference between the words and the things they represent, for it flaunts the fact that language and print are reversible, whereas the movement of life and the movement of the plot that mirrors life are not. It reminds us that the rules of the text are distinct from the rules of life. The teleology of the plot is impeded by the compulsive reversal of language dictated by the rhetorical system. The chiasmus is a pure linguistic exercise or game—the grammatical, written counterpart of the tongue twister. It functions as a microcosm of language used not in the service of the mimesis of an action but in order to capture various grammatical possibilities. In the chiasmus, grammatical parts of the sentence—the subject and object, the active and the passive voice—change places, like partners in a dance.

This interest in verbal play is apparent throughout the "Aeolus" chapter. The interchangeability of the parts of a sentence applies not only to the proliferation of syntactic rearrangements but also to the interchangeability of parts of speech. The sentence "The ghost walks, professor MacHugh murmured softly, biscuitfully to the dusty windowpane" (p. 123) is listed in Gifford's catalogue of figures as an example of anthimeria, "the substitution of one part of speech for another."[22] In addition, the neologisms created in the headings of "Aeolus" are examples of a corresponding interest in playing with lexical possibilities. In "Aeolus," various syntactical, grammatical, and lexical rearrangements occur, as language advertises its powers of combination.

The verbal antics in "Aeolus" adumbrate the play of language in subsequent chapters. The use of rhetorical figures in "Aeolus" inaugurates in the novel both the activity of cataloguing linguistic resources and the activity of a particular kind of verbal play. The exercise of language as a game appears increasingly in the writing of the succeeding chapters. In "Scylla and Charybdis," for example, the narrative

[22] Gifford and Seidman, *Notes for Joyce*, p. 520.

style is infiltrated by just such verbal games: "He came a step a sinkapace forward on neatsleather creaking and a step backward a sinkapace on the solemn floor" (p. 184) is a direct descendant of the chiasmus in "Aeolus" (although it was actually written first). But it is in the "Sirens" chapter that these games of language culminate: "Miss Kennedy sauntered sadly from bright light, twining a loose hair behind an ear. Sauntering sadly, gold no more, she twisted twined a hair. Sadly she twined in sauntering gold hair behind a curving ear" (p. 258). Like the letters of an anagram, the words in these sentences are interchangeable. As in the chiasmus in "Aeolus," the linearity of the prose is destroyed. The movement from words to things encounters resistance as the sentence rearranges itself in its various permutations.

Many of the rhetorical tropes and schemes in "Aeolus" are to be found in the dialogues and monologues of the characters. Lenehan's palindrome ("Madam, I'm Adam. And Able was I ere I saw Elba" [p. 137]), and Stephen's "underdarkneath" (p. 138) are examples of verbal games that can be naturalized as the words and thoughts of the characters. But it is important to point out the presence of such examples in "Aeolus" because these linguistic games increasingly infiltrate the initial style of the later chapters. The insertion of a word in the midst of another word found in "underdarkneath," for example, becomes in "Sirens" the insertion of the sound of a fart into the word "epitaph": "eppripfftaph" (p. 257). The compound words abundant in the third-person narration of "Scylla and Charybdis," such as "eglintoneyes" and "softcreakfooted" are extensions of the verbal games in "Aeolus." The playfulness of the resident verbal game players is translated into the pleasure of the text in "Aeolus" and increasingly in the later chapters as well.

In fact, one finds in "Aeolus" a complex relationship between the rhetoric in the writing of the chapter (including the headings) and the rhetoric in the speeches of the characters. The ideal of eloquence is the subject of the discussion in the newspaper office; the favorite activity is oratory. While the characters quote to each other examples of model rhetoric, however, the rhetorical play in the narration reminds us of language as play, a function of pleasure rather than belief. The rhetorical schemes, like Lenehan's puns, leaven and at times deflate the high tones in the news office. And while all the characters, including Stephen, are "wooed by grace of language," the reader is invited to look at the rhetorical system, the tools of the speaker's art.

But it is the headings, composed of rhetorical figures, that function most emphatically to mock the eloquence of the dialogue of the characters. The headings condense the dramatic action into flashy, trite phrases; they offer a variety of stale commonplaces, debased forms of legitimate rhetorical figures: epithets ("GENTLEMEN OF THE PRESS"), synecdochic pairs ("THE CROZIER AND THE PEN"), metonymy ("THE WEARER OF THE CROWN"), metaphor ("THE CALUMET OF PEACE"). They use literary and biblical allusions—a way to get metaphoric richness without working ("THE GRANDEUR THAT WAS ROME," "KYRIE ELEISON!")—coinages ("DEAR DIRTY DUBLIN"), and neologism. Perhaps the favorite rhetorical device in the headings is alliteration, the easiest rhetorical figure to cheapen into flashy and empty titles like "A POLISHED PERIOD," "ERIN, GREEN GEM OF THE SILVER SEA," "LENEHAN'S LIMERICK," "THE GREAT GALLAHER," "RHYMES AND REASONS," etc. The headings, then, represent facile slogans and easy eloquence in a variety of forms.

Their tendency is to level the examples of eloquence that they circumscribe: no matter what the degree of eloquence in the various speeches (either in the formal speeches or in dialogues), the speeches are summed up in the facile rhetoric of the headings. Occasionally the headings comment in some way on the speeches. Stephen's exploration of the origins of poetry is entitled "RHYMES AND REASONS," O'Molloy's speech is dubbed "A POLISHED PERIOD," MacHugh's nostalgic speech against the Roman conquerors of England is "translated" into the heading "THE GRAN-DEUR THAT WAS ROME." The strategic effect of the headings is to destroy the sanctity of the rhetorical occasions, to mimic and therefore mock the language of the characters. They encourage a skepticism about the serious purposes of rhetoric, a tendency to parody any expression of emotion or belief. The mockery of the ideal of eloquence and the mimicking repetitions anticipate the narrative behavior of parts of "Scylla and Charybdis," "Sirens," and "Cyclops," those other public chapters in which we hear Dublin talk.

This mockery of eloquence found in the headings of "Aeolus" is echoed in the dialogue of the characters in this chapter and anticipated in the dialogue of previous chapters. Again, what begins as a principle of a character's behavior emerges as a narrative principle at some point in the text. Throughout *Ulysses*, the characters mock and mimic elo-quence. From Martin Cunningham in "Hades," who mimics Tom Kernan's idea of "trenchant singing" (see pp. 90-91), to "Puck Mulligan" parodying Synge in "Scylla and Cha-rybdis," their penchant for mimicry is apparent. In "Aeolus" especially, the characters mock each other: Miles Crawford mocks MacHugh with a few lines of "The Rose of Castille," MacHugh in turn mimics the pomposity of Dan Dawson's speech ("A recently discovered fragment of Cicero's, pro-fessor MacHugh answered with pomp of tone" [p. 124]). This is the type of inflation that could easily be found in a heading. A chain of mimicry is established: the characters mock the language of Dan Dawson in the morning news, the headings mock the eloquence of the characters.

Occasionally, however, one feels the debased rhetorical tropes momentarily revitalized—for example, while reading the rendition of Taylor's speech, we too are "wooed by grace of language." In 1923 when Joyce was asked to record a portion of *Ulysses*, he selected the passages of Taylor's

73

speech in "Aeolus" (based on an actual speech given by John Taylor). He felt they were the most rhetorical passages in *Ulysses* and therefore the most reproducible for recording.[23] In "Aeolus," the context of the speech, its circumscription by the headings, tends to undercut it, but the power of the language that Joyce admired survives.

In fact, the dramatic action survives the process of distillation in the headings in other ways as well: it refuses to be totally summed up in their crude formulations. The headings offer a written distillation of the dramatic action in the newspaper office; they attempt to reduce the "hot stuff" of the dramatic interaction, including the dialogue among the characters, to "cold print." ("All very fine to jeer at it now in cold print but it goes down like hot cake that stuff," says Bloom [p. 126].) The dramatic action (the "reality") in the novel is "frozen" in the headings. But the relationship between the headings and the micro-narrative dramatizes how, to quote Hugh Kenner in another context, "something living has been imperfectly synthesized" in writing.[24] The story we have been reading in the preceding chapters of the novel continues beneath the headings and functions as the "reality" of the chapter; the headings, however, have a different ontological status from the narrative and function as the sign of writing. The headings act as a kind of signifier, the plot as the signified, and the relationship between them reveals the wealth of the signified with respect to the signifier. The story always exceeds the attempts of the headings to encompass its meaning—the wealth of life exceeds its representation in writing.

The obvious arbitrariness of the summaries presented in the headings further suggests life's resistance to classification and closure. As I mentioned previously, the particular detail of the narrative italicized in the heading appears to be arbitrarily chosen. For example, in a paragraph in which both

[23] See Gilbert, *James Joyce's Ulysses*, p. 182n.

[24] Hugh Kenner, *The Stoic Comedians: Flaubert, Joyce, and Beckett* (Berkeley: University of California Press, 1962), p. 47.

Jesus Christ and Lord Salisbury are mentioned, it is Salisbury who is given top billing in the heading ("LOST CAUSES NOBLE MARQUESS MENTIONED" [p. 133]). Another title, "WHAT WETHERUP SAID," elevates to the status of a heading a passing comment in Bloom's stream-of-consciousness. ("Entertainments open house. Big blow out. Wetherup always said that. Get a grip of them by the stomach" [p. 126].) It is as if the kind of private and random associations found in the stream-of-consciousness of the characters became a narrative principle in "Aeolus." The sudden presence of the unknown Wetherup in Bloom's stream-of-consciousness exemplifies Bloom's habitual way of drawing on the prevailing lore on any given subject. However, the boldfaced heading does not represent a character classifying the data of his world; it represents, instead, the book classifying its own data in a deliberately arbitrary and misleading way. Each heading seems like a joke played on the reader. What the italicizing of such trivial remarks suggests is that almost any sentence in the narrative passage could serve just as adequately as a heading. Each heading is only one randomly chosen sentence within numerous possibilities. Thus the arbitrariness of writing is suggested: any number of headings could be generated out of the passage and still not exhaust it completely. Any sentence is an arbitrary foreclosure that halts the play of life; writing is an act of circumscription and exclusion, an act of creation not *ex nihilo* but, as Milton believed it to be, out of excess. The sentences within the novel, and the text itself as an extended "sentence," transform and reduce reality into a linguistic equivalent, but in the process, there is always something left over that asserts its resistance to the formal restrictions placed on it. The headings parody this exclusion and arbitrariness. They show that life cannot be reduced to a heading, a sentence, or a text.

In their arbitrariness, the headings also parody the idea of an "event" in capital letters; specifically, they parody the notion of "events" to which the novel as a genre generally subscribes. The elevation of a trivial detail in the headings is paralleled in a strange narrative passage in "Aeolus," one that treats explicitly the kind of claims of significance seen in the creation of the headings:

> I have often thought since on looking back over that strange time that it was that small act, trivial in itself, that striking of that match, that determined the whole after-course of both our lives. (P. 140)

The note for this passage in Gifford's and Seidman's *Notes for Joyce*[25] refers the reader to Dickens's *David Copperfield*. The passage can be read as the thought of Stephen Dedalus, as we are in Stephen's mind in a passage that precedes this one, but this explanation fails to account for the strangeness of the passage's sudden appearance in the text. A piece of another novel displaces the novel we are reading, as if, for one moment, the text were rewritten as a nineteenth-century novel. For parodied in this strange passage is a nexus of assumptions about meaning upon which the traditional novel is constructed. The passage parodies the way the traditional novel "shapes" experience through retrospective revelation. The ludicrously heavy-handed "whole after-course" and the muddle produced by the strained effort to relate this trivial act to the whole of life expose the way in which plot is always a kind of overdetermination of aleatory experience. (This strain is reflected grammatically in the overworking of the pronoun "that," which serves, to the point of exhaustion, as both relative and demonstrative pronoun.) No one moment or event determines the meaning of a life; no heroic act of consciousness can encompass it. In this passage, Joyce anticipates Roland Barthes's criticism of the novel, which "transforms life into destiny" and "duration into an oriented and meaningful time."[26] Joyce's re-

---

[25] Gifford and Seidman, *Notes for Joyce*, p. 115.

[26] Roland Barthes, "Writing and the Novel," in *Writing Degree Zero*, trans. Annette Lavers and Colin Smith (1967; reprint ed., New York: Hill and Wang, 1968), p. 39.

jection of this kind of overdetermination is implicit in his decision to write about one typical day in the life of Dublin; but this emphasis on the significance of specific events is parodied directly in the "flashback" recorded in the passage from Dickens and in the flashy, boldfaced headings.

In "Aeolus," destiny and plot are revealed as "novelistic constructs."[27] In rejecting the theory of significance parodied in the headings and in the Dickens passage, Joyce presents its opposite: he shows that all of life is significant, that all things are, in a sense, "newsworthy." For Joyce, the shaping of the details of life into the plot of the traditional novel falsifies life precisely because it overemphasizes certain events while failing to acknowledge that all life has meaning. It is the overemphasis on certain events that is parodied in the headings, not the idea of the general significance of the quotidian details of life. Joyce's solution to a central problem of the English novel from Fielding to James—that is, how to transform, in James's words, "the splendid waste" of life into the "sublime economy of art"[28]—is to replace the ethic of economy with an ethic of inclusiveness. As much as possible of the "splendid waste of life" is included in the text.

In *Ulysses*, Joyce moves away from the traditional idea of the economy of the novel in two major ways: the first is the inclusion in the text of the details of life that other writers traditionally have chosen to exclude from their novels. In *Tom Jones*, Fielding provides a classic description of the ethic of economy that Joyce rejects, the principles of summary and selection upon which most realistic novels are based:

> We intend in it [the novel] rather to pursue the method of those writers who profess to disclose the revolutions

[27] See Jonathan Culler, *Flaubert: The Uses of Uncertainty* (London: Elek, 1974), p. 145.

[28] Preface to "The Spoils of Poynton," reprinted in *The Art of the Novel: Critical Prefaces by Henry James* (New York: Charles Scribner's Sons, 1962), p. 120.

of countries than to imitate the painful and voluminous historian, who, to preserve the regularity of his series, thinks himself obliged to fill up as much paper with the details of months and years in which nothing remarkable happened as he employs upon those notable eras when the greatest scenes have been transacted on the human stage.

Such histories as these do in reality, very much resemble a newspaper, which consists of just the same number of words whether there be any news in it or not. (Book 2, Chapter 1)

As if in answer to Fielding, in "Aeolus," Joyce gives us the newspaper that Fielding disdains. He gives us the most trivial details of life rather than the "great scenes transacted on the human stage." In fact, the presence of details becomes increasingly prominent in the text, as Joyce deliberately includes random details that lie outside the symbolic form he himself creates. These details resist recuperation as a part of the symbolic schema and thus dramatize the innate recalcitrance that materiality presents to the shaping imagination. They represent the wealth of life that cannot be assimilated to literary purposes. The second aspect of Joyce's "profligate" assault on the ethic of economy is his inclusion of a plurality of styles, which destroys the economy of one artistic perspective.

Yet what the seemingly limitless number of details and styles suggests is the awareness that no matter how comprehensive the text, it can never exhaust reality. Any sentence, any linguistic form (and this of course includes the form of the novel) excludes the wealth of possibilities in life. Any text is exceeded by the "play" of reality, the resources of life out of which it carves its territory. In eschewing the traditional economy of the novel, Joyce reveals that any fiction, any beginning, middle, and ending, is an arbitrary interruption of life. To quote J. Hillis Miller, "The putting into language of man's 'experience' of his life, is in writing or reading a hiatus in that experience."[29] This knowledge of the arbitrariness of writing itself becomes problematic in the text. The problem is dramatized most explicitly by Joyce in the lengthy catalogues, sentences, and questions and answers of "Cyclops," "Eumaeus," and "Ithaca," respectively. In these chapters, Joyce deliberately creates a narrative that seems to have lost the ability to know when to stop. He purposely includes excesses and irrelevancies to demonstrate the arbitrariness of closure.

One can view the encyclopedic nature of *Ulysses* as both a liberation from the constraints of the traditional novel form and a defensive strategy against the knowledge of the limitations of all writing. On the one hand, if any number of sentences can be generated and any number of styles can be used, then the text becomes a playground of experimentation. The play of the text begins to exceed the form of the novel it contains—the text opens up to include other formal and stylistic possibilities besides those traditionally used in the novel, as well as details that deliberately flout the idea of coherent plot. If it disrupts the conventions of the novel, "Aeolus" also opens up the book to the subliterary—the newspaper—and the language of the narrative incorporates into the province of literature what it has generally chosen to exclude. "Aeolus" initiates this process of expansion and experimentation; in subsequent chapters, Joyce tries out many different formal and stylistic possibilities. But on the other hand, this bravura performance is itself created out of anxiety. The compulsiveness of the inventories of possibilities reveals this anxiety: it is a defense against the knowledge that all of life can never be contained within the book.

[29] J. Hillis Miller, "Ariadne's Thread: Repetition and the Narrative Line," *Critical Inquiry* 3 (Autumn 1976): 72.

IV

"Wandering Rocks" and "Sirens": The Breakdown of Narrative

In a letter to John Quinn, Joyce pointed out that "Scylla and Charybdis" was the ninth chapter of eighteen, the last chapter of the book's first half.[1] Indeed, this division has more than numerical significance, for both "Lestrygonians" and "Scylla and Charybdis" concern themselves primarily with developing our knowledge of the two main characters, the kind of novelistic enterprise paramount in the first six chapters. After the strange intrusive headings in "Aeolus," the return to the narrative mode in these chapters restores a comforting novelistic convention. Although rhetorical play continues in both chapters, and even some typographical play in "Scylla and Charybdis," it is not until "Wandering Rocks" and "Sirens" that we witness the breakdown of the initial style and a departure from the novelistic form of the book's first half. "Lestrygonians" and "Scylla and Charybdis," then, are less relevant to our discussion of style than the succeeding chapters.

However, before proceeding to "Wandering Rocks" and "Sirens," I would like to comment briefly on a specific aspect of the literary self-consciousness in "Scylla and Charybdis," namely, Stephen's public display of his theory on Shakespeare. In its own way, Stephen's verbal fancywork is as showy and attention-getting as the headings of "Aeolus," and, with his literary theory, as with the headings, the book

<hr />

[1] 3 September 1920, *Letters of James Joyce*, Vol. 1, ed. Stuart Gilbert (New York: The Viking Press, 1957), p. 145.

can be said to turn back on itself to comment on its own creation. Like the headings, which call into question the idea of the origin of the writing, Stephen's theory deals with the relationship between creating consciousness and creation. The important distinction, however, is that the primary vehicle for the literary criticism in "Scylla and Charybdis" is character rather than narrative, and the comment on origins is given a naturalistic, dramatic context. The showmanship primarily attaches to Stephen: "Speech, speech. But act. Act speech. They mock to try you. Act. Be acted upon" (p. 211), Stephen directs himself during his strategic, experimental performance. Even the greater rhetorical play in the third-person narration seems closely linked to Stephen's theatricality. As Robert Kellogg has noted, much of the verbal play in the narrative seems to be an extension of Stephen's "powerfully patterned imagination."[2] This relationship between the theatrics in the narrative and the theatrics of the character is more exaggerated than, but still in keeping with, the kind of "borrowing" between character and narrative seen in the earlier chapters.

Stephen's critical premise—that the writer reveals his psychological obsessions in disguised and multiple forms in his work—can be applied to Stephen's literary theory itself, for his elaborate reading of Shakespeare is, of course, an expression of his own feelings about paternity, betrayal, and the relationship between the artist and his work. The basic image of the artist fathering himself is a comfort to a young writer who scorns his natural parents and thinks of himself as "made not begotten" (p. 38). Aside from the light it sheds on Stephen, however, the literary theory has important implications for *Ulysses* as a whole. One could relate Stephen's theory to the revelation of Joyce's own psychological obsessions in *Ulysses*, as Mark Schechner does in his book

[2] Robert Kellogg, "Scylla and Charybdis," in *James Joyce's Ulysses: Critical Essays*, ed. Clive Hart and David Hayman (Berkeley: University of California Press, 1974), p. 159.

Joyce in Nighttown: A Psychoanalytic Inquiry into Ulysses.[3]
For our purposes, however, a more relevant application of
the theory is to Joyce's deliberate use of rhetoric and style
to reveal and disguise himself in his work. In its broadest
implications, Stephen's theory represents more than a
straight biographical approach to literature: it recognizes
the subtle, intricate relationship between the artist's self-
exposure and disguise in his work. One is reminded of Stanislaus's comment that Joyce's style is such that he seems to
confess "in a foreign language."[4] As Stephen shows with
Shakespeare, the consciousness of the artist is fractured in
his work; it can be dispersed, however, not only among
multiple characters but among multiple styles as well. In
a sense, Joyce reveals himself in the rhetorical masks of the
second half of *Ulysses* as well as in the "signature style" of
the early chapters, and, paradoxically, it is in the gestures
of imitation and disguise that we come to recognize him.

In later chapters of *Ulysses*, self-referential literary criticism is conveyed largely by rhetorical display in the narrative
rather than by the verbal grandstanding of the characters.
In fact, Stephen's literary pyrotechnics pale next to the
book's showpiece of literary criticism, "Oxen of the Sun."
Once again in *Ulysses*, we find that what begins on the level
of character reemerges on the level of narration later on. It
is in "Oxen" that Stephen's parable will give way to parody
and his craftiness will be transferred to the craft of the writing.

"WANDERING ROCKS"

From the highly charged psychological dramas of Stephen
Dedalus and William Shakespeare in "Scylla and Charybdis," we move to the dispassionate, almost deadpan narration

[3] Mark Schechner, *Joyce in Nighttown: A Psychoanalytic Inquiry into Ulysses*
(Berkeley: University of California Press, 1974), pp. 15-49.

[4] *The Dublin Diary of Stanislaus Joyce*, ed. George Harris Healey (London:
Faber and Faber, 1962), p. 81.

in "Wandering Rocks." Jackson Cope has called the narration of this chapter "meticulous," and observes that the "drastic shift in stylistic technique" in "Sirens" is "all the more marked for coming upon the heels of the meticulous narration of 'Wandering Rocks.' "[5] But the simplicity of the narrative is deceptive and its "meticulousness" excessive. Although the familiar techniques of narration in the book's first half continue—interior monologue, free indirect discourse, dialogue, and the initial style of third-person narration—something strange happens nonetheless.

Like Gradgrind, the narrative spews forth a compendium of facts. Streets are named, the characters' courses are charted; the chapter ostentatiously creates that "complete picture" of Dublin from which the city itself could be reconstructed. But a seeming paradox arises from the way in which this is accomplished. While establishing the sense of fact in the text, the "meticulous" documentation suggests the strangeness of reality. Reality is "defamiliarized," to borrow a phrase from the Russian formalists, a process due to the type of narrative mind in the chapter. This narrative mind exhibits what I would call a "lateral" or paratactic imagination: it catalogues facts without synthesizing them. It documents the events that occur but fails to give the causal, logical, or even temporal connections between them. The discontinuity of the sections of "Wandering Rocks" is the most obvious example of this lack of synthesis. The temporal connections between the events presented in successive sections are deliberately obscured. For example, successive sections often refer to events occurring simultaneously, but there is no reference to this simultaneity in the text.[6] Indeed, within a single section, strange juxtapositions

---

[5] See Jackson Cope, "Sirens," in *James Joyce's Ulysses: Critical Essays*, ed. Clive Hart and David Hayman (Berkeley: University of California Press, 1974), p. 218.

[6] See Clive Hart's chart of the temporal scheme of events in this chapter in "Wandering Rocks," in *James Joyce's Ulysses: Critical Essays*, ed. Clive Hart and David Hayman (Berkeley: University of California Press, 1974), p. 218.

occur. For example, the narrator documents Father Conmee's movement along Mountjoy square east and then suddenly interpolates a description of the movements of Mr Denis J. Maginni, professor of dancing—movements that occur presumably at the same time but in a different place (p. 220). Even within a sentence, two actions are associated whose connection is arbitrary by the standards of novel writing, for they have no connection besides the mere coincidence in time (and a whimsical connection between the types of movements described): "Corny Kelleher sped a silent jet of hayjuice arching from his mouth while a generous white arm from a window in Eccles Street flung forth a coin" (p. 225).

Time and space are the unifiers in the universe of the chapter: the characters moving through Dublin are related by *coincidence* in time and *proximity* in space. Instead of plot as conspiracy (as reflected in Stephen's theory on Shakespeare), or at least as motivated drama, we find the characters' actions plotted according to the coordinates of time and space. The apparently arbitrary and accidental connections between events and people in "Wandering Rocks" deepen the skepticism about any absolute idea of order introduced in "Aeolus."

But if the narrative confounds our expectations of plot by connecting two events arbitrarily, it also fails to acknowledge certain connections when they do occur. The narrator mentions a "onelegged sailor" in section one of the chapter ("A onelegged sailor, swinging himself onward by lazy jerks of his crutches, growled some notes" [p. 219]) and again in section three ("A onelegged sailor crutched himself round MacConnell's corner skirting Rabaiotti's icecream car, and jerked himself up Eccles Street" [p. 225].) The repetition is strange because there is no acknowledgment in the narrative that the sailor is the *same* one in both descriptions. The narrative inability to progress from the indefinite to the definite article illustrates a strange failing in the "narrative memory." A crucial component of the development of narrative is precisely this ability to synthesize knowledge while accumulating it. In the previous example, the kind of conceptualization and logical subordination of events that one would expect in narrative discourse is again strangely absent.

This absence of connective fiber is reflected in other curious examples of verbal repetition. The following piece of dialogue appears at two different points in the narrative (with the only difference being the addition of a comma after the word "answered" in the second version): "—Hello, Simon, Father Cowley said. How are things?" "—Hello, Bob, old man, Mr Dedalus answered stopping" (pp. 239-240 and 243). Similarly, in a phrase in the initial style of third-person narration, we are told that "the young woman abruptly bent and with slow care detached from her light skirt a clinging twig" (p. 224), and later in the same chapter this phrase is repeated with slight modification: "The young woman with slow care detached from her light skirt a clinging twig" (p. 231). Although the two narrative descriptions document the same event, there is no awareness of this congruence in the narrative.

This verbatim repetition imparts a curiously mechanical quality to the narrative, as if a writing machine, rather than a human imagination, produced it. As in the previous description, the minor characters in the novel are tagged with characteristic descriptions or epithets. This mechanical system of classification has an important effect upon characterization in the novel. Whereas the repetition of phrases from a character's interior monologue helped establish the density of the character's inner life, the repetition of phrases in "Wandering Rocks" signals an odd reversal. The phrases are no longer subordinate to a sense of character; rather, the minor characters are reduced to the status of phrases. The existence of the "young woman" seems to be totally contingent upon the particular phrase that identifies her, as if she and her linguistic tag were identical. Similarly, "Marie Kendall, charming soubrette," and "Mr Denis Maginni, professor of dancing, &c." are comically inseparable from their advertisements. It is as if these linguistic labels exhausted the potential of the characters, as if Thom's Dublin Dictionary were equated with the real life of Dublin. Sentences that would normally refer us to the world of external reality begin to seem like cross-references in a textbook. As in "Aeolus," the process of inventory emphasizes the artifice of the writing.

Thus, masses of facts accumulate in the text with either arbitrary conceptual links or no links provided by the lateral imagination of the narrative. This strange cataloguing activity is reflected in the syntax of the prose itself. Sometimes the prose is paratactic and choppy ("Father Conmee perceived her perfume in the car. He perceived also that the awkward man at the other side of her was sitting on the edge of the seat" [p. 222]). However, one of the most interesting stylistic phenomena in the chapter is the threading together of "facts" in long, winding sentences (either grammatically paratactic or hypotactic), such as the following:

> Lawyers of the past, haughty, pleading, beheld pass from the consolidated taxing office to Nisi Prius court Richie Goulding carrying the costbag of Goulding, Collis and Ward and heard rustling from the admiralty division of king's bench to the court of appeal an elderly female with false teeth smiling incredulously and a black silk skirt of great amplitude. (P. 232)

and

> An elderly female, no more young, left the building of the courts of chancery, king's bench, exchequer and common pleas, having heard in the lord chancellor's court the case in lunacy of Potterton, in the admiralty division the summons, exparte motion, of the owners of the Lady Cairns versus the owners of the barque Mona, in the court of appeal reservation of judgment in the case of Harvey ver-

sus the Ocean Accident and Guarantee Corporation. (P. 236)

Although formally connected, the clauses and phrases of the sentences often bear arbitrary and irrelevant conceptual connections to one another. Here are Jamesian sentences sorely lacking the interpretive intelligence to wrestle with subtle connections and relationships. In these particular examples, the lengthy clauses are initiated by the similar phrases "having heard" and "and heard." A Pandora's box opens up in the narration: not only are the activities and thoughts of the characters illustrious objects in the narrative catalogue but so too are the immediate past experiences of the characters, even if they have been documented previously in the narration. The narrative could then presumably continue to catalogue and recatalogue these experiences ad infinitum.

In fact, from that which was *actually heard* by the characters, the narrative passes to the *hearsay* meticulously documented in the last section of the chapter: "On Northumberland and Landsowne roads His Excellency acknowledged punctually salutes from rare male walkers, the salute of two small schoolboys at the garden gate of the house *said to have been admired* by the late queen when visiting the Irish capital with her husband, the prince consort, in 1849" (p. 255; my italics). And the documentation of what might have happened is complemented in the last section by the documentation of what failed to happen: the viceregal carriages pass "unsaluted," John Henry Menton holds "a fat gold hunter watch not looked at in his fat left hand not feeling it," and Mr Denis J. Maginni walks "unobserved." The mushrooming sentences comically undermine any sense of telos in the writing. As in a comic cartoon, the plot of the novel seems to grow uncontrollably; everything seems potentially related to, indeed contaminated by, everything else (a kind of contamination that reaches epidemic proportions in "Ithaca"). Instead of Aristotle's definition of plot as an imitation of an action, this narrative gives us plot as infinite potentiality. For in documenting what doesn't happen in the chapter, Joyce plays with the categories of potentiality: the sentences of the chapter present a story in which boy doesn't meet girl nor fall in love nor get married ("Heard melodies are sweet, but those unheard/Are sweeter . . ."). The limitations imposed upon novel writing by the exigencies of plot making are ignored, and the reader's expectation of the functional relevance of narrative details is undermined. In "Wandering Rocks," the text includes the possibilities of writing usually "ousted" by any particular linear movement of plot. This is the aesthetic transvaluation of Stephen's interest in "Nestor" in the "ousted possibilities" of history.[7] Plot is the novelistic counterpart of history; especially in "Aeolus," "Wandering Rocks," and "Ithaca," Joyce investigates the possibilities that are ousted by conventional novelistic plot.

But the grammatical counterpart of plot is syntax, and in revealing the infinite potentiality of the plot, the narrative also reveals the infinite expansibility of the sentence. The sentences parody the arbitrary structure of prose writing. The narrative's attempt to catalogue all the action of the chapter is comically outpaced by the possibilities that present themselves as potential members in the catalogue. The sentences themselves huff and puff in a futile attempt to say all that can be said. The taciturnity of the initial style is replaced by the over-eager attempt to include everything. Roland Barthes's analysis of Flaubert's sentences is comically illustrated in "Wandering Rocks":

> La phrase est un objet, en elle une finitude fascine . . .
> mais en même temps par le mécanisme . . . de l'expansion,

---

[7] Stephen considers the problem of the relationship between "an actuality of the possible as possible" and "infinite possibilities": "Had Pyrrhus not fallen by a beldam's hand in Argos or Julius Caesar not been knifed to death? They are not to be thought away. Time has branded them and fettered they are lodged in the room of the infinite possibilities they have ousted. But can those have been possible seeing that they never were? Or was that only possible which came to pass? Weave, weaver of the wind" (p. 25).

toute phrase est insaturable, on ne dispose d'aucune raison structurelle de l'arrêter ici plutôt que là. . . . Elle est comme l'arrêt gratuit d'une liberté infinie.[8]

If the headlines of "Aeolus" revealed the potentially limitless number of sentences about Dublin, the sentences of "Wandering Rocks" reveal the potentially infinite expansibility of the sentence itself. Conversely, they reveal the gratuitousness of any chosen terminus for the sentence, a gratuitousness also found in the narrative of "Eumaeus." The syntax of a sentence progressively limits the potential choices of that sentence—its beginning limits the possibilities of its end. However, in the sentences of "Wandering Rocks," Joyce plays against this expectation of narrowing possibilities and ultimate closure, as successive clauses follow each other exhaustively in the prose.

In "Wandering Rocks," the book continues the exploration of its own choices begun in "Aeolus." It prepares for the investigation of potentiality in later chapters: "Circe" (the psychic potentiality of the characters); "Sirens," "Oxen of the Sun," and "Eumaeus" (stylistic and syntactic potentiality); and "Ithaca" (the potentiality of the plot). It is interesting that all of the examples I have cited from "Wandering Rocks" that illustrate an interest in the categories of potentiality were *added* to the chapter after its publication in *The Little Review*.[9] Joyce interpolated these passages into the text while he was working on the later chapters of the book. Despite the chapter's apparent simplicity, it thus an-

---

[8] Roland Barthes, *Le Degré zéro de l'écriture suivi de nouveaux essais critiques* (Paris: Seuil, 1972), p. 143. The following is my own translation of this passage: "The sentence is an object in which finitude entrances . . . but at the same time by a mechanism . . . of expansion, every sentence is insaturable; there is no structural reason to stop here rather than there. . . . It is like the arbitrary limit to an infinite freedom."

[9] See the volume entitled *Ulysses: "Aeolus," "Lestrygonians," "Scylla and Charydbis," & "Wandering Rocks." A Facsimile of Placards for Episodes 7-10*, in *The James Joyce Archives*, ed. Michael Groden (New York: Garland Publishing, Inc., 1978).

89

ticipates the bizarre narrative activity of the chapters to come.

"SIRENS"

In the "overture" of the "Sirens" chapter, *Ulysses* abandons even the pretense of being a traditional novel. Here conventional units of narration are fractured: short lines of non sequitur replace the paragraph, and splintered phrases replace the sentence. In turning the page from the lengthy paragraphs that conclude "Wandering Rocks," the reader comes upon a kind of shorthand or code in which Joyce seems to be playing linguistic games of notation. In the overture, the reader is offered an incomplete and abbreviated transcription of reality.

I have used the term "overture" as a convenient label for the opening section of the chapter because it does function as a musical overture, introducing the phrases and themes that are "orchestrated" in the narrative. However, the analogy between music and language does not, to my mind, supply the raison d'être of this strange section, as critics have suggested in discussing the "art" of the chapter. For example, Stanley Sultan contends that the "justification" for the section is that it "imitates an operatic overture."[10] But to see the chapter merely as an imitation of a musical form is to ignore how the stylistic antics in "Sirens" are anticipated in previous chapters and continued in subsequent chapters. The breakdown of the logic of narration and the willful arbitrariness of the writing in "Sirens" are first seen in "Aeolus" and extended in "Wandering Rocks." In addition, the linguistic games in the overture are anticipated in the games of notation found in "Calypso" ("Mkgnao . . . Mrkgnao! the cat cried") and in "Aeolus" ("The door of Ruttledge's office whispered: ee: cree"). And, finally, the

[10] Stanley Sultan, "The Sirens at the Ormond Bar: *Ulysses*," *University of Kansas City Review* 26 (Winter 1959): 84-85.

variations played on the phrases of the overture in the narrative of "Sirens" illustrate a kind of rhetorical exercise
which becomes increasingly obvious in later chapters that
do not have music as their "art." The text as a *verbal composition* supersedes the text as an imitation of a musical
composition.

The relationship of music and writing can be most fruit-
fully regarded not as an airtight analogy but as a kind of
experimental premise in the chapter. The critical question
then becomes, How does Joyce play on this relationship,
that is, what happens to the text when this experiment is
conducted? In a sense, the "Sirens" chapter is Joyce's experimental and, I think, parodic answer to Walter Pater,
the tutelary genius of the chapter, who said that all art
constantly aspires to the condition of music. The chapter
shows us how language is and is not music—it plays a
number of variations on this basic idea. In the process, the
text displays its artifice, its status as a verbal composition.
The experimental premise of the chapter thus liberates the
stylistic behavior of the text. Joyce's experiments with the
relationship between language and music issue in particular
kinds of verbal antics that, in turn, have important implications for the reading of the text.

The overture attempts to reproduce literal music as well
as formally to imitate its structure, for the overture is largely
an encoded transcription of sound: it gives us the sounds
of a voice, a piano, a garter snap, a laugh, applause. In
"Sirens," Joyce turns the novel over to sound, that is, he
writes a chapter that focuses on the "music" of Dublin—on
its literal music (there is music played throughout the chapter), on its dialogue, and on its noises. In his games of
notation in the overture, Joyce plays with the idea of re-
ducing sound, verbal and nonverbal, to its written equivalent. For example, the phrase "Will lift your tschink with
tschunk" reproduces a toast—both the words of the toast
("will lift your glass with us") and the sound of clinking
glasses ("tschink with tschunk"). Perhaps the most famous

example of sound reduced to its written equivalent is the representation of flatulence at the end of the chapter ("Pprrpffrrppfff").

In the overture, Joyce exploits the distance between the printed word and the sound it represents. In *The Stoic Comedians*, Hugh Kenner has observed of Joyce's games of notation in *Ulysses* that "there is something mechanical, Joyce never lets us forget, about all reductions of speech to arrangements of twenty-six letters."[11] It seems to me that in "Sirens" there is a special poignancy to the gap between sound and written language: Joyce shows us in the chapter that no matter how hard the writing may try to capture the living music of Dublin, the text, like all texts, is silent. A crucial component of the chapter's irony is its revelation of the way in which writing is *not* music. One can say that the relationship between the transcriptions in the overture and real sound is like the relationship between a musical score and music. Like the musical symbols of a score, the signs of the overture remind us of what is lost in the transcription of sound.

As a kind of musical score, the chapter lays bare its inner workings. The overture in particular exposes the chapter's structure and composition by offering a "breakdown" of the narrative system into its constituent elements. Like a musical overture, the first section of "Sirens" offers an encapsulated version of the narrative. It provides a kind of table of contents, a chronological catalogue of what we can expect to find. The "contents" of the chapter are, as I have mentioned, the sounds of Dublin out of which the text will be constructed. In the overture, we are shown the elements before they are woven into a comprehensive semantic system. They are neither classified in narrative categories (like direct dialogue or third-person narration) nor developed into dramatic symbols (like "Jingle jingle jaunted jingling,"

---

[11] Hugh Kenner, *The Stoic Comedians: Flaubert, Joyce, and Beckett* (Berkeley: University of California Press, 1962), p. 47.

which becomes a symbol for Boylan's car, and then for Boylan, and then for the cuckolding of Leopold Bloom). It is as if Ibsen reduced Nora's door slam to the status of mere noise.

Behind their meaning as acoustic transcriptions, however, the lines of the overture are themselves words on a page: the overture breaks down the contents of the chapter even further into the autonomous words and phrases that constitute the chapter. In confronting the almost meaningless overture, we are reminded that the literary text is comprised not of characters, nor plots, nor philosophies, but words.[12] In this way, the overture calls attention to the writer's tools: ultimately, we are meant to marvel at the creation of a story out of such basic ingredients. Again, there is a reminder of the text as a rhetorical exercise, a narrative fiat. "Sirens" provides a more self-conscious beginning to the narrative than any other chapter, for in the overture, the chapter ritualizes its intention to begin. Explicitly announcing its own end with the word *"Done,"* the overture provides an introduction to the narrative proper with the word "Begin!" Because a novel tends to hide the laws of its composition so that we concentrate on what it is saying, this exposure of structure makes us aware of the text as a constructed system.[13]

Like "Aeolus," "Sirens" is a chapter that emphasizes the artifice of the text—the drama of the writing usurps the dramatic action. But the most interesting experiments in this chapter are the more local, verbal games played in the

---

[12] See William H. Gass, "The Medium of Fiction," in *Fiction and the Figures of Life* (New York: Alfred A. Knopf, 1970), pp. 27-28.

[13] The narrative itself mimics its own structure: it begins with the word "Begin!" and ends with the word *"Done."* This mimicry cannot be naturalized according to the conventions that usually govern novel writing and, of course, it emphasizes the constructed nature of the text. In fact, the conclusion of the chapter, Bloom's flatulence, can be regarded as a comic version of a "natural" conclusion, as Bloom is unable to prevent "nature" from taking its course. This too parodies the epiphanies of the early chapters that also end not with a whimper but a bang.

sentences of the narrative. A kind of breakdown of the style occurs that mirrors the anatomy of structure, for the narrative norm from the preceding chapters seems to be dissected and reassembled like a tinker toy. Phrases are repeated, rearranged, slightly distorted. Statements in the serious, literate, precise prose of the narrative norm suffer the indignities of constant revision—they are pulled apart and examined, their literacy and assertiveness collapsing under the scrutiny. As in "Aeolus," we are drawn in "Sirens" to the surface of the language: in "Sirens," however, the play of the language almost seems to interrupt the telling of the story.

Recognizable examples of the narrative norm can be found in "Sirens," serving their characteristic function of documentation. For example, "Miss Douce's brave eyes, unregarded, turned from the crossblind, smitten by sunlight" (p. 268) is identifiably in the initial style of the book. The precision and formality of its diction, its slight syntactic and semantic dislocations (that is, the awkward separation of the adjective "unregarded" and the figure "brave eyes"), and the obvious attention to sound are hallmarks of the initial style. However, rather surprisingly, an entire paragraph seems to "mushroom" out of this statement:

> Miss Douce's brave eyes, unregarded, turned from the crossblind, smitten by sunlight. Gone. Pensive (who knows?), smitten (the smiting light), she lowered the dropblind with a sliding cord. She drew down pensive (why did he go so quick when I?) about her bronze over the bar where bald stood by sister gold, inexquisite contrast, contrast inexquisite nonexquisite, slow cool dim seagreen sliding depth of shadow, *eau de Nil.* (P. 268)

The succeeding sentences in the paragraph combine interior monologue with continued third-person narration, a juxtaposition that occurs in other chapters. But what is strange about the passage is that the first narrative statement is immediately rewritten and explored: it gives birth to an

exuberant narrative excursus. The initial sentence generates
its own qualifications that are, in turn, repeated and qualified
at an accelerating pace. The second sentence (omitting the
word "Gone") explores the implicit pun in the first (Miss
Douce is both smitten with love for Boylan and struck by
the harsh light of the sun). Similarly, the third sentence
begins to repeat and expand on the second, when, quite
inexplicably, it fixates on producing variations of itself and
begins to rearrange the phrase "inexquisite contrast." This
narrative exuberance is made more comic because it is itself
based on a distorted echo of both a comment by Miss Kennedy ("Exquisite contrast," p. 257) and a narrative comment
about her and Miss Douce ("Ladylike in exquisite contrast,"
p. 258). The phrase "in exquisite" becomes "inexquisite";
through some rather deaf-eared transcribing, the phrase
becomes its opposite.

Thus, in the midst of the narrative, language circles back
on itself, as if, by some strange compulsion, three steps
backward must accompany any one step forward.[14] As in
the preceding example, the narrative excursus sometimes
involves an inaccurate repetition of a phrase already uttered.
Simon Dedalus asks Miss Douce for some whiskey and she
replies, "With the greatest alacrity." Suddenly, however,
the phrase is repeated in the narrative in slightly altered
form: "With the greatest alacrity" is transformed into "with
grace of alacrity," and an entire passage is spawned from
this distortion:

> With grace of alacrity towards the mirror gilt Cantrell
> and Cochrane's she turned herself. With grace she tapped
> a measure of gold whisky from her crystal keg. Forth from

[14] A similar example is the one to which I alluded in my discussion of
"Aeolus," the descendant of the chiasmus in that chapter: "Miss Kennedy
sauntered sadly from bright light, twining a loose hair behind an ear. Sauntering sadly, gold no more, she twisted twined a hair. Sadly she twined in
sauntering gold hair behind a curving ear" (p. 258).

the skirt of his coat Mr Dedalus brought pouch and pipe. Alacrity she served. (P. 261)

Here the sounds of phrases are repeated while their sense is ignored. As in the child's game of telephone, the original statement is lost in transmission, but the writing seems not to notice. (Instead of the absolute pitch we might expect to find in a chapter about music, we find less than perfect hearing. At times we seem to be in the same unfortunate predicament as Bald deaf Pat who "seehears lipspeech" [p. 283].)[15] This deaf-eared transcribing places the emphasis on the phonetic rather than the semantic characteristics of words. An interest in the sounds of words begins to dominate the writing. Throughout the narrative, we find rhetorical figures of sound, such as rhyme, assonance, alliteration, elision—sentences like "lightward, gliding, mild, she smiled on Boylan." If we have seen the language of "Sirens" imitate literal sound, we also see it here as itself a form of arranged sound. Aural associations guide the movement of the sentences: "Encore, enclap, said, cried, clapped all" (p. 276). A personal pronoun metamorphoses into a laugh right before our eyes (or ears, as the case may be): "Pat is a waiter who waits while you wait. Hee hee hee hee. He waits while you wait. Hee hee. A waiter is he. Hee hee hee hee" (p. 280). In experimenting with language as patterned sound, Joyce liberates all kinds of aural associations and combinations. The rhetorical schemes and aural poetry of the

---

[15] These errors of transcription in the text serve to remind us to what degree "reality" is mediated and at times distorted in the narrative. Static seems to be built into the narrative itself. The following passage plays upon this idea of distortion: "From the saloon a call came, long in dying. That was a tuningfork the tuner had that he forgot that he now struck. A call again. That he now poised that it now throbbed. You hear?" (p. 264). The question "You hear?" is worthy of the washerwomen in the Anna Livia Plurabelle section of *Finnegans Wake*, who can't hear each other's gossip because the water's running. (In fact, the narrative of "Sirens" has a gossipy quality to it.) It is in *Finnegans Wake* that the kind of local distortions in "Sirens" find their issue. It is not until *Finnegans Wake* that Joyce really explores the idea of the text as a distortion and liberates the aural associations of words.

initial style are now exaggerated into bizarre verbal behavior—sounds migrate within a sentence, as in the example "Mr Bloom reached Essex bridge. Yes Mr Bloom crossed Bridge of Yessex" (pp. 261-262).[16]

As the chapter experiments with the sounds of words, the machinery of narration begins to creak and groan. Joyce deliberately sabotages the devices of narration used so effectively in the early chapters of the novel. The third-person narration becomes deliberately awkward: the writing has a comic, gestural component, as if a drunken clowning were enacted by the language itself. The moment the narration attempts to walk a straight line, it begins to wobble. A confident narrative statement such as "From the saloon a call came, long in dying" suddenly gives way to the awkward strains of "that was a tuningfork the tuner had that he forgot that he now struck. A call again. That he now paused that it now throbbed" (p. 264). An excess of labor is needed for the simplest narrative functions (the reader is reminded of the comic style first glimpsed in "Telemachus"). With the punctiliousness and defensiveness of a drunk trying to prove he can still speak coherently, the narrative must labor to communicate even the simplest ideas: "He, Mr Bloom, listened while he, Richie Goulding, told him, Mr Bloom of the night he, Richie, heard him, Si Dedalus, sing *'Twas rank and fame* in his, Ned Lambert's house" (p. 277). Indirect discourse becomes increasingly indirect and awkward: "First gentleman told Mina that was so. She asked was that so. And second tankard told her so. That that was so" (p. 277). Narrative statements documenting external reality are misplaced, as if the narrative were a broken record telling us something we have already heard and no longer need to know: "Blazes Boylan's smart tan shoes creaked on the barfloor, said before" (p. 276).

---

[16] Sometimes, this aural liberation produces a kind of "Freudian slip" in the narration. The "Yessex" ("Yes sex") in this sentence is a punning reminder to the reader of what Bloom is trying to forget all day long, but especially at this hour.

(Boylan, we have been told already, has left the bar and is on his way to Molly's.)

In "Sirens," the book examines its own resources and plays with the kind of language it has once taken seriously. The third-person narration in the early chapters seems to have outlived its usefulness, and, indeed, it disappears after the "Sirens" chapter (as I said previously, I will discuss its brief reappearance in "Nausicaa"). The serious, literate documentation of reality becomes in "Sirens" almost an illiterate verbal gesture ("Bald deaf Pat brought quite flat pad ink" [p. 278]). And the lyrical strand of the initial style associated with Stephen Dedalus turns into a verbal fiasco of excessive alliteration. In the following passage (a description of Simon Dedalus singing an aria), Joyce gives us his most parodic interpretation of Pater's observation that all art aspires to the condition of music:

> It soared, a bird, it held its flight, a swift pure cry, soar silver orb it leaped serene, speeding, sustained, to come, don't spin it out too long long breath he breath long life, soaring high, high resplendent, aflame, crowned, high, in the effulgence symbolistic, high, of the ethereal bosom, high, of the high vast irradiation everywhere all soaring all around about the all, the endlessnessnessness. (Pp. 275-276)

In this passage, Joyce invokes the spirit of Walter Pater, plagiarizes Dan Dawson in "Aeolus" (see Dawson's speech in "Aeolus," p. 126), and parodies the lyrical flights to which both he and Stephen Dedalus have sometimes been prone (see the epiphany on the beach in *A Portrait* and the lyrical descriptions in "Telemachus"—"Woodshadows floated silently by through the morning peace from the stairhead seaward where he gazed. . . . White breast of the dim sea . . . . Wavewhite wedded words shimmering on the dim tide" [p. 9]). In *Ulysses on the Liffey*, Richard Ellmann suggests that this passage parodies the sentimentality of the characters listening to the music,[17] but it seems to me to go beyond parody of character to a parody of lyricism and all pretensions to fine writing, even the book's own. The book borrows from the highflown oratory of a character mocked in a previous chapter: excess infiltrates the writing.

In "Sirens," the play of rhetorical figures first seen in "Aeolus" leads to a more insistent verbal tinkering with the prose. If the verbal play and the headlines in "Aeolus" diverted us from the action in the micro-narrative, in "Sirens," the surface of the prose is even more absorbing, at times even obstructionist. In its self-delighted preening, the narration almost seems to ignore what is happening in the plot.[18] The play of the language is, in fact, a kind of linguistic diversion from the main event of the day, which occurs offstage: Molly's adultery with Boylan. For while the writing amuses itself with linguistic games, while the characters, including Bloom, amuse themselves with music, Boylan amuses himself with Molly. To put it another way, the reader is absorbed by the verbal surface of the prose just as Bloom momentarily escapes his loneliness, specifically his thoughts of his wife's adultery, by listening to music. The writing, like the music for the characters, is a form of play that substitutes pleasure for pain. The rhetorical play in part derives from the "gap" between reality and language: if language is basically defective as an instrument for transcribing the sounds and experiences of life, it still makes an exceptional tinker toy. If it can never really aspire to the condition of music for fear of becoming ridiculous, its patterns of sound can generate interesting distortions of sense.

[17] Richard Ellmann, *Ulysses on the Liffey* (New York: Oxford University Press, 1972), pp. 104-105.

[18] It must be noted that Bloom's interior monologue provides an anchor for the reader in the chapter. Even if the narrative no longer displays a stable narrating "self," a palpable sense of the human self is maintained by the interior monologue of the main character. In chapters like "Eumaeus," "Cyclops," and "Ithaca," we lose the sound of the character's inner monologue, which "defamiliarizes" the book even further.

The knowledge of the "gap" between reality and language leads, then, to a sense of liberation as well as loss.

And yet, paradoxically, the deliberately oblique treatment of the action functions as a strategy for capturing the pain being repressed. The avoidance makes us aware of the pain, just as Bloom's sudden reminder of Molly's meeting with Boylan (occasioned by the coincidence of his watch stopping at four-thirty) hits him with greater force because he has tried to forget it. An example of this oblique treatment is the sentence "Bloom looped, unlooped, noded, disnoded" (p. 274). Twisting language in a verbal imitation of Bloom's game with an elastic band, the writing expresses Bloom's pain not by direct statement but in the rhythms of the prose. The prose bides its time, Bloom bides his time; both gestures make us aware of what is *not* confronted, either verbally in the narration or mentally by Bloom. Another example of this oblique treatment of emotion is the following: "Under the sandwichbell lay on a bier of bread one last, one lonely, last sardine of summer. Bloom alone" (p. 289). In this example, the avoidance comes in the form of metaphoric substitution. In "Sirens," our sense of the emotional as well as the empirical reality is stubbornly maintained throughout the verbal machinations of the prose.

V

"Cyclops," "Nausicaa," and "Oxen of the Sun": Borrowed Styles

"Cyclops"

In "Cyclops," the initial style of narration disappears. Replacing the norm are two stylistic "masks": a narrative persona, a bard-cum-barfly who speaks in a low Dublin idiom, and a series of parodies that interrupt the narrator's verbal monologue. The first "mask" can be naturalized according to novelistic conventions and, in a book that has increasingly divorced itself from a narrator, the sudden appearance of this person is, for the most part, reassuring. No matter how "limited" a point of view he represents, the presence of a definitive narrative self is comforting. Despite the inevitable questions about the reliability and temporality of his narrative,[1] which do provide some discomfiture, the narrator provides relief after the fragmentation of "Sirens." For the first time in *Ulysses* we encounter an actual narrative persona.

But the parodies provide a much greater obstacle to the naturalizing process, for like the headings in "Aeolus" or the narrative excursus in "Sirens," these ballooning passages seem to arise out of nowhere. Like the language of the headings, the parodies in "Cyclops" are "written," anony-

---

[1] See David Hayman's discussion of the discomforting effect of the narrator in "Cyclops," in *James Joyce's Ulysses: Critical Essays*, ed. Clive Hart and David Hayman (Berkeley: University of California Press, 1974), pp. 244-265.

mous, and public—they too are difficult to read as the product of a second narrative voice in the text.[2] Clearly, the rules of the game have been radically altered in "Cyclops." The story appears to be told twice, once in the single voice of the narrator, once in the parodic forms of various literary and subliterary styles. The parodies themselves expand before our eyes: cataloguing and describing in exhaustive detail, the book now exploits its encyclopedic potential. Having stretched, bent, and broken the initial style in "Wandering Rocks" and "Sirens," Joyce created a chapter of multiple styles and encyclopedic detail. The narrative norm disappears; excess becomes the mode of writing.[3]

The relationship between the monologue and the interpolations is complex. In the schema of *Ulysses* that he sent to Carlo Linati, Joyce called the narrative technique of the chapter "alternating asymmetry,"[4] a term that aptly describes the skewed relationship between the narrative and the parodies. Like the headings in "Aeolus," the parodies seem to be generated in the text from some insignificant event or comment in the narrative. And like the headings, the passages give an exaggerated version of the "original" story, this time by expanding rather than encapsulating it. (In many cases, one can imagine the interpolated passages in "Cyclops" as the stories that could accompany the headings in "Aeolus.") The language and the length of the passages are both inflated. For example, Joe's question to the citizen, "And how's the old heart, citizen?" unleashes a torrent of hyperbolic language in a parody of epic description:

---

[2] Although Marilyn French acknowledges these characteristics of the parodies, she describes them as representing a second narrator (an "off-scene narrator"). This seems to me to falsify our experience of the heterogeneity of the parodies. See French, *The Book as World: James Joyce's Ulysses* (Cambridge, Mass.: Harvard University Press, 1976), p. 141.

[3] According to Michael Groden, the germ of the chapter was the series of parodies rather than the first-person narration. See *Ulysses in Progress* (Princeton: Princeton University Press, 1977), p. 118.

[4] Reprinted in Richard Ellmann, *Ulysses on the Liffey* (New York: Oxford University Press, 1972), Appendix.

"In rhythmic resonance the loud strong hale reverberations of his formidable heart thundered rumblingly" (p. 296). Likewise, the citizen's plea to "save the trees" suddenly spawns a society page report of the coniferous wedding of Miss Fir Conifer and Jean Wyse de Neaulan (p. 327).

Through this inflation, the interpolated passages parody aspects of the original story. They satirize the excesses of the characters and, by extension, of Irish society. The citizen's sentimental patriotism is mocked when his plea for reforestry is transformed into the chic wedding of the trees, an event that will insure a new tree population. Bob Doran's sentimentality over Dignam's death is mocked in the epic passage "And mournful and with a heavy heart he bewept the extinction of that beam of heaven" (p. 303). Irish patriotism, romanticism, and sentimentality are the primary targets in the parodies. "Cyclops" is the most satiric and "Irish" of the chapters in *Ulysses*, that is, the parodies are directed against specific aspects of Irish society.

But characteristically in *Ulysses*, Joyce focuses on society's discourse, that "anonymous voice" of culture that codifies the culture's received ideas (or "myths," as Roland Barthes has called them).[5] The parodies represent a kind of travestied choric expression of Irish consciousness, which includes, among others, the collective voice of the contemporary press (found in "Aeolus") and the collective voice of the epic. The parodies in "Cyclops" are double-tiered: they parody society by parodying its forms of discourse. If Joyce exposes "myths" of culture, he does it by showing the rhetoric that perpetuates the deception. In "Cyclops," he parodies the voices of culture—the styles used to tell Irish stories, past and present.

The passages parody the various forms of Irish propaganda—language that romanticizes and simplifies the Irish past and present. Hugh Kenner has said that the passages

[5] Roland Barthes, *Mythologies*, trans. Annette Lavers (New York: Hill and Wang, 1972), especially pp. 109-159.

parody "varieties of nationalistic literature" such as "Ireland's idyllic past, the Ossianic hero, a journalistic version of an Ossianic *geste*."[6] But the passages parody language that is political and propagandistic in a broader sense: they parody a language that is a ready-made deception, a kind of sloganeering. Instead of a picture of Ireland, this kind of language offers a glossy print. The glossy print is, of course, exactly what *Ulysses* refuses to be; in it, Joyce reveals Dublin and Dublin's citizens, warts and all. In "Cyclops," Joyce parodies Ireland's mythic self-image, incorporated in a language that inflates its glories and suppresses its faults. We have seen other romanticized self-images in Joyce's writing, largely through the use of free indirect discourse in stories like "Clay" in *Dubliners* or in Father Conmee's free indirect discourse in "Wandering Rocks" ("He was humane and honoured there" [p. 223]). In "Cyclops," it is Ireland seen through its language that concerns Joyce. The parodies present what Hugh Kenner has called "pseudo histories" of Ireland. In lieu of the history of "force" and "hatred," we find a myth of "an idyllic past"; instead of the anti-Semitism and divisiveness of the present, we find the myth of "real Irish fun without vulgarity" (p. 307).

The two major narrative forms of "myth making" in the passages are the epic, the narrative form of the past, and the newspaper item, the narrative form of the present.[7] These

---

[6] Hugh Kenner, *Dublin's Joyce* (1956; reprint ed., Boston: Beacon Press, 1962), pp. 254-255.

[7] Other forms in the parodies include baby talk, novelese, graffiti, and the Apostles' Creed, among others. The newspaper item, however, is the most pervasive. Marilyn French says that "the chapter contains a newspaper in miniature, with a sports column (the boxing match); reports of a debate, a hanging, an earthquake, and a religious ceremony; special features on a famous handkerchief, ancient Gaelic sports, and physical culture; a literary column on canine verse; a society page devoted to a wedding and a farewell ceremony; and a science page devoted to the findings of Bloom alias Herr Professor Luitpold Blumenduft" (*The Book as World: James Joyce's Ulysses*, p. 148). According to Phillip Herring, Joyce drew on newspapers from around June 16, 1904, for many incidents in "Cyclops." See *Joyce's Notes and Early Drafts*

forms are not always separated from each other. In fact, some of the comedy of the chapter depends upon the degeneration of one form into another. A closer look at specific passages will illustrate the way both past and present narrative forms are parodied.

In the first epic parody, we are offered a description of the Dublin area of St. Michan's parish traversed by the nameless narrator and Joe Hynes on their way to Barney Kiernan's. The narrator summarizes the walk: "So we went around by the Linenhall barracks and the back of the courthouse talking of one thing or another" (p. 293). This is all the description he gives, but it immediately engenders a parody that begins "In Inisfail the fair there lies a land, the land of holy Michan." The Dublin area is seen through the rosy-colored glasses of epic and romance. In its epic manifestation, the Dublin market is "a shining palace." The glory of the past is resuscitated. But what is interesting about this passage and most of the other epic parodies in the chapter is that it is a parody of an attempted *revival* of an archaic, literary form. In their *Notes for Joyce*, Gifford and Seidman gloss almost all of these medieval or epic passages as parodies of modern (nineteenth- and twentieth-century) translations or reworkings of Irish myth.[8] The twentieth century looks at nineteenth-century adaptations of dead forms. According to *Notes for Joyce* and Thornton's *Allusions in Ulysses*, the preceding example parodies James Clarence Mangan's translation of "Aldfrid's Itinerary," "a poem in Irish by Aldfrid, a seventh-century king of Northumbria."[9]

---

for Ulysses: Selections from the Buffalo Collection, ed. Phillip F. Herring (Charlottesville: University Press of Virginia, 1977), p. 146. The importance of "journalese" strongly links the "Cyclops" chapter with "Aeolus," and, in fact, Joyce originally envisioned much the same cast of characters in both episodes. See Groden, *Ulysses in Progress*, pp. 133-134.

[8] See Don Gifford and Robert J. Seidman, *Notes for Joyce: An Annotation of James Joyce's Ulysses* (New York: E. P. Dutton Co., Inc., 1974), p. 258-311.

[9] Gifford and Seidman, *Notes for Joyce*, pp. 259-260. See also Weldon

Even if one is deprived of the benefit of these notes, the internal incongruity of the passage is evidence that a rather inept revival is taking place. After the "straight" imitation of Irish legend at the beginning of the passage just mentioned, comic exaggeration begins with the catalogue of fish in the streams. Soon the diction shifts drastically: "And there rises a shining palace whose crystal glittering roof is seen by mariners who traverse the extensive sea in barks built expressly for that purpose" (p. 294). The levels and kinds of diction comically clash, as if a present-day writer rather unskillfully attempted to resuscitate the dead phrases of an obsolete genre. A phrase such as "extremely large wains" sounds like a student's attempt to use the poorly digested contents of a lecture on Irish history and myth.[10] The epic catalogues are transformed into a tourist catalogue: "In the mild breezes of the west and of the east the lofty trees wave in different directions their first class foliage, the wafty sycamore, the Lebanonian cedar, the exalted plane-tree, the eugenic eucalyptus and other ornaments of the arboreal world with which that region is thoroughly well supplied." Irish epic modulates into the selling of Ireland. The parody displays the same hybridization of romantic literature and glossy postcard first seen in some of the headings in "Aeolus" (for example, "ERIN, GREEN GEM OF THE SILVER SEA").

Thornton, *Allusions in Ulysses: A Line-by-line Reference to Joyce's Complex Symbolism* (1961; reprint ed., New York: Simon and Schuster, 1973), pp. 256-257.

[10] The degeneration of pastiche into parody in these passages is reminiscent of what happens when Don Quixote attempts to use the language of romance:

> Scarce had the ruddy Apollo spread the golden threads of his lovely hair over the broad and spacious face of the earth, and scarcely had the forked tongues of the little painted birds greeted with mellifluous harmony the coming of the rosy Aurora who, leaving the soft bed of her jealous husband, showed herself at the doors and balconies of the Manchegan horizon. . . .

See Cervantes, *The Adventures of Don Quixote*, trans. J. M. Cohen (Baltimore: Penguin Books, Inc., 1950), Part 1, Chapter 2, p. 36.

While the citizen talks "in his best Fenian style"[11] about past glories, the deteriorated epic passages parody the attempt to revive old myths. As if by incantation, the dead heroes of the past are summoned in the epic catalogues. Indeed, everything is revived in the chapter: from Paddy Dignam to the Irish language, from Gaelic sports to the "ranns of ancient Celtic bards" (to which the dog-poet's verses bear "striking resemblance"). If the Irish Literary Revival is the specific object of parody here, the Irish penchant for "embalming" the past, as Kenner puts it, is the general object. And, as Kenner has said, it is through his language that the Irishman preserves the past.[12]

But Ireland's "mythic self-image" is perpetuated by the contemporary Irish voices as well as the archaic voice of the epic. Nostalgia for the past is only one form of sentimentality parodied in the chapter. Joyce parodies the language of the present that is just as inflated and deceptive as the styles of the past. He parodies a journalistic account of an execution, a form of verbal whitewash that makes the execution sound like a picnic: "Special quick excursion trains and upholstered charabancs had been provided for the comfort of our country cousins" (pp. 306-307). He parodies the fastidious voices of "civilization": the story of a fight is told in the civilized language of a legal contract; the hanged man's erection is disguised underneath pseudoscientific mumbojumbo; British persecution of the Irish is masked in religious ceremony. The emblem of this myth-making contemporary voice is the newspaper, the genteel "allembracing" voice of the press that legitimizes society's clichés. But all of the "discourses" of Irish society—the medical, legal, religious, scientific, and social—conspire in this deception.

---

[11] See Joyce's letter to Frank Budgen, 19 June 1919: "The chapter of the *Cyclops* is being lovingly moulded in the way you know. . . . He [the Fenian] unburdens his soul about the Saxo-Angles in the best Fenian style." In *Letters of James Joyce*, Vol. 1, ed. Stuart Gilbert (New York: The Viking Press, 1957), p. 126.

[12] See Kenner, *Dublin's Joyce*, p. 9.

All of these discourses are a kind of propaganda or encoded language that propels itself forward without the necessity of an individual speaker. The length of the parodies (particularly the gigantic catalogues) contributes to this feeling that the discourse is a machine without a driver, which will stop only when it runs out of fuel. But the mechanistic feeling of the discourse is also a function of its precoded language. Much of the comedy of the parodies in "Cyclops" depends upon the language riding like a steamroller over the content: the rhythms of the Apostles' Creed are intact, gliding over a totally inappropriate content. Similarly, the serviceable pseudointellectual literary criticism of the Literary Revival is hilariously applied to the works of Garryowen, the dog.

The mélange of styles in "Cyclops" has two important philosophical implications. First, it expresses Joyce's skepticism about any one mode of writing. Arnold Goldman says of this catalogue of styles in "Cyclops": "As in the *Wake* the incipient encyclopaedism promotes a sense of randomness and arbitrariness of any one particular 'interpretation' of the action, or direction of the narrative. Where so many are available at all times, the choice of one mode of vision . . . is demoted in importance."[13] Secondly, the interpolated passages demonstrate the problem of the modern writer: the styles of the past are available only as parody and the discourse of the present only as cliché. To quote Joyce in a different context, the styles are "scorched," no longer a possible medium.[14]

And yet, paradoxically, while he tells us through parody that the dead styles cannot be resuscitated, Joyce revitalizes old forms. In "Cyclops," comedy and stylistic energy infuse the parodies. The zest of the parodies takes over their function as literary criticism. While showing us the limitations of language, the writing looses its comic power. For ex-

[13] Arnold Goldman, *The Joyce Paradox: Form and Freedom in His Fiction* (London: Routledge & Kegan Paul, 1966), p. 93.

[14] Letter to Harriet Weaver, 20 July 1919, *Letters*, Vol. 1, pp. 128-129.

ample, the sudden capitulation of the epic into the tourist catalogue deliberately acts out a comic misfiring in the writing, as if the style, like a child's wind-up toy, were winding down. In the parodies of "Cyclops," Joyce plays games with genre, superimposing one on the other, mixing styles of discourse in deliberately incongruous ways. More Rabelaisian in "Cyclops" than in any other chapter, Joyce deliberately flouts notions of decorum and norm. His nose-thumbing at convention is very much like Rabelais' in *Gargantua and Pantagruel*, both in its mélange of discourses[15] and its exorbitant catalogues. In "Cyclops," Joyce gives us the literary equivalent of Bloom's fart. One finds in "Cyclops," as one does not in "Oxen of the Sun," a kind of slapstick craziness in the writing; more than any other chapter, "Cyclops" is meant to seem improvisational, as if the lid keeping down excess and craziness in the preceding chapters had been lifted. There is a deliberate arbitrariness to the writing that is very different from the more craftsmanlike performance of "Oxen of the Sun."

The various catalogues of Irish heroes (p. 296), of clergy (p. 317), and of the scenes of the Irish landscape (p. 332) in the chapter are the most obvious dramatizations of this sudden erratic behavior in the narrative, as if the writing were seized with some mad compulsion. Many of the Gargantuan catalogues begin in ostensible rationality, only to explode the bonds of the category they establish. What begins as a principle of ordering becomes a vehicle of illogic; the category of Irish heroes that commences with Cuchulin suddenly includes the world ("... Goliath, Horace Wheatley

---

[15] See, for example, the battle of the monks and guards in *Gargantua and Pantagruel*, in which the discourse of romance and the discourse of a medical treatise are superimposed. "Whipping it out in a trice, he brought it down upon the archer on his right. The blow severed the jugular veins and the parotid arteries and the throat to the uvula, split the thyroid glands and, hacking further, opened the spinal marrow between the second and third vertebrae. The first archer fell dead at his feet." (See *Gargantua and Pantagruel*, trans. Jacques LeClercq (New York: Modern Library-Random House, 1944), Book 1, Chapter 44, p. 126.

. . . Dante Alighieri . . ." [pp.296-297]). But there are other more subtle examples of the slapstick quality that results from Joyce's use of the literary and subliterary machinery. The following passage, describing Bloom's exit from the pub, illustrates this farcical quality as well as the comic use of the epic style:

> The milkwhite dolphin tossed his mane and, rising in the golden poop, the helmsman spread the bellying sail upon the wind and stood off forward with all sail set, the spinnaker to larboard. A many comely nymphs drew nigh to starboard and to larboard and, clinging to the sides of the noble bark, they linked their shining forms as doth the cunning wheelwright when he fashions about the heart of his wheel the equidistant rays whereof each one is sister to another and he binds them all with an outer ring and giveth speed to the feet of men whenas they ride to a hosting or contend for the smile of ladies fair. Even so did they come and set them, those willing nymphs, the undying sisters. And they laughed, sporting in a circle of their foam: and the bark clave the waves. (P. 341)

The passage, of course, describes Bloom's exit in mock-epic style, but the particular way that Joyce uses the mock-epic is worth noticing. The passage itself is magically spawned by a passing metaphor of the narrator's: "And he got them out as quick as he could, Jack Power and Crofton or whatever you call him and him in the middle of them letting on to be *all at sea* up with them on the bloody jaunting car" (my italics). The "scene," then, is a dramatic projection of a figure of speech. The passage begins in ceremony, the "milkwhite dolphin" and "golden poop" suggesting that we are witnessing the departure of Cleopatra Bloom. The first sentence is meticulous in its nautical description. But it is in the next sentence that things begin to happen in the writing: "to starboard and to larboard" sounds suspicious, a case of a rhyme unresisted, a purely verbal diversion (of the kind we find with another sailor at the end of "Ithaca"—"Sinbad the Sailor and Tinbad the Tailor and Jinbad the Jailer"). The Homeric simile that follows clinches the case, as the narrative is carried away by its own stately grandeur. By the end of the sentence, the "vehicle" of the metaphor has become a literal vehicle that takes us back to the "tenor" of the metaphor. Comparing the maidens around the ship to the spokes of a wheel, the simile suddenly has the wheels traveling toward the maidens ("ladies fair"). Although the passage does parody the inept revival of Homeric poetry, it is itself a funny "revival," inspired by the drop of a metaphor, degenerating into the tangle of its own metaphoric language.

In revealing the parodic state of language, Joyce paradoxically opens up the novel to a virtuoso exhibition and expands the limits of the text. Although the passages represent the limitations of various modes of writing, they are narrative excursuses that allow for an investigation of both linguistic and dramatic possibilities. For in the chapter, Joyce flaunts the arbitrariness of style, trying out various stylistic possibilities from the flotsam and jetsam of linguistic resources. The parodies are narrative excursuses in which various possibilities of writing are explored while the forward motion of the linear narrative is halted. These ballooning narrative interludes are prepared for in the shorter linguistic passages of "Sirens" that rewrite and revise the narrative. As in "Sirens," the parodic revision exists out of the space and time of the action of the story, as if the narrative were frozen while the writing took a journey of its own. The writing of a history continues, but the history of the writing is of primary interest. Robert Scholes, speaking of the catalogues in the parodies, says that in them "displaced possibilities are allowed to sport themselves."[16] It seems to me that this is what happens in the parodic interludes themselves. A strange linguistic "space" opens up as the parodies

[16] Robert Scholes, "*Ulysses*: A Structuralist Perspective," in *Ulysses: Fifty Years*, ed. Thomas F. Staley (1972; reprint ed., Bloomington: Indiana University Press, 1974), pp. 168-169.

demonstrate (paradoxically) something that is no longer possible. For the dead styles of the past and present are used by the modern text as parody. In "Cyclops," Joyce demonstrates the "failure" of style with more energy than many writers display its success.

This use of other styles in "Cyclops" reveals Joyce's particular brand of "self-exposing plagiarism," a term coined by Geoffrey Hartman to describe the self-conscious derivativeness of certain works of literature, modern literature in particular: instead of making a claim for its originality, Hartman says, these works flaunt the derivativeness of their language.[17] In "Cyclops," the book's initial style, the author's stylistic signature, disappears. It is drowned out by the texts of culture, the voices of the Irish past and present. In essence, private signature is blotted out by rubber stamp. But Joyce's parodies are rhetorical masks, lavishly and extravagantly donned; the borrowed styles are mined for their comic potential. The chapter presents Joyce as "bricoleur," the writer who can create nothing original.[18] In a way, "Cyclops" spells the end of the image of the Romantic artist with which Stephen (and one must assume Joyce) flirted, the artist, that is, who could create from his personal anguish alone. "Cyclops" demonstrates with a flourish that the writer indeed creates out of other writers. He is a parasite, a user of other men's language.[19] What saves the "plagiarism" from expressing the kind of nihilism that Hartman links to this type of derivativeness is precisely the mileage Joyce gets out of the borrowed forms and styles. By using the stylistic

[17] Geoffrey Hartman, Letter, *PMLA* 92 (March 1977): 307-308.

[18] For a discussion of Joyce as "bricoleur" in *Finnegans Wake*, see Margot Norris, *The Decentered Universe of Finnegans Wake: A Structuralist Analysis* (Baltimore: The Johns Hopkins University Press, 1974), pp. 130ff.

[19] "Have you ever noticed, when you get an idea, how much *I* can make of it?" Joyce asked Budgen, and this image of Joyce as what Richard Ellmann calls "an inspired cribber" applies to his use of language even more than to his thought. See Ellmann's introduction to Stanislaus Joyce's *My Brother's Keeper: James Joyce's Early Years*, ed. Richard Ellman (London: Faber and Faber, 1958), pp. 19-20.

and generic resources of the past and present, he continues his story of Dublin and expands the form of the novel.

The narrative excursuses in "Cyclops," however, develop dramatic as well as stylistic possibilities. They offer a dramatic interlude that allows an expansion of the possibilities of plot. The slightest verbal suggestion in the narrative can lead to a dramatization (like the metaphor "at sea" mentioned previously). The nameless narrator calls Bloom the "prudent member," and an epic passage follows in which Bloom is metamorphosed into "O'Bloom, the son of Rory ... Impervious to fear ... Rory's son: he of the prudent soul" (p. 297). The dramatization of things suggested in the narrative points forward to "Circe," a place in the text where an imaginary stage rises in the midst of the novel. In fact, Paddy Dignam's spirit, which communes with the living in a parody in "Cyclops" and asks, rather incongruously, for a quart of buttermilk, pops up in "Circe" to inform us that "That buttermilk didn't agree with me" (p. 473).[20] Black Liz, who makes her debut in "Cyclops," also appears in the drama of "Circe." In his discussion of "Cyclops," David Hayman introduces the notion of pantomime. He says that the passages operate like little "skits."[21] Indeed, the characters don costumes in these episodes, as they participate in a pantomime: Bloom becomes "Herr Leopold," Martin Cunningham and Jack Power become trusty knights. Again, the parodies are an artistic strategy to expand the limits of the novel form.

This kind of actualization of a possibility is a common modern literary theme: one can instructively compare Joyce with T. S. Eliot in this respect. In "Burnt Norton," the poet asks how the modern poem can present vision in the

[20] The report of this scene, including Dignam's request for buttermilk, resembles Don Quixote's report of his adventure in the Cave of Montesinos. The common element is, of course, farce. See *Don Quixote*, Part 2, Chapter 23, pp. 614-624.

[21] Hayman, "Cyclops," p. 273.

language available to it, and his first answer is that vision is impossible: "What might have been is an abstraction/ Remaining a perpetual possibility/ Only in a world of speculation."[22] But, paradoxically, the poem opens up, "abstraction" becomes vision, and the rose garden appears. For Joyce, possibility is actualized not as vision but as parody and farce, which rescue the modern text just as they destroy the writing of the "novel." As his career developed, Joyce grew skeptical of rose gardens. Whereas Eliot believed that "moments of inattention" could lead to vision, Joyce comically shows (especially in "Eumaeus") that these moments are just as likely to produce cliché.

The parodies in "Cyclops," however, have two "objects": as well as parodying literature and literary styles, they parody the actions and the words of the characters. They rewrite not only other literature but also the plot of the story. Almost every verbal expression of feeling or belief on the part of the characters automatically generates its own parody: the citizen's declaration of patriotism, Bloom's expressions of sympathy and his definition of love. As in "Aeolus," every attempt to be eloquent is debased, and every attempt to conclude ends in stupidity. All language is treated as the words of Dan Dawson in "Aeolus" and "Sirens"—it is parodied and mimicked, its excesses exposed. "Cyclops" illustrates that there is no "privileged" style. In it, no language is allowed to stand unparodied. Just as no "scrupulous meanness" prevents the narrative from lapsing into apparent sentimentality and stupidity, no prudence or taciturnity can protect the characters from the same fate.

In certain parts of the text, this can lead to what seems like a ruthless and defensive retraction of eloquence and feeling. Despite the theoretical and artistic justifications for the parodies, one feels that in certain instances, they are angrier than any previous "demonstrations" of the stupidity

---

[22] T. S. Eliot, *Four Quartets*, in *The Complete Poems and Plays: 1909-1950* (New York: Harcourt, Brace & World, Inc., 1958), p. 117.

or inadequacy of language. The primary example of this is the passage that mocks Bloom's definition of love. Bloom says, "Force, hatred, history, all that. That's not life for men and women, insult and hatred. And everybody knows that it's the very opposite of that that is really life. What? says Alf. Love, says Bloom. I mean the opposite of hatred" (p. 333). The mimicking passage that follows turns Bloom's statement into a kind of childish chant: "Love loves to love love. Nurse loves the new chemist. Constable 14A loves Mary Kelly. Gerty MacDowell loves the boy that has the bicycle." Bloom's definition is transformed into an exercise in conjugating the verb "love" (a kind of conjugation already seen in "Aeolus" and "Sirens"). The last sentence of the passage sums up the clichés present in the chapter. "Everybody loves somebody" encapsulates romantic clichés and society's mythic self-image (that is, the tidy fictions about the love and kindness in Irish society presented in the journalistic "texts"). And "God loves everybody" parodies religious clichés.

This passage is one of the most explicit examples in *Ulysses* of the debased currency of language. Words like "love" are so contaminated by overuse and misuse that they become meaningless. More specifically, Joyce represents in the passage the inadequacy of language to convey *emotion*; the language of feeling has degenerated into sentimental cant. The parody illustrates what Flaubert says in *Madame Bovary*, that "the human tongue is like a cracked cauldron on which we beat our tunes to set a bear dancing when we would make the stars weep with our melodies."[23] But Joyce's parody ignores the qualification that Flaubert makes in his novel after the above quotation: that despite the prostitution of language, one should be able to distinguish between sincere and hypocritical expressions of feeling. The parody in *Ulysses* ignores Bloom's sincerity; Bloom's definition is, in

[23] Gustave Flaubert, *Madame Bovary*, ed. Paul de Man (New York: W. W. Norton, 1965), p. 138.

fact, neither a deception nor a cliché. The mocking words of the citizen lead the way to the parody by transforming Bloom's words into slogan and cliché: "A new apostle to the gentiles . . . Universal love" and "He's a nice pattern of a Romeo and Juliet." But the point is that Bloom's words do not offer the sentimentalized version of history displayed in the interpolated "texts," for they acknowledge instead the nightmare of history ("Force, hatred, history . . . insult and hatred"). Unlike other parodies of the characters' rhetoric and sentimentality, this passage mocks a statement that is sincere and unsentimental. There is a difference between Bloom's statements and others parodied in the chapter. For example, the citizen's exclamation: "*Sinn Fein! . . . Sinn fein amhain*! The friends we love are by our side and the foes we hate before us" (p. 306) becomes "the last farewell was affecting in the extreme," a parody that mocks the kind of specious "love" of friends who gather to watch an execution. This chauvinistic sloganeering is already a simplified view of life in language, a form of propaganda. Similarly, the mock eighteenth-century novelistic dialogue between Bob Doran and Bloom parodies Doran's sloppy, drunken sentimentality. In contrast, Bloom's words are unsentimental and forthright.

The effect of the parody is a moral leveling much more aggressive than the one engendered by the headings of "Aeolus." One senses here that the theoretical basis for this mockery or belief might be accompanied by Joyce's defense against his own feeling, a defense that is transferred to the behavior of the text. Bloom offers a "conclusion" about human nature, the kind of conclusion that easily can be parodied, and Joyce believes, I think, with Flaubert, that to conclude is an act of stupidity. But the parody seems excessively harsh, as if Joyce were retracting his own statement, as if he felt he had confessed *not* in a foreign language. One has difficulty distinguishing here between an implied philosophy of language and a fear of sentimentality, between the mechanical component of parody and cliché and the author's need to mock his own feelings.[24]

In any case, Joyce's skepticism about eloquence and sentimentality is funneled through the persona of the narrator as well as the parodies (a technical device he relinquishes in "Eumaeus"). The misanthropic yet comedic narrator spends much of his time sneering at the "eloquence" and the sentimentality of other characters, and his skepticism anticipates the parodic commentary that follows. The narrator scorns Bob Doran's maudlin reaction to Paddy Dignam's death: "And Bob Doran starts doing the weeps about Paddy Dignam, true as you're there" (p. 302). Doran's "eloquence" ("The finest man, says he, snivelling, the finest purest character") occasions the narrator's derision: "The tear is bloody near your eye. Talking through his bloody hat." The parody that follows shortly is an extension of the narrator's mockery. In it, both Doran's exaggerated emotion and the hyperbole of his language are parodied: "And mournful and with a heavy heart he bewept the extinction of that beam of heaven" (p. 303).

Bloom's sentimentality and rhetoric are a favorite target of the narrator's scorn, and again his comments serve as a cue to the emergent parody. The narrator says:

> And of course Bloom had to have his say too about if a fellow had a rower's heart violent exercise was bad. I declare to my antimacassar if you took up a straw from the bloody floor and if you said to Bloom: *Look at, Bloom. Do you see that straw? That's a straw.* Declare to my aunt he'd talk about it for an hour so he would and talk steady. (P. 316)

A parodic inflated report of the "most interesting discussion" and "magnificent oration" follows. The narrator's scorn of strong nationalistic feelings as well as his mockery of the

---

[24] This is a question that cannot be answered definitively. Joyce's philosophy of language is consistent, whether the personal defensiveness is involved or not. His belief in the inherent vulnerability of language justifies the parody.

rhetoric used in the service of this nationalism is translated into parodic form.

Since dialogue as well as events is filtered through the critical consciousness of the narrator, he can choose to report the dialogue indirectly rather than verbatim—he can place a screen between the reader and the characters. Some of the discussion on capital punishment, for example, is summarized by the narrator: "So they start talking about capital punishment and of course Bloom comes out with the why and the wherefore and all the codology of the business" (p. 304). Bloom's speech is at first quoted directly by the narrator: "That can be explained by science, says Bloom. It's only a natural phenomenon, don't you see, because on account of the . . ." (the ellipses occur in the text). Suddenly, the narrator aborts the direct quotation with an ellipsis that is then followed by indirect discourse: "And then he starts with his jawbreakers about phenomenon and science and this phenomenon and the other phenomenon." Then the parody of Bloom's pseudoscientific knowledge begins: "The distinguished scientist Herr Professor Luitpold Blumenduft tendered medical evidence to the effect that. . . ." The narration moves from direct reporting to indirect reporting in the first-person narration and then to parody. In the ellipsis, the narrator transforms Bloom's words into predictable clichés, as if to say we need not hear what he is saying because it is all formulaic. He turns Bloom into a cliché-dispensing lecturer, a transformation in turn exaggerated in the parody. (This is a fate that befalls Bloom in "Eumaeus" as well.) Because of his "control" over the narrative, the narrator's presence prepares for the indirect reporting of "Eumaeus" and the alienation of "Ithaca." In "Cyclops," the interior monologue of Leopold Bloom disappears along with the initial style of narration. Whereas in "Sirens" the consciousness of the main character acts as an anchor to the reader in the face of the bizarre narrative antics, in "Cyclops," the sound of Bloom's mind thinking is gone, and his dialogue is vulnerable to the narrator's "rewriting." The new hostility toward Bloom is reflected technically in the shift from direct to indirect reporting. In this sense, the increasing alienation from the character is compounded rather than introduced in the parody.

"Cyclops" is a chapter in which conventions and norms are flouted and parodies lead to the expansion of the text. The destruction of order seems to me to represent both Joyce's skepticism about the ordering of experience in language *and* a personal desire to be above the constraints that writing usually imposes. If in *Ulysses*, paragraph yields to non sequitur, and convention to parody and exaggeration, this signifies both Joyce's philosophy of writing and a kind of fantasy of omnipotence, a desire to transcend all logical, formal, and emotional constraints.[25]

"Nausicaa"

The overused and misused language of feeling parodied in the "Cyclops" passage, "Love loves to love love" (p. 333), is given its due in the sentimental language of the next chapter.[26] To begin the "Nausicaa" chapter is to feel that one has stumbled into a bad Victorian novel: "The summer evening had begun to fold the world in its mysterious embrace" (p. 346). In the second sentence of the chapter, however, the "fine writing" of the romantic novel is exaggerated

[25] Richard Ellmann says that "Joyce's politics and aesthetics were one. For him the act of writing was also, and indissolubly, an act of liberating." See *The Consciousness of Joyce* (New York: Oxford University Press, 1977), p. 90. The connection between the act of writing and the act of liberation is very complex in *Ulysses*. It derives, it seems to me, both from defensive needs and philosophical beliefs. And, too, liberation from the past and an almost oppressive connection with the past are intertwined.

[26] In its widest application, the "Love loves to love love" passage parodies not only the language of feeling but all language that is tainted by overuse. It is in "Eumaeus" that Joyce undertakes to write an entire chapter of his book using only this battered language. If "Nausicaa" is his *Madame Bovary*, "Eumaeus" is his *Bouvard et Pécuchet*.

into its purplest shade. Here one finds the unmistakable signs of parody:

> Far away in the west the sun was setting and the glow of all too fleeting day lingered lovingly on sea and strand, on the proud promontory of dear old Howth guarding as ever the waters of the bay, on the weedgrown rocks along Sandymount shore and, last but not least, on the quiet church whence there streamed forth at times upon the stillness, the voice of prayer to her who is in her pure radiance a beacon ever to the stormtossed heart of man, Mary, star of the sea.

The excessive alliteration and the precious diction first introduced in Dan Dawson's speech and the cheap rhetorical tricks of the headings in "Aeolus" are generously applied in this passage.

What Joyce presents in the first half of "Nausicaa" is the indirect monologue of Gerty MacDowell, translated into a language appropriate to her; he parodies her sentimental mind by parodying the second-rate fiction that has nurtured it. As in *Dubliners* (and in the description of Father Conmee in "Wandering Rocks"), the self-image of the character dominates the narrative account. Here is the description of that "specimen of winsome Irish girlhood," Gerty MacDowell: "The waxen pallor of her face was almost spiritual in its ivorylike purity though her rosebud mouth was a genuine Cupid's bow, Greekly perfect. Her hands were of finely veined alabaster with tapering fingers and as white as lemon juice and queen of ointments could make them though it was not true that she used to wear kid gloves in bed or take a milk footbath either" (p. 348).[27] Gerty wonders at one point why "you couldn't eat something poetical like violets

---

[27] In Flaubert's *Dictionary of Accepted Ideas*, next to the word "alabaster" is written: "Its use is to describe the most beautiful parts of a woman's body." See *Dictionary*, trans. Jacques Barzun (New York: New Directions, 1954), p. 14. (Published with *Bouvard and Pécuchet*.)

or roses" (p. 352), and it is clear from her description that she has ingested a complete diet of romantic clichés.

The close connection between character and style seen in the free indirect discourse of *Dubliners* and in the first part of *Ulysses* is restored. In "Nausicaa," however, the prose is more exaggerated and obviously parodic than in *Dubliners*, the linguistic case against the character is more damning. The description of Gerty is a classic example of what Wayne Booth calls "stable irony"—irony that depends upon the fact that some incongruity in the statement acts as a clue to the reader that the passage cannot be taken "straight."[28] The description of Gerty incorporates clichés of romantic fiction such as "finely veined alabaster," but it implicitly contrasts them with phrases like "lemon juice" and "queen of ointments" which come from the advertisements in ladies' magazines. The pretense behind Gerty's self-image is exposed. If Gerty, like Emma Bovary, aspires to turn life into literature, her romantic model is literature once removed, filtered through the magazines.

In fact, Gerty is a kind of poor man's Emma Bovary; it is as if Joyce selected a Félicité rather than an Emma to sit for his ironic portrait. Although the parody in the chapter is well done and often very funny, its object is a particular character who is far less interesting than others we have seen in *Ulysses*, and its technique is one that has been used more radically in previous chapters. Increasingly, parody and irony have been used to expose the stupidity inherent in language. The parodies of "Cyclops," culled from a variety of sources, testify to the limits of style. But no such theoretical basis for parody is found in "Nausicaa." If the level of Gerty's diction declines in the chapter and the "two little curlyheaded boys" suddenly become the "snottynosed twins," the loss of refinement is more social than linguistic. It is not language's inability to refine itself into an accurate

[28] Wayne C. Booth, *A Rhetoric of Irony* (Chicago: The University of Chicago Press, 1974), p. 10.

representation of reality but Gerty's inability to sustain the pretense of refinement that we witness. In "Nausicaa," Joyce seems to take up the cudgel that he laid to rest when he completed *Dubliners*, returning once again to a member of the "submerged population."

The interpretive problem which results from this section of the "Nausicaa" chapter is that the use of style in the narrative would seem to lead to an interpretation that the book has rejected. The succession of styles in "Cyclops" and the different styles in the book as a whole imply that all language is, in a sense, inherently stupid, that all styles are arbitrary. But by choosing a member of the "submerged population" as the object of his parody and by allowing his prose to "formulate her in a phrase," Joyce allowed the reader and the writer to be exempt from the indictment of Gerty. If the book has demonstrated that all styles are, in a sense, equal, the parody here seems to say that some are more equal than others. The kind of obvious stable irony deployed in the narrative of "Nausicaa" narrows the scope of the parody.

The trouble with this section of "Nausicaa" is not that it represents a technical reversion but that it suggests an idea about language that the text has already rejected. It is true that in a book which deliberately sets out to destroy the concept of linear development, one cannot expect each chapter to contribute to the progressive "development" of a theme, even one as broad as "language" itself. Indeed, from chapter to chapter Joyce goes to great pains to vary the stylistic experiment, sometimes, as in the use of the first-person narrator in "Cyclops," reverting to a simpler technique of narration. But the use of a particular technique—the return to a kind of simplicity—should not work against the larger philosophical implications of the text. The first half of "Nausicaa" seems to vitiate the pluralism of the text: by condescending to the mind and style of Gerty Mac-Dowell, it suggests that there is some Olympian ground upon which the writer and reader can stand to be exempt from the charges of stupidity.

This kind of reversion in technique in the first half of "Nausicaa" is different from the temporary reappearance of both Bloom's interior monologue and the "initial style" in the chapter's second half. The latter part of the chapter is mainly interior monologue, while the former is indirect discourse. Thus the second half of "Nausicaa" affords us one last familiar look at material reality;[29] it provides a reminder in the text of that which Stephen discovered in "Proteus": the world is "there all the time without you . . . world without end" (p. 37). In the midst of the parodic second half of the book, we are reminded of the mimetic project that continues throughout the book. Just as "Aeolus" provided a proleptic view of the book's second half, this part of "Nausicaa" affords a glance backward to the book's earlier conventions by providing a look at the kind of narrative so conspicuously absent from "Oxen of the Sun," "Eumaeus," and "Ithaca."

Not only the denotative prose of the norm but also the direct interior monologue of Leopold Bloom will be missed in the succeeding chapters of increasing indirection. But here, between the mocking parody of Bloom's definition of love in "Cyclops" and the transformations of his monologue (and dialogue) in "Oxen of the Sun," "Circe," "Eumaeus," and "Ithaca," we see the Leopold Bloom of the early chapters. "All that old hill [Howth] has seen. Names change: that's all. Lovers: yum yum" (p. 377), Bloom thinks in "Nausicaa," assuming an unsentimental, mocking view of love clearly different from the one attributed to him in the parody of "Cyclops." Anticipating his transformation into "Sir Leopold" of "Oxen of the Sun" and "the elder gentleman" of "Eumaeus," the book offers us a look at the character we have known thus far.

---

[29] Sentences like "Mr Bloom effaced the letters with his slow boot" (p. 381) represent the documentation of reality in the "initial style."

"*Cyclops*," "*Nausicaa*," and "*Oxen*"

The cryptic phrases that begin the "Oxen of the Sun" chapter ("Deshil Holles Eamus. . . . Send us, bright one, light one, Horhorn quickening and wombfruit" [p.383]) are reminiscent of the overture in "Sirens." Instead of acoustic transcription, however, these phrases represent the language of ritual, a fertility prayer to the sun god. Indeed, both a bouncing baby boy and yet another inventory of prose styles are summoned into existence in the chapter. By this point in *Ulysses*, stylistic experimentation is not unexpected, but the obscurity and abundance of the language in the chapter exceed that of anything we have yet experienced.

Although the syntactic patterns of the prose become more manageable after the first two pages, our initial impression of obscurity remains throughout the chapter. The volume of language is overwhelming; the periphrasis and obfuscation that characterize the execrable Latinate jumble in the beginning of the chapter continue. At least some of the reader's uncertainty is caused by the rapid succession of styles, which prevents him from adjusting to one style long enough to concentrate on the dramatic events reported. Depending on how annoyed or lulled we are by the screen of language, we can read right past certain events that *do* occur in the chapter (or, at least, miss salient aspects of these events): a birth, a peal of thunder followed by rain, numerous discussions of birth and birth control, the first prolonged contact between Stephen and Bloom in the book. Often, when we finally do see through the fog of periphrastic language to the scene or object described, as happens when we realize that the "vat of silver with the strange fishes withouten heads" (p. 387) is a tin of sardines, we are struck by the incongruity between style and object and the deliberate overkill in the writing.

The effect of linguistic abundance is also produced by the obvious literariness of the styles and their oratorical quality. The various styles in the chapter (from the Anglo-Saxon

sentence "Before born babe bliss had" [p. 384] to the nineteenth-century fustian style of Thomas Carlyle) are examples from literature, some of which are parodies (exaggerations of styles), most of which are pastiches (imitations
rather than exaggerations). We pass from one oratorical high
to another: the rhetorical abilities of Seymour Bushe are
child's play compared to what we find in the full-blown,
high-style, literary gems in "Oxen." In a letter to Frank
Budgen, Joyce offered one of his many clues for interpreting
his "chaffering allincluding most farraginous chronicle," a
phrase from "Oxen of the Sun" that self-consciously applies
both to the chapter and the book: the narrative, Joyce says,
imitates the development of English prose style, from Anglo-Saxon through the nineteenth century to "the frightful
jumble" of twentieth-century dialect and slang.[30] In the letter, Joyce names some of the specific authors he planned
to use as models, among them Malory, Bunyan, Pepys, and
Newman. The letter is one of the most often quoted of Joyce
epistles, probably because it provides what seems to be the
skeleton key to a most exasperating chapter. Almost every
critic makes reference to it. Indeed, the paragraphs of the
letter have become almost as sacred a part of the "text" of
Ulysses as the paragraphs of the chapter itself.

Many interesting questions regarding Joyce's use of specific models arise, and I will deal subsequently with Joyce's
imitation of specific writers, but the "key" the letter offers
only supplements our basic impressions of the literariness,
imitativeness, and protean nature of the chapter's styles.
Even if we fail to identify Malory as the author of a line like
"But sir Leopold was passing grave maugre his word by
cause he still had pity of the terrorcausing shrieking of shrill
women in their labour and as he was minded of his good
lady Marion" (p. 390), we know from its diction and syntax
that this is medieval romance literature. Even if we have not
discovered that Thomas Browne once wrote something sim-

---

[30] 13 March 1920, *Letters*, Vol 1, pp. 138-139.

ilar to the words "Assuefaction minorates atrocities" (p. 394), in the paragraph that includes this sentence we recognize oratory and sermonizing—based on the elaborately Latinate diction, a pre-eighteenth-century variety.

And even if we fail to recognize the specific models, the "gesture" of borrowing from specific models is obvious. The presence of many styles in quick succession, the difference between these styles and the ones we have already seen, the archaism of most of the styles, and our sense that some, at least, are singularly inappropriate for the language of a novel, ensure that we recognize, not for the first time in *Ulysses*, that stylistic models are being quoted. In "Circe," too, this gesture of quotation appears. In that chapter, Bloom shamelessly cribs from other characters: he tells Lenehan's riddle, recites the dialogue of a stage Irishman, and is accused of plagiarism by Philip Beaufoy. This gesture of quotation represents Bloom's characteristic defense—his refuge in imaginative identities (like Henry Flower). In "Circe" and in "Oxen," the *act* of borrowing is more important than the particular source.

The cumulative impact of this compendium of rhetorical models transcends the influence of any one model: the text demonstrates that there is no neutral rhetoric, no basic style or prose from which all depart. The theories of Dryden's creation of a "literary norm" in his prose or of the neutral prose of the realistic novel (Defoe's, for example) are belied in the comparative mode of the chapter.

The predominant kinds of literary models Joyce employs in the chapter are the didactic models of the essay and sermon, forms in which the writer seeks to persuade. Certain narrative forms do serve as models—Malory's romances and the novels of Dickens, Defoe, and Sterne—but much more common is the form of the essay as practiced by Browne, Burke, Addison, Steele, Pepys, Lamb, Landor, Macaulay, Newman, Ruskin, Carlyle.[31] One might argue that Joyce

[31] In *My Brother's Keeper*, Stanislaus Joyce says that in James's youth he wrote essays that were "deliberate imitations of Carlyle, Newman, Macaulay,

would logically select these prose models because the history of English prose before the eighteenth century is largely the history of the essay, sermon, and anatomy; the genre of the novel did not exist. But this argument does not satisfactorily account for Joyce's selection of so many didactic models, even from the eighteenth and nineteenth centuries.

If in "Cyclops" we had our ears bent by the garrulous, opinionated barfly of a narrator, here, in the voices of some of the most distinguished essayists, we and our characters are judged, flattered, reproached, exhorted. The sermons of Browne and Newman, the homilies of Burke, the satires of Swift provide an excellent opportunity for Joyce to play with the resources of the essay form, one of the literary forebears of the novel. Joyce's selection of models allows him to play with the intrusive, philosophical, explanatory voice that characterizes the essay form. This ruminating voice is particularly appropriate to a chapter in which very little happens to advance the plot. Like the musical rhythms of "Sirens" and the epic inflations of "Cyclops," the discursive models of "Oxen" allow a new narrative relationship between writer and reader and writer and character. And, like the headings of "Aeolus," the pastiches of "Oxen" allow for previously suppressed comment and judgment. The judgment, however, comes to us through stylistic masks; we make an error if we interpret the voices as the direct pronouncements of Joyce. The Junius-like castigation of Bloom, for example, presents only one face of the character and one judgment of him. Like the great swing from romantic self-glorification to romantic self-deprecation in Gabriel Conroy after Gretta has told him of Michael Furey ("He saw himself as a ludicrous figure, acting as a pennyboy

---

De Quincey and others. He knew by heart long passages from the stylists he most admired. When Ruskin died my brother's essay on him, entitled, 'A Crown of Wild Olive,' was, as the title implies, a studious imitation of the deceased author" (p. 104). For the aspiring young writer, these authors would have provided not only model styles but also the formal model of the essay, an appropriate genre for the expression of a young man's idea about life and art.

for his aunts, a nervous well-meaning sentimentalist, orating to vulgarians"), the oscillation of judgments and styles in "Oxen" admits no one definitive reading of the character.

Some of the strangest effects in the chapter result from the application of these essayistic models to storytelling. A deliberate awkwardness arises in the representation of consciousness; the discursive styles place a barrier of words between us and the characters. Here are Bloom's thoughts, narrated in the eighteenth-century style of Burke, the conservative political philosopher:

> . . . he had passed through the thousand vicissitudes of existence and, being of a wary ascendancy and self a man of rare forecast, he had enjoined his heart to repress all motions of a rising choler and . . . foster within his breast that plenitude of sufferance which base minds jeer at, rash judgers scorn and all find tolerable and but tolerable. To those who create themselves wits at the cost of feminine delicacy . . . to them he would concede neither to bear the name nor to herit the tradition of a proper breeding. . . . To conclude . . . the issue . . . now testified once more to the mercy as well as to the bounty of the Supreme Being. (Pp. 407-408)

This is Bloom as eighteenth-century, rational man, someone who can "enjoin" his heart to "repress all motions of a rising choler" and who accords the utmost respect to tradition and breeding. The style of the man is the style of the language; the balanced repetition of the sentences and the formal conclusion express this studied approach to emotions. The comedy of the application of this style to Bloom's consciousness stems from the disparity between so polished a period and the style (emotional and linguistic) that we usually associate with Bloom. If in "Aeolus" the rapid-fire thoughts of Bloom act as a counter to the often overblown oratory in the newsroom, in "Oxen," the minds of the characters, as well as the dialogue and narration, become periphrastic. Here the narrative gives us Bloom's thoughts in grand summation, complete with moral example and conclusion. And yet, despite the basic incongruity between this elaborate style and Bloom's fast-paced consciousness, the style does capture one aspect of Bloom: his habit of defensive rationalization. To this extent, the periphrasis of the style characterizes the elaborate avoidance mechanisms of the man.

This circuitous representation of thought often has the consequence of casting the character himself in the role of rhetorical poseur, as in the following example:

> Singular, communed the guest with himself, the wonderfully unequal faculty of metempsychosis possessed by them, that the puerperal dormitory and the dissecting theatre should be the seminaries of such frivolity, that the mere acquisition of academic titles should suffice to transform in a pinch of time these votaries of levity into exemplary practitioners of an art which most men anywise eminent have esteemed the noblest. But, he further added, it is mayhap to relieve the pentup feelings that in common oppress them for I have more than once observed that birds of a feather laugh together. (Pp. 408-409)

The staccato of Bloom's interior monologue—the shorthand rendering of a character's relationship to himself in his own mind—is replaced by this pompous self-communion. And the pomposity is emphasized by the surfacing of a Bloomian cliché at the end of the ornate passage, a comedown that makes it seem as if Bloom (like Gerty MacDowell) cannot keep up the pretense. Here, too, the circumlocution of the style is not wholly unsuitable, for Bloom is sometimes prone to defensive pomposity as well as defensive rationalization. In fact, the pretense implied by Bloom, "singularly communing with himself" over the disrespect of the medical students, is itself exposed in the Junian invective that succeeds it in the text, a passage in which Bloom is castigated for the unspoken homilies he has not dared to express: "But with what fitness, let it be asked, of the noble lord, his patron, had this alien . . . constituted himself the lord paramount of our internal polity?" (p. 409).

It is not only interior monologue, however, that falls prey to the oratory of the narrative but also the dialogue. Like "Aeolus," "Scylla and Charybdis," and "Cyclops," "Oxen" is full of the talk of its characters. Like "Scylla and Charybdis," especially, a chapter in which Stephen carefully orchestrates the intellectual discussion about literature, "Oxen" includes Socratic discussion and formal discourse on various themes. Much of the action is verbal. During the scene in the hospital, the characters line themselves up to take positions on the topics of birth, sex, love. They orate to one another, sometimes borrowing (without acknowledgment, of course) literary models: Dixon speaks dialogue from Swift's *Complete Collection of Genteel and Ingenious Conversation;*[32] à la Addison and Steele, Mulligan delivers a homily on the virtues of his Farm for Fertilization. The characters speak as well as think in the language of the narration, in this case, the language of particular literary models.

This "convention" is different from indirect reporting in which the narrator paraphrases the speech of a character, and it is the converse of free indirect discourse in which the narrator borrows the language of his characters. Here the character "borrows" (directly) the particular style of narration, even in what (misleadingly) appears to be direct quotation. For example, although the narrative begins to quote the characters indirectly, it slips into what appears to be direct quotation: ". . . he wondered what cry that it was whether of child or woman and I marvel, said he, that it be not come or now. Meseems it dureth overlong" (p. 387). This is Bloom's speech translated into the idiom of romance, but it purports to be a direct transcription. This mediated discourse given in the guise of direct quotation continues in both "Circe" and "Eumaeus." In these three

---

[32] See Gifford and Seidman, *Notes for Joyce*, p. 350.

chapters, we get a translation, a narrative equivalent of speech and thought.

We have witnessed this translation of dialogue in "Cyclops," for example, in a polite, Victorian exchange between Bloom and Bob Doran:

—Let me, said he, so far presume upon our acquaintance which . . . is founded . . . on a sentiment of mutual esteem, as to request of you this favor. But, should I have overstepped the limits of reserve let the sincerity of my feelings be the excuse for my boldness.

—No, rejoined the other, I appreciate to the full the motives which actuate your conduct. (P. 313)

This dialogue displays, perhaps, a more radical disruption of the conventions of quoted dialogue than the example from "Oxen," since the dash employed is Joyce's usual convention for designating direct quotation. But, like many of the parodies in "Cyclops," this one has the appearance of a skit— a little fictional rendition of a conversation in the midst of the first-person narration. In "Oxen," one finds no principle of contrast by which to judge the dialogue. There is no progression, as there seems to be in "Cyclops," from direct quotation (admittedly, the dun's quotation of his fellow barmates), to indirect reporting, to parody. "Oxen" presents us with one dialogue after another, one scene after another, from various types of literature, all funneled through the particular style chosen.

In fact, although the narrative components of dialogue and interior monologue can be discussed separately for the purposes of analysis, they are part of the larger transformation of the characters that occurs in the chapter. Unlike the Victorian dialogue in "Cyclops" which occurs in a kind of "timeout" in the forward progression of the narrative, the dialogue and monologues of "Oxen" form the action itself: the costume changes in the chapter are all we have. Joyce is at pains to show that style confers a role on character; when the style changes, a new fictional role is created.

This link between style and fictional role is forged, of course, elsewhere in the text. "Nausicaa," for example, provides us with our only sustained view of Bloom as romantic hero and "dream husband," compliments of Gerty Mac-Dowell and the styles of the Victorian novelette and ladies' magazine. "Cyclops," too, anticipates the role changes in the skits that give us, among others, Herr Blumenduft and Rory, Son of the Prudent Member. And, of course, it is in "Circe" that we will find the culmination of the dramatization of the characters' potential roles. But it is the "Oxen" chapter that gives us the most complete and systematic look at the way style creates a certain type of fictional role for the character, and, in a larger sense, creates a particular type of fictional world in which the character belongs. In a chapter concerned with birth and conception, we are given a series of "conceptions" (or misconceptions) of the scene, as the narrative gives birth to various manifestations of the characters.

So the scene changes: the same hospital is "Hornes house" in Middle English, a castle in the fourteenth-century style of medieval travel books, and the land of "Phenomenon" in Bunyanesque allegory. The roles change: Bloom is alternately the traveller Leopold, sir Leopold, Mr Cautious Calmer, Leop. Bloom of Crawford's journal, the alien and traitor, the embryo philosopher; Stephen is "young Stephen" and "Boasthard," among others, and the cast of minor characters changes as well. In this sense, "Oxen" actualizes a principle that operates throughout the book: the creation, by means of suggestion and allusion, of symbolic parallels between the characters and literary or mythic figures. Although the characters' various incarnations are explicitly cited in the narrative, like the basic parallels between Bloom and Odysseus and Stephen and Telemachus, the new roles are conferred without the characters' knowledge. Bloom has no more idea that he is sir Leopold than that he is Odysseus. It is for the reader's benefit that Bloom receives his knightly dubbing (or drubbing, as the case may be).

"Cyclops," "Nausicaa," and "Oxen"

The role change, of course, affects the way we interpret events, for each role has its attendant "myths" or ways of explaining the world. In a Middle English rendition (and schematization) of the plot of the *Odyssey*, we see "that man, Bloom," who had been living "with dear wife and lovesome daughter that then over land and seafloor nine year had long outwandered" (p. 385). This particular version of events transforms the emotional and physical estrangement of Bloom from Molly into forced exile, an explanation acceptable in the world of the *Odyssey* and the romance. Similarly, when we read that "sir Leopold . . . bore fast friendship to sir Simon and to this his son young Stephen and for that his languor becalmed him there" (p. 388), we have stumbled upon a fiction about the Odyssean traveller. Like Odysseus, sir Leopold must pause temporarily in his return home to perform a necessary deed.

This description of events contradicts our previous knowledge of the modern version of the story. No knightly fellowship exists between Bloom and Simon Dedalus, although we know Bloom has looked at Simon and has envied him his son (p. 89). In this hale and hearty world of jolly good fellows, envy becomes friendship. This type of fiction is continued in the style of Malory, as Bloom looks at Stephen: ". . . and now sir Leopold that had of his body no manchild for an heir looked upon him his friend's son and was shut up in sorrow for his forepassed happiness and as sad as he was that him failed a son of such gentle courage (for all accounted him of real parts) so grieved he also in no less measure for young Stephen for that he lived riotously" (pp. 390-391). Again, Bloom's sense of loss and his budding protective instincts toward Stephen find expression in a particular type of fiction, a romance in which Stephen is universally praised, a good kid who has fallen under bad influences.

This description of Bloom and Stephen is not totally false; it merely selects certain details while omitting others. If, upon occasion, we have seen Stephen display "gentle courage," he more frequently displays rudeness and arrogance. And, as Michael Groden points out, gentleness and courage are not the qualities Bloom admires in Stephen.[33] If we see Leopold nostalgic for his past happiness, we also see him resolutely face the present and the living ("Feel live warm beings near you. Let them sleep in their maggoty beds" [p. 115]). The style presents only a certain view of the characters' experience, and because we have seen other views in this chapter and in previous chapters, we cannot accept one rendition as absolute.

Yet the pathos of Bloom's search for his lost son is momentarily conveyed in this fusion of his self-pity with the sentimental style of Malory: it *is* poignant that there is no manchild in the promised land to whom Bloom can show the way. The desire of the character is expressed in a genre of wish fulfillment, the romance. For one moment, we see a glimpse, not only of Bloom's growing interest in Stephen (part of the naturalistic plot), but of a fiction of grief and sorrow that promises, according to its generic context, some relief. Bloom regards Stephen's profligate ways, and we feel the makings of a rescue in progress.

Other recognition scenes between the two characters also reveal the determinate pressure of a particular style. When Joyce reaches the nineteenth-century Romantics, nostalgia again suggests a connection between Stephen and Bloom. In an imitation of Lamb, the narrative asks philosophically, "What is the age of the soul of man?" and proceeds to present a flashback, a "retrospective arrangement" of Bloom as a young man, a version that transforms the workaday "staid agent of publicity and holder of a modest substance in the funds" into a young, energetic "knighterrant," the child as father of the man (p. 413). It is also a piece of magic that anticipates the sudden appearances and disappearances of the characters in "Circe." But the vision changes to the present. The hope is held out that those about him might

[33] Groden, *Ulysses in Progress*, p. 50.

be his sons—"Who can say?" the narrative asks, as Bloom thinks of a former fling with Bridie Kelly that might have produced one of these strapping young men. We teeter on the brink of the kind of ingenious revelation found in Victorian novels—Will the dissolute, rowdy youth turn out to be the true heir of the lonely hero? "Nay, fair reader. . . . She dare not bear the sunnygolden babe of day. No, Leopold! Name and memory solace thee not. That youthful illusion of thy strength was taken from thee and in vain. No son of thy loins is by thee. There is none now to be for Leopold, what Leopold was for Rudolph" (pp. 413-414). Here is an updated version of the "dark destiny" presented in the romance according to Malory (p. 390), archaic language enacting in prose the nostalgia for a better time. This is reality shaped as it might be in a certain kind of novel.

If the recognition scenes lend themselves to romantic models, the peal of thunder in the chapter lends itself to allegorical treatment. It is interpreted allegorically, first in Anglo-Saxon style, then in Bunyanesque imitation. Stephen and his friends have been discussing creation and the working of the universe, Punch Costello sings Stephen's song of creation (based on a parody of a nursery rhyme), and, suddenly, the peal of thunder is heard. "A black crack of noise in the street here, alack, bawled, back. Loud on left Thor thundered: in anger awful the hammerhurler. Came now the storm that hist his heart" (p. 394). The narrative combines Stephen's earlier definition of God as a "shout in the street" (p. 34) and the sounds of his rendition of resurrection ("Hired dog! Shoot him to bloody bits with a bang shotgun, bits man spattered walls all brass buttons. Bits all khrrrklak in place clack back" ["Proteus," p. 42]) with Anglo-Saxon substantive and alliterative style. The thunder is first said to signify the voice of that Norse hammerhurler, Thor ("Loud on left Thor thundered"). In the midst of the imitation of seventeenth-century style, the narrative reverts to its most primitive style: the atavism emphasizes the primitive, symbolic potency of this natural event.

The characters, too, get into the act of interpreting the significance of the thunder. Lynch tells Stephen that God is punishing him for his "hellprate and paganry," while Stephen, who is trying to regain his composure, offers his own literary explanation. Cavalierly, he offers a drunken "Nobodaddy," Blake's version of God and one that he has previously mentioned in another chapter of debate and role playing, "Scylla and Charybdis" ("Whether these be sins or virtues old Nobodaddy will tell us at doomsday leet" [p. 205]). Bloom, too, offers an interpretation: the thunder is merely a "natural phenomenon" (like the hangman's erection in "Cyclops," for which he uses the same expression), but Stephen's fear is not allayed. It is then that the narrative launches into a Bunyanesque allegory of "young Boasthard's" spiritual condition. The passage is a cross between a seventeenth-century moral drama and Mulligan's bawdy parody, "Everyman his own wife" (also from "Scylla and Charybdis"). The style in this case seems to be humorously incongruous with the subject, and yet, again it presents one "face" of Stephen—prodigal son and sinning pilgrim.

The point is that the various styles contain their own systems of values; because events are narrated in certain styles, they are apt to be altered by the style chosen. If the crack of thunder had been narrated in the "scientific style" of Huxley that Joyce adopts later on in the chapter (see p. 418), it would have been interpreted as a "natural phenomenon," or perhaps it would not have been interpreted at all. But the assumption of divine significance endemic to the allegorical styles allows Joyce to stage a kind of climax, a dramatic interruption of the blasphemous discussion, which leads into an exploration of Stephen's fear and guilt. Again, style carries with it a system of values—it affects both the plot and the interpretation of the plot.

That is why it is difficult to accept Stanley Sultan's categorical reading of the end of the Bunyan passage as Joyce's serious statement to the reader: "O wretched company, were ye all deceived for that was the voice of the god that was in a very grievous rage that he would presently lift his arm and spill their souls for their abuses and their spillings done by them contrariwise to his word which forth to bring brenningly biddeth" (p. 396). Despite the ironic presentation of the passage, Sultan reads it as the voice of the author, basing his reading, again, on Joyce's letter on the chapter in which he describes the theme of "Oxen" as "the crime against fecundity." According to Sultan, "the author condemns 'the carnal concupiscence' of the company, but his statement is addressed to the reader, and the characters continue as they are."[34] On the contrary, I think the impact of the changing styles prevents us from assigning one style as the voice of the author or from giving it a privileged position. After the pious address to the company, the style changes abruptly to a recording of quotidian details in imitation of Pepys. This kind of abrupt switch helps create a structure of anticlimax in the chapter, as one "translation" of events succeeds another. Bunyan's idea of the world is presented as no "better" or more accurate than Pepys'.

As in "Cyclops," the compendium of styles makes it impossible to identify the one which tells the truth—all the styles offer different versions of the story. As many critics have observed, "Oxen" provides a microcosm of the method of the book: the notion of the relativity and potentiality of all styles that informs the succession of styles in the book as a whole provides the principle for this most literary of chapters. As Hugh Kenner says, "Pastiche and parody, these are modes which test the limits of someone else's system of perception. Any 'style' is a system of limits; pastiche ascribes the system to another person, and invites us to attend to its

---

[34] Stanley Sultan, *The Argument of Ulysses* (Columbus: Ohio State University Press, 1964), p. 287.

recirculating habits and its exclusions."[35] Stylistic and dramatic possibilities are mined, but the actual significance of any one event becomes impossible to state given the constant shifting of ground rules and obvious narrative mediation.

By "dramatic possibilities" I mean not only that Leopold Bloom in some strange sense becomes "sir Leopold" and acts accordingly but that the connections between characters can be said to occur as *potential* connections. Bloom looks at Stephen and, for the first time, is reminded of Rudy. This is an important element of the plot of the story. But just what this recognition signifies about their relationship is left in doubt, partly due to the melodrama of the style and partly to the structure of anticlimax implicit in the succession of styles. Although an event occurs, the significance of the event is difficult to determine at this crucial first meeting between the modern-day Telemachus and Odysseus. Although we may want to point to Bloom's paternal feelings toward Stephen and his identification of Stephen and Rudy as a particularly important point in the chapter, we should recognize that the whole machinery of the chapter offers this "recognition" scene most obliquely and in an ironic structure that inhibits our ability to point to one event and to say "here is a high point" or "here is the climax or the heart of things." As Clive Hart says, "Stephen and Bloom are revealed in a succession of different lights and their potential significance is revealed for past times as well as for the present."[36] The "potential significance" is revealed for the present and is again explored amid the carnival atmosphere of "Circe," the assorted clichés of "Eumaeus," and the "no-nonsense" questions and answers of "Ithaca."

It might be worthwhile to comment on the idea of the "pastness" of the past mentioned by Hart, for it is not easy to state the sense of the past conveyed in "Oxen." We do

[35] Hugh Kenner, *Joyce's Voices* (Berkeley: University of California Press, 1978), p. 81.

[36] Clive Hart, *James Joyce's Ulysses* (Sydney: Sydney University Press, 1968), p. 69.

see the characters portrayed in the terms of older forms of literature: they are transformed into romance heroes, allegorical personages, Victorian moral crusaders and sinners. The protean transformations of the style, too, suggest a general historical development, a theme sounded early in the book by Stephen Dedalus in the "Proteus" chapter. But as J. S. Atherton has recently shown, the "progression" through the history of prose style is not as neat as Joyce's letter would suggest—anachronisms, for example, are found throughout.[37] And although the characters think and speak in the particular style being imitated, they bring with them certain literary associations that upset the forward chronological progression of the styles. For example, the pastiche of Elizabethan writers, via the literate mind of Stephen Dedalus, includes some lines from both William Blake and W. B. Yeats: "His words were then these as followeth: Know all men, he said, time's ruins build eternity's mansions. What means this? Desires wind blasts the thorntree but after it becomes from a bramblebush to be a rose upon the rood of time" (p. 391).

This is a strange mélange of literary quotations, and one that intentionally discourages our evaluating the styles strictly according to the historical periods that produce these models.[38] Two effects are produced by Joyce's intentional "swerving" from strict adherence to a particular period. The first is that we think in the looser categories of types of fictions—melodramatic, romantic, bourgeois, religious— rather than specific historical periods. And, second, this mélange contributes to our overriding sense of an abundance of language, of all sorts of words converging rather than of

[37] J. S. Atherton, "The Oxen of the Sun," in *James Joyce's Critical Essays*, ed. Clive Hart and David Hayman (Berkeley: University of California Press, 1974), esp. pp. 320-321 and p. 325.

[38] In his admirable study of the chapter, Wolfgang Iser attributes too much significance to the idea of historicity. See *The Implied Reader: Patterns of Communication in Prose Fiction from Bunyan to Beckett* (Baltimore: The Johns Hopkins University Press, 1974), esp. pp. 192-193

particular periods displayed. The progression of styles affords us less of a walk through time than a patchwork of textbook examples.[39] Indeed, Atherton has shown that Joyce relied on handbooks of style for his model passages, even though he was familiar with "the originals." He used George Saintsbury's *History of English Prose Rhythm* and W. Peacock's *English Prose: Mandeville to Ruskin*.[40] Joyce wrote twentieth-century pastiche or parody of earlier styles, based on excerpts selected by historians of prose—this kind of archeological layering in the composing process intrigued him. It also contributes to our sense of a more erratic narrative movement than Joyce's neat historical scheme would suggest.

This mixture of sources is subtle, but I believe it is part of the point of the chapter, for Joyce often deliberately plays with the whole notion of sources. An example of such play is the following: "Assuefaction minorates atrocities (as Tully saith of his darling Stoics) and Hamlet his father showeth the prince no blister of combustion. The adiaphane in the noon of life is an Egypt's plague which in the nights of prenativity and postmortemity is their most proper *ubi* and *quomodo*" (p. 394). Gifford and Seidman identify the exact source of the two words "Assuefaction minorates" (not a typical lexical duo) as Thomas Browne's *Christian Morals*,[41] and Atherton shows that this particular example came to Joyce by way of Saintsbury: "Forget not how assuefaction unto anything minorates the passion from it, how constant objects lose their hints, and steal an inadvertisement upon

[39] See Hugh Kenner's fine discussion of the prose parodies in *Joyce's Voices*, pp. 48-49.

[40] See Atherton, "The Oxen of the Sun," p. 315. Atherton also observes that the always meticulous Joyce relied on a handbook of grammatical errors as well, W. B. Hodgson's *Errors in the Use of English* (p. 332). He used it to help him compose the one passage in "Oxen" that resembles the prose of "Eumaeus," the passage that begins "However, as a matter of fact though" (*Ulysses*, p. 416).

[41] Gifford and Seidman, *Notes for Joyce*, p. 345.

us."[42] Aside from altering the sense of Browne's admonition
to suit the purposes of Stephen's lecture, Joyce has Stephen
attribute the line to Tully (and Gifford and Seidman dig
up a possible referent in Marcus Tullius Cicero's *Tusculan
Disputations*[43]). The style of the passage is, as Atherton says,
a "caricature" of Browne's Latinate style. Stephen speaks
in a parody of Browne's style while attributing his words
to Tully rather than Browne. Joyce gives us quite a comical
line of transmission: Browne's words, via Saintsbury's book,
attributed to Tully by Stephen (who is made to parody
Browne's style), in a book written by James Joyce. In the
remainder of the paragraph, the "issue" is compounded even
further, as Stephen quotes, in Brownian prose, Aristotelian
ideas about which he ruminates in "Proteus."

The characters often quote themselves in "Oxen": Haines
quotes his own "history is to blame," Stephen alludes to the
Edenville and Tophet of his reverie on the beach—all in-
terwoven with a narrative that is itself a pastiche of words
and rhythms already written by someone else. As in "Aeolus," Joyce plays with language as quotation, a field of repetition that includes: the characters unwittingly, wittingly,
and sometimes, wittily quoting themselves, each other, and
literature, and the book quoting lines from its own previous
pages and from other writers. Increasingly, the characters'
memories and the narrative memory fuse—at a certain level,
all the "memories" in the book are fictions created out of
other fictions for the purpose of this fiction. All are quotations or citations, iterative events, linguistic and dramatic,
including the title of the book that prepares us to encounter
a retelling of a very old story.

The swerving from a model is sometimes reflected in the
imitation of a particular author as well as a period. Hugh
Kenner illustrates this point with the example of the imitation of Macaulay in the chapter. He calls the passage "a

---

[42] Atherton, "Oxen of the Sun," p. 322.
[43] Gifford and Seidman, *Notes for Joyce*, p. 345.

systematic deviation from Macaulay's method," which produces a sense of "words, arranged" and rearranged.[44] This
is true as well of the prose imitation of the style of Cardinal
Newman, who is, according to Stephen in *A Portrait*, the
finest prose writer in English:

> There are sins or (let us call them as the world calls them)
> evil memories which are hidden away by man in the dark-
> est places of the heart but they abide there and wait. He
> may suffer their memory to grow dim, let them be as
> though they had not been and all but persuade himself
> that they were not or at least were otherwise. Yet a chance
> word will call them forth suddenly and they will rise up
> to confront him in the most various circumstances, a vision
> or a dream, or while timbrel and harp soothe his senses
> or amid the cool silver tranquillity of the evening or at
> the feast at midnight when he is now filled with wine.
> Not to insult over him will the vision come as over one
> that lies under her wrath, not for vengeance to cut off
> from the living but shrouded in the piteous vesture of the
> past, silent, remote, reproachful. (P. 421)

The notion of secret sin is found in Newman's *Parochial
and Plain Sermons*. The closest model passage for Joyce's
imitation that I can find describes the "reckless mirth" of
a profligate group of merrymakers and includes some of the
specific diction Joyce uses in his passage but with some
crucial differences: "Chance words and phrases of her [the
Church's] services adhere to their [sinners'] memories, rising up at moments of temptation or of trouble, to check or
to recover them."[45] Joyce altered Newman's "chance phrases"

---

[44] Kenner, *Joyce's Voices*, p. 107 and p. 49.

[45] The passage continues:
And hence it happens, that in the most irreligious companies a distinction
is said to be observable between those who have had the opportunity of
using our public Forms in their youth, and those whose religious impressions
have not been thus happily fortified; so that amid their reckless mirth, and
most daring pretence of profligacy, a sort of secret reverence has attended

of the Church that aid the sinner in his trials with temptation so that they remind the sinner not of his devotion but of his sins (a thematic reversal appropriate to Stephen Dedalus). Despite this idiosyncratic use of the model, the feeling of the passage is Newmanesque. Reflected are the antitheses, parentheses, and qualifying phrases Newman uses to capture subtle moral and intellectual distinctions in his prose. The first part of the third sentence, especially, displays the vigorous strength and "manly" prose that Joyce admired: "Yet a chance word will call them forth suddenly and they will rise up to confront him." But the remainder of the third sentence displays the deviation: the sentence seems to get lost in its own lyrical catalogue of sensuous pleasures—the timbrel and harp, the cool tranquillity of the evening, the feast at midnight. Newman might have presented sensual pleasure, but the presentation would have led to a reminder of God. At a certain point in Joyce's imitation, the style departs from its model, and, again, the "swerve" makes the model recede into a wash of words.

Despite the deviation from particular models and historical periods, however, one must make distinctions between the kind of quotation found in "Oxen" and that in "Cyclops" and "Eumaeus." All three chapters suggest that language is an immense repository to be raided and cited; all three reveal the artist as "self-exposing plagiarist," a writer creating his art deliberately out of the phrases of others. But despite the fact that "Oxen" is not rigid in its progressions and imitations, the reader's general sense of the chapter is of Joyce borrowing specific models. Although he does play with the notion of sources in the chapter to reveal the "archeological" levels of language, the chapter as a whole still dramatizes the idea of specific literary models. This is what is more misleading about "Oxen" than the two other chap-

---

the wanderers, restraining them from that impiety and profaneness in which the others have tried to conceal from themselves the guilt and peril of their doings.

John Henry Newman, Sermon XX: "Forms of Private Prayer," in *Parochial and Plain Sermons* (London: Longmans, Green, and Co., 1894), 1: 267.

ters in terms of the use of language in the book as a whole. It plays down the idea of the general citationality of language in favor of the narrower idea of literary models. In "Eumaeus," Joyce will show us that citation is the way of all language, not just of literary texts, and in *Finnegans Wake*, he shows us language as a corporate enterprise at its most extreme.

Perhaps this narrower conception of imitation also leads to a greater sense of discipline and less spontaneity in "Oxen" than in "Cyclops," the chapter that it most closely resembles. One can find comic incongruity in "Oxen" (the sardine tin is an example), but in general the emphatic exuberance and spontaneity of the early chapter are rare in "Oxen," which seems more craftsmanlike in its execution. "Oxen" seems like a chapter Stephen Dedalus would like to have written, and, indeed, it is, as I have said, the *book's* piece of literary criticism that complements Stephen's own fancywork in the library. Other writers, too, have seen it as a literary tour de force; Anthony Burgess labeled it "an author's chapter, a dazzling and authoritative display of what English can do,"[46] the chapter he most would have wanted to write. And yet one can admire with Burgess the technical brilliance while missing the greater exuberance of the "Cyclops" and "Eumaeus" chapters.

One of the functions of all this discipline and craft in the chapter is to provide a veritable anatomy of style and a classic demonstration of the provisional nature of any one style. Referring to *Ulysses* in general and probably to "Oxen of the Sun" in particular, T. S. Eliot said that Joyce had exposed "the futility of all the English styles,"[47] a judgment that suggests that style has failed to live up to its claims. For Eliot, who himself had demonstrated the desire to find

[46] Anthony Burgess, *Re Joyce* (New York, W. W. Norton & Co., Inc., 1965), p. 156.

[47] Quoted in Virginia Woolf's *A Writer's Diary: Being Extracts from the Diary of Virginia Woolf*, ed. Leonard Woolf (New York: Harcourt, Brace and Company, 1953), p. 49.

"*le mot juste*," Joyce's inventories of style revealed the failure of such a stylistic absolute. Indeed, "Oxen of the Sun" does show the naiveté of assuming that any one style can convey the way things really are, but I would prefer to regard it as a demonstration of the inevitable *limitations* rather than the *failure* or futility of style.

Even the word "limitation," however, tends to ignore the other aspect of Joyce's stylistic tour de force in the chapter. For in treating the styles of the past as fuel for the modern writer, he makes capital of the styles while revealing their limitations. Eliot also said that bad poets borrow and good poets steal—Joyce was an expert thief who could create something new out of old materials. To borrow a phrase from *Finnegans Wake*, "Oxen of the Sun" is "the last word in stolentelling," a chapter fashioned out of the signature styles of other writers. In "Oxen," Joyce attempted to outdo his predecessors by encompassing them and to expand the limits of his own text by importing, cataloguing, and displaying others. "Oxen" is the last stand for literary plagiarism in *Ulysses*. From now on the book will pillage most mercilessly its own resources.

VI

"Circe": The Rhetoric of Drama

The rambunctious pantomimic skits of "Cyclops" and the role playing and scene changes in "Oxen of the Sun" are the closest we have come in *Ulysses* to the drama of "Circe." In these two earlier chapters, imitation, impersonation, and rhetorical flamboyance are narrative principles; the role playing of the characters is a function of the general pomp and ceremony of narrative style.

Impersonation and rhetorical excess also characterize "Circe," but the convention of the chapter is that it is a dramatic script rather than a narrative. The staginess of the narrative in the preceding chapters yields to a stage, as everything is acted out instead of mediated through narration. The oratory of English prose styles gives way to a new kind of rhetorical extremism, integrally related to the dreamlike quality of the chapter. This extremism depends upon two dominant rhetorical modes: metaphoric substitution and hyperbole.

The entire chapter is, in a radical sense, figurative: its fantastic scenes and dialogues function as dramatized conceits or metaphors for the characters' suppressed desires, fears, and guilt. In "Circe," as in a dream, metaphoric substitution operates as a basic principle. But what is radical about the treatment of dream symbolism in the chapter is its dramatic and literal presentation: that which is private and internalized in a dream becomes public spectacle, as metaphors for feelings become literal actors on the stage. And, as in a dream, the figures are presented with extravagance and exaggeration. In the dramatic context of the chapter, this extravagance is manifested in the broad gestures of vaudeville and burlesque. Hidden feelings are not merely acted out in disguised form—they are overacted. This symbolic, indeed hyperbolic, projection of feelings contributes to the "pathopoeia" of the chapter, a rhetorical term for pathos making—emotional, hyperbolic expression in speech and gesture. In "Circe," characters and objects alike orate, exhort, and mimic.

I will say much more about the rhetoric of the Circean drama, particularly the dominance of metaphor and hyperbole in the chapter, but first I want to trace briefly some of the antecedents of the theatrics we find there. The roots of the Circean drama can be found in both the stream-of-consciousness of the characters and the narrative style in earlier chapters. For example, the kind of drama staged in "Circe" is adumbrated in two passages of "Wandering Rocks," in which the characters give free rein to their imaginations. The first describes Bloom at the bookstall, reading a passage from *Sweets of Sin:*

> He read where his finger opened.
> —*All the dollarbills her husband gave her were spent in the stores on wondrous gowns and costliest frillies. For him! For Raoul!*
> Yes. This. Here. Try. . . .
> —*You are late, he spoke hoarsely, eyeing her with a suspicious glare. The beautiful woman threw off her sable-trimmed wrap, displaying her queenly shoulders and heaving embonpoint.* . . .
> Mr Bloom read again: *The beautiful woman.*
> Warmth showered gently over him, cowing his flesh. Flesh yielded amid rumpled clothes. Whites of eyes swooning up. His nostrils arched themselves for prey. Melting breast ointments (*for him! for Raoul!*). Armpits' oniony sweat. Fishgluey slime (*her heaving embonpoint!*). Feel! Press! Crushed! Sulphur dung of lions! (P. 236)

We move from Bloom reading, "flesh cowed," to Bloom

cheerleading for Raoul as he will be for Boylan in "Circe." Bloom's imagination embellishes the pornographic scene from the book. His reverie brings us to the borderline between stream-of-consciousness and dramatized fantasy. This particular fantasy is transformed in "Circe": the sable-trimmed wrap appears on the shoulders of Mrs Yelverton Barry, one of the fantasized sadistic women of "Circe" (p. 465); Molly (Marion), in her "pelt," addresses Boylan as "Raoul" (p. 565); and the smells and sweat that Bloom pictures as the "Sweets of Sin" abound in the sadomasochistic drama. (Even the emotional excess is adumbrated in "Wandering Rocks," when Bloom is so carried away by the vision that he has "trouble" mastering his breath to say that he wishes to buy the book.)

Stephen, too, indulges in fantasies that anticipate the drama of the later chapter. For example, he gazes through the lapidary's window: "She dances in a foul gloom where gum burns with garlic. . . . She dances, capers, wagging her sowish haunches and her hips, on her gross belly flapping a ruby egg" (p. 241). Like Bloom's fantasy, Stephen's anticipates the lurid drama of "Circe." In the later chapter, however, these kinds of images appear with a difference: the present tense that signals a fantasy in the earlier chapter appears instead in the actual stage directions for the drama; and a descriptive phrase like "sowish haunches" gives way to symbolic transformation. In "Circe," instead of the "sowish haunches" in Stephen's imagination, we find Bella raising her hoof and placing it on Bloom. Simile gives way to literal representation, as human characters are transformed into animals.

By the time we get to "Circe," then, two important changes have occurred. First, impressionism is replaced by expressionism: imaginative coloration of the landscape is no longer tied to the private point of view of a particular character. It is, rather, both communal and externalized. Whole landscapes and situations symbolically express feelings and sensations: the Nighttown setting given at the beginning of the chapter, before the appearance of any character, is a general projection of the murky, clandestine, sordid world of the unconscious to be charted in the chapter as a whole. The setting is thus the externalization of the unconscious— a stage set which need not conform to the norms of naturalistic representation but which nevertheless gives materiality and substance to fear and desire. With its "danger signals," "skeleton tracks," and "stunted men and women," Nighttown is both the literal setting of the plot of the chapter and the expressionistic equivalent of the feelings of guilt and trespass that are experienced by the characters.

Second, analogy gives way to dramatized conceit. The transformations in "Circe" are bizarre and literal extensions of the figurative language in the narration of the earlier chapters. These preceding chapters are replete with somewhat strange metaphoric descriptions of characters and landscapes that anticipate the dramatized conceits of "Circe." For example, in the "Aeolus" chapter (which has no thematic relation to animals), the use of animal metaphors suddenly turns the newspaper office into a virtual barnyard: "An instant after a hoarse bark of laughter burst over professor MacHugh's unshaven black-spectacled face"; "The inner door was opened violently and a scarlet beaked face, crested by a comb of feathery hair, thrust itself in" (p. 126).[1] In fact, even the animation of objects like hooves, fans, and buttons can be regarded as an extreme version of earlier narrative tendencies, specifically, of the strange use of synecdoche in the narrative of "Wandering Rocks" and "Sirens," chapters in which the breakdown of the initial style occurs. Bloom follows the bag of Richie Goulding into the restaurant in "Sirens": "The bag of Goulding, Collis, Ward led Bloom by ryebloom flowered tables" (p. 266). If this bag can lead Bloom into the bar in "Sirens," why can't Bella Cohen's fan lead him on in "Circe"? Similarly, the sturdy

---

[1] Ann Rafferty and Fern Chertkow first made me aware of the presence of these metaphors in "Aeolus."

trousers that salute the viceregal procession at the end of "Wandering Rocks" (p. 255) anticipate the gesturing objects of "Circe."

Thus, the roots of the Circean drama are found in the impressionism of the characters' view of the world and the rhetorical habits of the third-person narration in the earlier chapters. The play staged in "Circe" is an extension of the play of language earlier on. In fact, both the stage directions and the role playing in the chapter are anticipated in the staginess of the naive narrative style of "Telemachus," with its clear demarcation of action and style of action: "Stephen said with energy and growing fear" (p. 4), "Buck Mulligan cried with delight" (p. 11), "Buck Mulligan's gowned form moved briskly about the hearth to and fro" (p. 11). The naive style gives us dialogue or action and the style of performance (for example, with fear, quickly, merrily); the stage directions, too, tell us about the style and gesture accompanying the action. In the "Hades" chapter, this dramatic notation continues in a different vein: "All waited. . . . All waited. . . . They waited still" (p. 87); "All watched awhile through their windows caps and hats lifted by passers" (p. 88); "All raised their thighs" (p. 89); "All walked after" (p. 101). This chorus of actions, transposed into the present tense, resembles the stage directions of "Circe," and the sense of orchestration and of characters put through their paces anticipates the directorial mode of the chapter. Finally, in "Scylla and Charybdis," the narrative briefly gives way to dramatic script, an extension of the general staginess of both the language of narration and the resident literary critics (especially Stephen).

This brief glance backward is meant not only to illustrate the continuity among the chapters but to establish that the "Circe" chapter provides a release of certain energies that have emerged earlier in the text in milder, tamer form. Thus, what is true for the characters is true for the book in a larger sense: all kinds of suppressed energies, narrative as well as psychological, are tapped in this antic chapter. "Circe" provides a stage for a libidinous release of tendencies in the language and in the characters. The chapter's general carnival atmosphere, with its puns, wisecracks, and burlesque, represents the dramatic eruption of the unconscious of the characters and of rhetorical energies in the language. The book's previously suppressed or "censored" material now surfaces.[2] The offstage and "ob-scene" are now spotlighted—scenes merely hinted at previously are now given center stage. Exhibitionism abounds in the gestures of the language and the characters.

It is through the mechanism of the dream that the link between the rhetorical extremism of the chapter and the dramatic representation of the characters' hidden feelings is forged. Many critics have observed that there is much of dream logic and mechanism in the chapter.[3] As in a dream, in which the unconscious communicates in disguised forms, in "Circe," scenes, dialogue, even the stage directions, function as metaphors for the characters' feelings. Metaphoric substitution, synecdoche, hyperbole abound precisely because, as Freud and, recently, Jacques Lacan have shown, the dream communicates by means of rhetorical figures. In "Circe," it is as if the book itself were staging dreams for the characters by means of symbol and verbal and visual play. The dramatic script brims over with signs to be deciphered; even the italicized names of the speakers (that is, *MARION* instead of Molly) are symbols of hidden feelings.

It is important to stress that the "dream of the text" is not equivalent to the fantasies or dreams of the characters.

[2] Mark Schechner discusses this release in psychoanalytic terms. He says that "Circe" "celebrates Joyce's power over himself—specifically, his power over taboo and repression." See *Joyce in Nighttown: A Psychoanalytic Inquiry into Ulysses* (Berkeley: University of California Press, 1974), p. 104.

[3] See Arnold Goldman, *The Joyce Paradox: Form and Freedom in His Fiction* (London: Routledge & Kegan Paul, 1966), pp. 96-99, for a discussion of "Circe" as the dream of the author, and Hugh Kenner, "Circe," in *James Joyce's Ulysses: Critical Essays*, ed. Clive Hart and David Hayman (Berkeley: University of California Press, 1974), p. 356, for a discussion of the dream of the text.

For the psychological boundaries of the characters' minds are wildly, extravagantly transgressed in the chapter; that is, the narrative memory of the book provides the resources for this extraordinary drama, often in violation of the *actual* memories and associations of the characters. Motifs from different chapters appear in new forms to reveal something about the characters: Black Liz, straight from her appearance in a parody in "Cyclops" materializes in "Circe" to show how henpecked and motherly Bloom is. According to the stage directions, Bloom feels his "occiput," dubiously, "with the unparalleled embarrassment of a harassed pedlar gauging the symmetry of her [Zoe's] peeled pears" (p. 500), a line that refers us back to the spelling bee conundrum offered in "Aeolus." Kitty, the whore, appears, cloaked in the style of Gerty MacDowell: "Kitty unpins her hat. . . . And a prettier, a daintier head of winsome curls was never seen on a whore's shoulders" (p. 521). As in a dream, the elements of the past reappear in new forms, often severed from the context that would explain them, but it is the *book's* past that provides the material for the drama.

Thus, as C. H. Peake has observed, we are by no means given "filmed records" of the unconscious.[4] Instead, we have the book staging dramas for the reader that could not exist in their present form in the conscious minds or dreams of the characters. The distorted, composite dramas of "Circe" afford the reader yet another look at the possibilities lodged within the characters and the world of Dublin. Like the other distortions or "misconceptions" provided in the book's second half—the "static" in "Sirens" or the masquerades in "Cyclops" and "Oxen"—the bizarre speeches and actions of "Circe" reveal to the reader further aspects of the characters. "A man of genius," Stephen says, "makes no mistakes. His errors are volitional and are the portals of discovery" (p.

[4] C. H. Peake, *James Joyce: The Citizen and the Artist* (Stanford: Stanford University Press, 1977), p. 268.

190). The distortions of "Circe" are "portals of discovery" for the reader. The curtain rises.

The material that we discover in "Circe" differs from that in previous chapters, however, because of its deeply sensitive nature. In "Circe" it is as if we dive into the ellipses of the stream-of-consciousness passages of the early chapters. We see the fears, wishes, and guilty feelings that the characters have tried all day to suppress. "Circe" symbolically dramatizes those painful thoughts that we have learned of obliquely, by means of the characters' avoidance or narrative omission. All day long Bloom has been troubled by the crucial events relating to three primary relationships in his life: his father's suicide, his son's death at eleven days old, and his wife's adultery. When thoughts of these events come to Bloom's mind, he tries to repress them, and the narrative, obligingly, complies. The concept of the stream-of-consciousness is honored; if the character represses a painful thought or memory, we see the act of repression but cannot look through him to what lies beneath. The text stays with Bloom in the Ormond Hotel rather than shifting the scene to 7 Eccles Street. Only verbal echoes—the haunting refrain "at four" and the jingle of Boylan's car—remind us of what is occurring.

But in "Circe," primarily through symbolic dialogues, Bloom and Stephen are made to play out scenes that express and make public these hidden feelings. The omitted is now committed. These latent feelings include their desires and need for approval (for example, Bloom's stint as Lord Mayor of Dublin), their guilt and need for punishment (for example, Mrs Yelverton Barry's accusations). Although the naturalistic action progresses in the chapter—Bloom and Stephen visit Bella Cohen's brothel, Stephen loses his money and self-control, and Bloom comes to the rescue— most of the chapter is taken up with the public dramatization of the kinds of internal conflicts that we have seen the characters suffer in private all day long.

Many of the dramatized scenes in the chapter involve

elements from the characters' *pasts*. In fact, the dialogue spoken and the roles played in the chapter differ in this respect, too, from those in "Cyclops" and "Oxen of the Sun," both chapters in which, for the most part, *present* scenes and conversations among the characters are written according to the conventions of a particular style. In "Circe," the "sins of the past" are recapitulated; the characters' spoken confrontations with specters from their pasts symbolize the inescapable relationship between past and present. We have seen the psychic wounds before—now we see them in relation to the experiences of the past. As Bloom says at one point in the chapter, "Past was is today" (p. 514).

In dramatizing the relationship between past and present, "Circe" provides a very strange kind of exposition, literally an exposure of some of the antecedent conditions that have made the characters what they are on June 4, 1904. To alter one of Stephen's pet phrases, we see what was there all the time within them. In "Oxen of the Sun," Stephen is cowed by a clap of thunder, which he interprets as "Nobodaddy's" disapproval of his apostasy; in "Circe," May Dedalus rises from the dead to chastise him for the same thing, and we see how the son has introjected the voice of parental authority. In a sense, "Circe" provides a counterpart to the exposition of the characters' pasts that appears in "Ithaca." Both chapters present an inventory of the near and distant pasts of the characters and the book, but they differ in their temperament and temperature. The mode of "Circe" is hyperbolic drama; the mode of "Ithaca" is understated catechism. "Circe" is the past served "hot"; "Ithaca" is the past served "cold."

Precisely because the material in "Circe" is so psychologically charged, the "sins of the past," like everything else in the chapter, are presented metaphorically. As I have previously stated, we are given *conceits* or expressive equivalents for the characters' psychic secrets rather than actual replays of past scenes in their lives. In keeping with the rhetoric of the dream, metaphoric substitutions, puns, synecdoches are used to reveal and disguise feelings. For example, Mrs Yelverton Barry's accusation of Bloom for improper advances made at 4:30 is an instance of displacement, a key process involved in dream-formation. She functions as a substitute for Molly and, as such, provides a vehicle for Bloom's fears about Molly's adultery and his guilt about his own masturbation on the beach. The "raincaped watch" who call to Bloom (and whose description first appears in his memory of Bridie Kelly in "Oxen") similarly function metaphorically: they represent Bloom's self-accusations. They "watch" his actions disapprovingly, authoritatively, their "raincape" representing the forces of Bloom's own repression, the prophylaxis that protects him from his sexual desires. In an interesting discussion entitled "Watchwords in *Ulysses*: The Stylistics of Suppression," Margaret McBride discusses the complex pun on the word "watch" in the chapter, which, she says, symbolizes Bloom's sexual guilt over his own voyeurism (his "watching"), his cuckoldry (his watch stops at 4:30), and his masturbation (the phallic clock in "Circe," which Canon O'Hanlon "elevates and exposes" is a transformed version of the clock on the mantlepiece whose chimes conclude the hour of Bloom's masturbation). As McBride observes correctly, these painful feelings surface in "Circe," but they are represented in disguised form.[5]

In the dialogue as well as in the stage directions and actions of the characters, rhetorical devices such as puns appear and the process of displacement occurs. For example, in his discussion with Mrs Breen, Bloom displaces his painful feelings onto innocuous dialogue, with certain code words protruding through the fabric of trivial gossip to reveal the pain, desire, and guilt underneath. In the conversation, Bloom promises to divulge a secret to Mrs Breen if she swears to "never tell" Molly that she has seen him in Nighttown. The discussion functions as a conceit for

[5] Margaret McBride, "Watchwords in *Ulysses*: The Stylistics of Suppression," *The Journal of English and Germanic Philology* 77 (July 1978): 364-365.

Bloom's present misgivings about being in Nighttown, his deeper guilt over his voyeurism and other sexual peculiarities (it follows Gerty's chiding of Bloom because he saw "all the secrets" of her "bottom drawer" [p. 442]), and his sexual inadequacy with Molly. The words "never tell" become code words signifying Bloom's guilt about his relationship with Molly and his pain over her adultery; the word "Nevertell" is the name of the horse that Molly bet on the night Bloom and Mrs Breen flirted with each other and applies to the secrets he and Molly keep from each other. The conversation continues: Bloom reminds Mrs Breen of the day when Molly won the money and a Mrs Hayes falsely "advised" Mrs Breen to wear an unbecoming new hat. Mrs Breen says, "She did, of course, the cat! Don't tell me! Nice adviser!" (p. 449).[6] And then Bloom says, lapsing into female chitchat: "Because it didn't suit you one quarter as well as the other ducky little tammy toque with the bird of paradise wing in it that I admired on you." Then "(Low, secretly, ever more rapidly)" he says: "And Molly was eating a sandwich of spiced beef out of Mrs Joe Gallaher's lunch basket. Frankly, though she had her advisers or admirers I never cared much for her style." The dialogue includes the key words "advisers" and "admirers," which were revealingly interchanged in Bloom's Freudian slip earlier in the evening (see "Cyclops," p. 313). The superficial dialogue about clothes is itself a coy digression, a rhetorical strategy that reflects an attempt to avoid sensitive material. Nevertheless, the displaced secrets leak through in the key words. The conversation continues briefly but gets too close to the telling of secrets for Bloom's comfort. Mrs Breen fades away just at the point when the secret might be divulged. Thus, the obvious strategy of avoidance in the dialogue of the character merges with the sudden shift of scene.

The rhetorical devices in the stage directions and actions,

---

[6] Here again, in Mrs Breen's colloquial Irish exclamation, "Don't tell me!" we find a form of the code word "Nevertell."

then, cannot be distinguished functionally from those found in the characters' dialogue, since all contribute to the dream of the text—that is, to the book's symbolic exploration of its own significant themes. The rhetorical devices within individual speeches are only part of a larger rhetorical strategy in the chapter: even the very structure of the speeches combines rhetoric with obsession, as the text's rhetorical strategy facilitates both exhibition and disguise. This larger sense of rhetorical structure and its relationship to psychology is illustrated, too, in the dominant motif of courtroom drama and formal debate in the chapter. For the debates and trials themselves symbolize the characters' internal conflicts (their "courts of conscience," as it is called at one point). These dramatic dialogues represent a kind of "splitting," an exhibition of the character as *agon* to himself. In various manifestations, the "sins of the past" rise to confront the characters. The energetic trials involving Bloom thus symbolically represent *both* his self-accusation and self-defense. The judicial branch of rhetoric and various rhetorical forms of proof, especially, receive strenuous exercise, as the characters become orators. In defining himself, Bloom uses rhetoric with an ingenuity that could rival Seymour Bushe's: he tries to prove his innocence by persuading his accusers of his good character, by playing on their sympathy, and by logically disproving their accusations—he employs, that is, the three main types of rhetorical proof: ethos, pathos, and logos (or logic).[7]

Hyperbole, gesture, and imitation are among Bloom's favorite tools for pleading his case, and he is not above borrowing his eloquence if that will help. In answer to Mary Driscoll's charge of sexual harassment (which represents Bloom's own sexual guilt), he makes a "long unintelligible speech," rendered indirectly as a stream of clichés, such as "he wanted to turn over a new leaf" and to "lead a homely

---

[7] This "proof" anticipates some of the demands and responses in the catechism of "Ithaca." See, for example, the imperative to "Prove that he [Bloom] loved rectitude from his earliest youth" (p. 716).

life in the evening of his days" (p. 462). He defends himself with plagiarism and claims of mistaken identity. He borrows (and bungles) Lenehan's joke, for example, symbolizing his attempt to evade responsibility for his thoughts and actions. He admits plagiarizing from Philip Beaufoy's story but uses the very act of plagiarism as a defense; just as the pseudonym Henry Flower is an excuse for his long-distance flirtation, his plagiarism is meant to excuse him from even greater crimes. After being burned by the mob, Bloom seeks refuge in a parody of the stage Irishman, "Let me be going now, woman of the house" (p. 499), and then tries even harder to defend himself with Shakespearean words, "To be or not to be." "Talk away till you're black in the face," Zoe says; Bloom's eloquence and plagiarism represent two of his pet defenses.

Thus, the rhetorical flamboyance and the theatrics of the chapter are a function of the struggle between exhibition and inhibition in the text. Scenes are overacted, the characters impersonate, mug, gesticulate wildly, and, in part, the melodrama functions as defense; it allows the characters to exhibit themselves and yet hide behind the excesses of their performances. One thinks yet again of Stanislaus's comment about his brother's confession "in a foreign language."[8]

But the melodrama of the chapter functions in another way as well. It is, finally, an expression of the conventional nature of the unconscious, which, after all, contains the stuff of melodrama. In the unconscious, we see ourselves in terms of the basic drama of victory and defeat; we are protagonists and antagonists, the damned and the redeemed. Beaufoy accuses Bloom of leading "a quadruple existence! Street angel and house devil" (p. 460). One of the points implied by the melodrama of "Circe" is that these roles and more are a part of the unconscious. The paradox of "Circe" is that

---

[8] See Stanislaus Joyce, *The Dublin Diary of Stanislaus Joyce*, ed. George Harris Healey (London: Faber and Faber, 1962), p. 81.

we do not move beneath convention to the "real" original selves of the characters or through rhetoric to "sincerity." What we realize in the mode of "Circe" is that the unconscious *is* conventional and rhetorical: in the unconscious, myth and melodrama, archetype and stereotype merge. We play the roles basic to all four: parents, children, lovers, daemons. Somewhere in the dark recesses of his psyche, Stephen is a rebel and redeemer, Bloom a betrayed martyr. "Circe" helps us to see that the symbolic parallels between the characters and past literary figures are part of the role playing in the unconscious itself.

Now that the significance of the rhetoric of the drama has been explored, at least one important question remains: What is the relationship between the madcap drama of "Circe" and the plot and theme of the story? What Joyce chooses to do in "Circe" is to blend the melodrama of the unconscious with the surface melodrama of the plot. For at this point in the book the naturalistic plot is itself highly melodramatic: amid the lurking evils of the seamy underside of Dublin life, the older character rescues the younger from deceit and brutality. Here is the potential climax of the plot. Instead of writing *against* sentimentality, against the notion of climax as he does in "Ithaca," he milks the melodrama of both the naturalistic and the psychic plots for all they're worth. The pathopoeia of the chapter provides a chance for the *book* as well as the characters to act out—to try on yet another outmoded literary formula, to elaborate on it, to parody it and yet to get mileage out of it at the same time. One of the most interesting aspects of the melodrama in "Circe" is how exaggeration becomes yet another mode of possibility *and* skepticism. Acting *out* (that is, expression of the unconscious) and *acting* out (that is, theatricality) are one and the same: although uncensored impulses are dramatized in the chapter, it is within a *context* of uncertainty, disguise, and obvious theatrical illusion. Even more so than in the skits of "Cyclops" and the scenes in "Oxen of the Sun," in "Circe," we find the playing out of *possible* relationships among the characters. The climaxes that are staged in the chapter are often more of a suggestion to the reader than a decisive event (physical or psychological) for the characters.

For example, at the end of the chapter, Joyce stages such a climax: the appearance of Rudy. Nothing could be more sentimental than a pantomime vision of Rudy "in mauve and lambswool." Nothing could be more stagy than suggesting that the chapter could end climactically, with Bloom rescuing Stephen and finding in him a substitute for his dead child. As in the pastiche of Charles Lamb in "Oxen of the Sun," where the romantic style seems to hold out the possibility of a happy ending, in the pathetic, even bathetic vision of Rudy, we feel a potential climax.

What the vision of Rudy does at the end of the chapter is to dramatize a lost possibility—that is, to project one of Bloom's deepest wishes at a strategic moment in the text. The vision of kidnapped Rudy is a symbolic projection of Bloom's desire and his loss. Earlier in the day he thinks to himself: "If little Rudy had lived. See him grow up. Hear his voice in the house. Walking beside Molly in an Eton suit. My son. Me in his eyes. Strange feeling it would be. From me. Just a chance" (p. 89). At the end of "Circe," Bloom almost gets his wish. We see the lost possibility dramatized: Rudy appears, eleven years, instead of eleven days old.

But unlike the visions of Bloom's mother, father, and wife, the vision of Rudy does not speak to him. Rudy is conjured up in the magic of "Circe," but the wish fulfillment is not totally successful—reality seeps in, the vision is incomplete. The sense of irretrievable and premature loss is expressed in the incompleteness of the dialogue. The vision of Rudy as Little Lord Fauntleroy and a Yeatsian stolen child (the stereotypical Celtic child kidnapped by the fairies) expresses Bloom's desire for and loss of the perfect male child in the family romance. The vision of Rudy at this particular time suggests not that Bloom recovers his son

Rudy in Stephen but that Bloom *acts* like a father to Stephen.

Hugh Kenner says that in the pantomime vision of Rudy, Joyce is playing a game by creating "a parallel to the old-fashioned novel with a happy ending. In life," he continues, "things are not transformed like that overnight, though it was a convention of fiction, once, that they might be, as it is a convention of pantomime."[9] The symbolic action of the chapter thus represents not so much a radical change in the characters as a charged exploration of their latent desires and fears and their origins expressed in a series of possible scenes. It allows us to feel where the climax *would have been* in a more conventional novel. Like all the other chapters, "Circe" is Joyce's experiment with stylistic and novelistic possibilities. The melodrama, the histrionics, offer a type of resolution and climax that other books have given decisively and unequivocally—how many naive writers have resolved their plots by resorting to fantasy and dream?

Here Joyce plays with these same devices in a highly sophisticated way. The "highs" in this chapter are more *allusions* to climaxes than climaxes, for a number of reasons. First, the context of theatrical illusion and *trompe-l'oeil* (or deceit of the eye) in the chapter makes it impossible to determine the relationship between the dramas being staged and the psyches of the characters. How can "moments" like the vision of Rudy, or Bloom looking through the keyhole at Boylan and Molly, really be decisive when we are uncertain of the degree to which they represent the character's experience? This confusion is compounded, of course, by the fact that most of the dramas in which the characters participate are *composite* dramas that recombine elements from the book's past, transgressing the boundaries of the psyches of the characters. It is difficult to say what is mere theatrical magic produced for the reader's benefit. Finally, the structure of anticlimax—that is, the undermining of the

---

[9] See Kenner, "Circe," p. 359.

seeming decisiveness of events—also undercuts the idea of crisis and radical change.

That is why it is difficult to accept fully Hugh Kenner's idea that Bloom, at least, undergoes a "psychic purgation,"[10] or James Maddox's thesis that Bloom confronts "his own sense of worthlessness and futility" (an "inheritance from his father"). "Circe" dramatizes, Maddox says, Bloom's ability to absorb his sense of impotence and despair, "to accept his own feelings of futility and yet still commit himself to the world of broken lampshades. Insofar as Bloom is able at least to accept the unhappy circumstances of his father's death, he is able to move tentatively toward the vision of himself as a father."[11] Well, yes and no. Bloom does act like a father in "Circe," from his entrance into Nighttown to search for Stephen, "the best of the lot," to his defense of him and his literal "rescue" at the end of the chapter. But it is impossible to pinpoint the relationship between the expressionistic dialogues and these naturalistic events. The direct relevance of Bloom's confrontation with his father to his relationship with Stephen is also less obvious than Maddox suggests. (Besides, the most "dramatic" of all the episodes is Bloom's confrontation with Bella/Bello rather than with Virag, and the most psychologically revealing is, as Maddox acknowledges, Bloom's vision of Boylan and Molly.) More importantly, Maddox overlooks the fact that Bloom's confrontation with his own worthlessness is a process that occurs *continually*, all day long. The symbolic and dramatic projection of previously repressed content reveals something about the psyches of the characters: it demonstrates that crisis is coextensive with their lives. They are constantly fighting the battles they fight in "Circe"—constantly, in Bloom's case, acknowledging and then repressing their feelings. "No one is anything. This is the very worst hour of the day," Bloom thinks in "Lestrygonians" (p. 164),

[10] See Kenner, "Circe," p. 356.

[11] James H. Maddox, Jr., *Joyce's Ulysses and the Assault upon Character* (New Brunswick: Rutgers University Press, 1978), p. 142.

and then gets on with his physical and mental wanderings. "Circe" presents a stunning image of Bloom's ability to survive, but it is an ability that we have seen all day.

The mounting excitement of "Circe" cannot be denied, but the whole of *Ulysses* makes us suspicious of the decisiveness of one event, physical or psychological. The aggressively overt symbolism in the chapter sometimes amounts to a kind of mock peripety. For example, as many critics have observed, Bloom's button snaps and he faces up to Zoe, evidently realizing "who wears the pants." The popping of the button is a real occurrence (Bloom is missing his button later on), and it symbolically expresses Bloom's sudden assertiveness: momentarily, he reasserts his masculinity. But the symbol itself is comic and burlesque—one would expect the popping of a button, even a back trouser button, to suggest the possibility that the pants might fall down—and some of this enters into the symbol to color its potential as a serious symbol of the reemergence of masculine dominance. The symbol here is a leaky vessel—for all its overt meaningfulness, it reminds us of its opposite. Furthermore, soon after this seemingly climactic reversal, the height of Bloom's masochistic fantasies are dramatized as he welcomes Boylan to Molly's bed. And if Bloom's troubles are acknowledged and conquered in the chapter, why does he continue to suppress the thought of Molly in the Cabman's shelter? ("Suppose she was gone when he? . . ." [p. 653]). The structure of anticlimax and the painstaking detail in *Ulysses* have shown us that if people do change, it is inch by inch rather than all at once, and in the dark rather than in a flash of blinding light.

The indeterminacy of events in "Circe" is further revealed in an interesting allusion in "Ithaca" to one of the Circean dialogues:

Why did Bloom refrain from stating that he had frequented the university of life?

Because of his fluctuating incertitude as to whether this

observation had or had not been already made by him to Stephen or by Stephen to him. (P. 682)

The "fluctuating incertitude" is a telling phrase, appropriate to our own uncertainty about how to treat the "events" of "Circe." Bloom has "spoken" this phrase, not to Stephen but to Philip Beaufoy, in defense of his own practical education. The question and answer in "Ithaca" imply that Bloom has a hazy recollection of the thought, as if some of the dialogue in "Circe" represented thought that hovers between the subconscious and the conscious. The significance of the dialogues and tableaux in "Circe" cannot be pinned down more explicitly than this. Hugh Kenner speaks of the "accidental psychoanalysis" that occurs in the chapter in an attempt to explain how a character can *change* without ever becoming conscious of his painful thoughts as he would in psychoanalysis. The stress of the physical surroundings does produce a kind of psychological climax in the characters, but, finally, the climax is literary—the latent problems of the characters are given form in the symbolic landscape of the chapter, just as their actions and conscious feelings are expressed in musical phrases in "Sirens."

The stylistic strategy of histrionics and catharsis in "Circe" fails as a "key" to the book. The talky, desultory style of "Eumaeus" is an intentional letdown for the reader after the explosives in Nighttown. Finally, if the peripety were placed firmly, unequivocally, in "Circe," there would be no need for the "Ithaca" chapter, which recapitulates and sorts out the events of the day yet once more.

VII

"Eumaeus": The Way of All Language

By the time he reaches "Eumaeus," the reader is prepared for outrageous experiments in *Ulysses*; after "Cyclops," "Oxen of the Sun," and "Circe," he no longer expects the relative tameness of the initial style. The first sentence of the chapter informs him of the book's return to narrative after the expressionistic drama of "Circe." In this first sentence, we recognize the sound of other chapter openings in *Ulysses*, such as "Stately, plump Buck Mulligan came from the stairhead" and "By lorries along Sir John Rogerson's Quay Mr Bloom walked soberly," where the physical action is described in faintly pompous, inaugural tones. But in "Eumaeus," precision is exaggerated into punctiliousness, the literate diction cedes to faded elegance and cliché.

> Preparatory to anything else Mr Bloom brushed off the greater bulk of the shavings and handed Stephen the hat and ashplant and bucked him up generally in orthodox Samaritan fashion, which he very badly needed. (Pp. 612-613)

Circumspect, in a succession of phrases, the sentence seeks to modify and amplify its subject. Beginning portentously with the phrase "preparatory to anything else," it betrays its pretensions with slang expressions ("buck him up"). Redundant, idiomatic, it finally collapses into anticlimax. Although the reader no longer expects to find the initial style, he might wonder why this sentence would be produced by a man who could write, "Two shafts of soft day-light fell across the flagged floor from the high barbicans: and at the meeting of their rays a cloud of coalsmoke and fumes of fried grease floated, turning" (p. 11).

As the first sentence indicates, the language of "Eumaeus" is pretentious, verbose, and clichéd. It displays a love of elegant variation, convoluted phrases, and Latinate diction: "Possibly perceiving an expression of dubiosity on their faces, the globetrotter went on adhering to his adventures" (p. 628). Where one word will do, it insists on a phrase ("his expression of features"). But its most salient characteristic is its commonplaces, idioms, proverbs, and clichés:

> . . . on his expressed desire for some beverage to drink Mr Bloom, in view of the hour it was and there being no pumps of Vartry water available for their ablutions, let alone drinking purposes, hit upon an expedient by suggesting, off the reel, the propriety of the cabman's shelter, as it was called, hardly a stonesthrow away near Butt Bridge, where they might hit upon some drinkables in the shape of a milk and soda or a mineral. (P. 613)

As can be seen from the previous examples, the style has pretensions to elegance. Sometimes the writing tries to be coy and cute: "The keeper of the shelter in the middle of this *tête-à-tête* put a boiling swimming cup of a choice concoction labelled coffee on the table and a rather antediluvian specimen of a bun, or so it seemed" (p. 622). It specializes, however, in little verbal twists on clichés ("gone the way of all buttons," "on the tapis," "ventilated the matter thoroughly"), or in coinages ("Sherlockholmsing it") and forced puns ("Telegraphic, Tell a graphic lie") of a type Lenehan would offer in "Aeolus." The style, in fact, is not the "namby-pamby" style of a Gerty MacDowell but a style that exaggerates the qualities of the more educated, garrulous talk of the storytellers, would-be rhetoricians, and resident Dublin wits at their worst moments: "So, as neither of them were particularly pressed for time, as it happened, and the temperature refreshing since it cleared up after the recent visitation of Jupiter Pluvius, they dandered along past by where the empty vehicle was waiting without a fare or a jarvey" (p. 614). The elaborate use of classical allusion to describe rain ("the visit of Jupiter Pluvius"), and then the slight twist on the accepted phrase ("visitation"), plus the word "dandered," could originate with a Lenehan but not with a Gerty MacDowell. "Looking back now in a retrospective kind of arrangement" (p. 651), the narrator says, and this recalls the pretentious critical vocabulary of Tom Kernan, as mocked by Mr Power: "—Trenchant, Mr Power said laughing. He's [Tom Kernan's] dead nuts on that. And the retrospective arrangement" (p. 91). Stanislaus once described the language of "Eumaeus" as "flabby Dublin journalese, with its weak effort to be witty,"[1] and there is something in "Eumaeus" of the headings (both the pomposity of the late Victorian headings and the smart slang of the "modern" headings) and of the conversation in "Aeolus." The common denominator of all these styles, including Gerty MacDowell's, is their pretense to some kind of fine writing.

The elegance is faded and the language misfires—all deliberately, of course, on Joyce's part. For in "Eumaeus," Joyce chooses the "wrong" word as scrupulously as he chooses the right one in the early chapters. Comedy arises from the narrator's misuse of language—"originality" enters through the back door of error. In phrases like "nipped in the bud of premature decay" and "redolent with rotten corn," we see the narrator's reach exceed his grasp. Language in the chapter glances off its object. A succession of phrases is offered, none of which captures meaning fully. In the following example, we see the narrator trying and failing to duplicate subtle novelistic description: "He displayed half solicitude, half curiosity, augmented by friend-

---

[1] Letter from Stanislaus to James Joyce, 26 February 1922, in *Letters of James Joyce*, Vol. 3, ed. Richard Ellmann (New York: The Viking Press, 1966), p. 58.

liness"—the mathematics of the situation (half and half, plus some more) tells us that too many phrases are needed. As in the language of "Cyclops" and "Nausicaa," sentences that begin with fanfare cannot maintain their high tone. In "Eumaeus," however, it is as if the sentences forget where they begin. (See the sentence beginning with the word "Accordingly" and ending with the words "Dan Bergin's" on page 613.) There is something vaguely senescent about this writing, from the wandering sentences to the half-remembered idioms. It is as if all the allusions, clichés, and idioms of a lifetime floated somewhere in the memory and were summoned forth for the sake of the story. The movement of the narrative mind is like the stream-of-consciousness of the early chapters slowed down, its associations grown fuzzy. It is as if the silent monologue of the early chapters had become a rambling and tedious after-dinner speech. The narrative is indeed the "narrative old" that Joyce described to Gilbert.[2]

But the "memory" invoked in the chapter is best regarded not as a personal but a collective one, specifically, a linguistic memory. The cumulative effect of all these clichés is to make "Eumaeus" into a kind of encyclopedia of received phrases. If the language of "Eumaeus" is enervated, it is not merely to reflect the fatigue of the characters or a narrator but to reveal that language is tired and "old," used and reused so many times that it runs in grooves. The language of "Eumaeus" is the public, anonymous "voice of culture" first heard in the headings of "Aeolus," a transpersonal repository of received ideas. Just as the narrative of "Aeolus" offers a compendium of rhetorical figures, the narrative of "Eumaeus" offers a compendium of clichés, from a catchword of popular melodrama ("balderdash"), to bureaucratic jargon ("embark on a policy," "Accordingly, after a few such preliminaries"), to proverbs ("as things always moved with

---

[2] See Stuart Gilbert, *James Joyce's Ulysses: A Study*, rev. ed. (New York: Vintage Books-Random House, 1952), p. 30.

the time"), to the low Dublin idiom of the dun in "Cyclops" ("hang it, the first go-off"). Although one can describe the habit of mind or the tone in the chapter, one's final impression of "Eumaeus" is of a body of language—as Gerald Bruns says, "a world of banal locutions within which both narrator and story struggle into being."[3] Clichés in "Eumaeus" are not relegated through indirect discourse to the mind of a character, as in "Nausicaa," or separated typographically from other writing, like the headings of "Aeolus." In "Eumaeus," all writing has become cliché. Joyce gives us, then, a picture of all language in the debased state of the word "love" in the parody of "Cyclops." More than Flaubert in *Bouvard et Pécuchet* or the *Dictionary of Accepted Ideas*, Joyce focuses on received *locutions*, the ready-made phrases that express the received ideas of society.

Both description and discourse pass through the crucible of cliché. Instead of the narrator's borrowing the language of the characters, as he does in free indirect discourse, in "Eumaeus" the discourse of the characters is assimilated to the language of narration (as it is also in "Oxen of the Sun"). "Mr Bloom, likely to poohpooh the situation as egregious balderdash" is a translation of Bloom's reactions into a language he would never use. Neither the prissy "poohpooh the situation" nor the blustery "egregious balderdash" could possibly originate with Leopold Bloom. Similarly, the following passage of Bloom's thoughts is paraphrased:

It was a subject of regret and absurd as well on the face of it and no small blame to our vaunted society that the man in the street, when the system really needed toning up, for a matter of a couple of paltry pounds, was debarred from seeing more of the world they lived in instead of being always cooped up since my old stick-in-the-mud took me for a wife. After all, hang it, they had their eleven

[3] Gerald L. Bruns, "Eumaeus," in *James Joyce's Ulysses: Critical Essays*, ed. Clive Hart and David Hayman (Berkeley: University of California Press, 1974), p. 368.

and more humdrum months of it and merited a radical change of *venue* after the grind of city life in the summertime, for choice, when Dame Nature is at her spectacular best, constituting nothing but a new lease of life. (P. 627)

We recognize this as having elements of Bloom's thought, in its plans for the welfare of society, in its use of the formulae of public wisdom, even in its getting its clichés confused (compare "lease of life" with Bloom's "out of the land of Egypt and into the house of bondage" [p. 122]). But this is not the sound of Bloom's mind—from its beginning in the tones of a newspaper editorial, to its shift to the low Dublin idiom, to its conclusion in the tones of a pretentious advertisement in a travel magazine. (Its anger is also alien to Bloom.) This is a picture of Bloom's mind cheated of all its vitality and curiosity. One has only to compare this passage with a passage of stream-of-consciousness in an earlier chapter to see the distortion:

The chemist turned back page after page. Sandy shrivelled smell he seems to have. Shrunken skull. And old. Quest for the philosopher's stone. The alchemists. Drugs age you after mental excitement. Lethargy then. Why? Reaction. A lifetime in a night. Gradually changes your character. Living all the day among herbs, ointments, disinfectants. All his alabaster lilypots. . . . Enough stuff here to chloroform you. Test: turns blue litmus paper red. Chloroform. Overdose of laudanum. . . . Paragoric poppysyrup bad for cough. Clogs the pores or the phlegm. Poisons the only cures. Remedy where you least expect it. Clever of nature. ("Lotus-Eaters," P. 84)

The depiction of the act of imagination here is different from the one in "Eumaeus," even though in both passages Bloom relies on the formulae in his memory. In "Lotus-Eaters," his manipulation of these formulae is creative, intelligent, funny. "Eumaeus" gives us a travestied form of Bloom's stream-of-consciousness, a reduction of it to its least common denominator.

What the stream-of-consciousness technique and the third-person narrative norm in the early chapters had in common was that they purported to present "reality" directly, either psychological or material "reality." In "Eumaeus," this pretense of unmediated vision is exposed once more. The chapter marks the climax of the increasing indirection of the narration seen in "Cyclops" and "Oxen of the Sun." The indirection is flagrantly advertised in various aspects of style: rhetorically in the technique of indirect discourse; semantically in the use of elegant variation, euphemism, and cliché; and syntactically in the circumlocutions of the sentence. In "Eumaeus," Joyce shows us language that is patently inadequate to the task of capturing the subtle nuances of behavior or even the quality of a physical action—a travesty, that is, of the initial style. Instead of language that is able to fix essences in confident phrases, this is language that casts a net of words in the forlorn hope of capturing meaning. It names rather than presents emotional and psychological behavior: "Mr Bloom, actuated by motives of inherent delicacy, inasmuch as he always believed in minding his own business, moved off but nevertheless remained on the *qui vive* with just a shade of anxiety though not funkyish in the least" (p. 616). The linguistic tools available are impediments to the capturing of the complexity and subtlety of reality: trying to capture nuance with phrases like "inherent delicacy" and "*qui vive*" is like trying to whittle with a sledgehammer. Wolfgang Iser's description of one of the styles in the "Oxen of the Sun" chapter is equally appropriate to "Eumaeus": "As language approached, reality seemed rather to withdraw than to come closer."[4] The twists and turns of the phrases, the elegant variation, the attempt of the writing to wrap itself around its object in

[4] Wolfgang Iser, *The Implied Reader: Patterns of Communication in Prose Fiction from Bunyan to Beckett* (Baltimore: The Johns Hopkins University Press, 1974), p. 191.

"Eumaeus" reveals the essential discrepancy between language and the reality it seeks to describe. If the circumlocution and the modifying phrases of Henry James's style convince us that language is a subtle and pliable enough instrument for capturing the nuances of life, the travestied style of "Eumaeus" reveals Joyce's essential skepticism about language. In "Eumaeus," he demonstrates once again that life is mediated through the abuses of language.

One can say that "Eumaeus" is a version of the writer's struggle to write with a language that is contaminated, a language that is no longer a transparent medium. In the preface to his *Essais critiques*, Roland Barthes discusses the writer's struggle with language, and I quote him at length because I think he describes the view of language Joyce expresses in "Eumaeus." According to Barthes:

> *La matière première de la littérature n'est pas l'innommable, mais bien au contraire le nommé; celui qui veut écrire doit savoir qu'il commence un long concubinage avec un langage qui est toujours* antérieur. *L'écrivain n'a donc nullement à «arracher» un verbe au silence . . . mais à l'inverse, et combien plus difficilement, plus cruellement et moins glorieusement, à détacher une parole seconde de l'engluement des paroles premières que lui fournissent le monde, l'histoire, son existence, bref un intelligible qui préexiste, car il vient dans un monde plein de langage. . . . [N]aître n'est rien d'autre que trouver ce code tout fait et devoir s'en accommoder. On entend souvent dire que l'art a pour charge d'exprimer l'inexprimable: c'est le contraire qu'il faut dire (sans nulle intention de paradoxe): toute la tâche de l'art est d'inexprimer l'exprimable, d'enlever à la langue du monde, qui est la pauvre et puissante langue des passions, une parole* autre, *une parole* exacte.[5]

---

[5] Roland Barthes, *Essais critiques* (Paris: Seuil, 1964), p. 14-15. The following is Richard Howard's translation of the passage from Barthes's preface: The primary substance of literature is not the unnamable, but on the contrary the named; the man who wants to write must know that he is beginning

"Eumaeus" represents "the world full of language," something that only Flaubert before Joyce had treated so fully in fiction. Through interruption and displacement in the early chapters of *Ulysses*, Joyce dramatized the struggle between writing and rewriting, personal signature and the world's language in "Eumaeus," he deliberately stages an "accommodation" to writing that is "previous."

There is no particular exponent of language who encroaches on the writer's ego: the "fear" of other writing in "Eumaeus" is generalized beyond individual predecessors (as in "Oxen of the Sun") or even generic models (as in "Cyclops"). Joyce does not display the "anxiety of influence" which Harold Bloom describes, that Freudian battle of Titanic egos; instead, he reveals a more general anxiety about writing as an echo of other writing[6] and language that has been tainted by its prior use. Joyce is quoted as having remarked to a friend: "I'd like a language which is above all languages, a language to which all will do service. I cannot express myself in English without enclosing myself in a tradition."[7] Again, one can see Joyce's desire to tran-

---

a long concubinage with a language which is always *previous*. The writer does not "wrest" speech from silence . . . but inversely, and how much more arduously, more cruelly and less gloriously, detaches a secondary language from the slime of primary languages afforded him by the world, history, his existence, in short by an intelligibility which preexists him, for he comes into a world full of language. . . . [T]o be born is nothing but to find this code ready-made and to be obliged to accommodate oneself to it. We often hear it said that it is the task of art to *express the inexpressible*; it is the contrary which must be said (with no intention to paradox): the whole task of art is to *unexpress the expressible*, to kidnap from the world's language, which is the poor and powerful language of the passions, another speech, an exact speech.

See *Critical Essays*, trans. Richard Howard (Evanston, Ill.: Northwestern University Press, 1972), p. xvii.

[6] See Bloom's *The Anxiety of Influence: A Theory of Poetry* (New York: Oxford University Press, 1973).

[7] Quoted in Stefan Zweig, *The World of Yesterday* (New York: 1943); reprinted in Richard Ellmann, *James Joyce* (New York: Oxford University Press, 1959), p. 410.

scend the limitations of language and the classifications of reality offered by his predecessors.

The problem posed by this linguistic inheritance, however, is not only that it is a threat to the writer's ego but also that it assaults intelligence and meaning. It is the Flaubertian language of stupidity. The clichés and proverbs, the public wisdom of "Eumaeus," exemplify the premature "conclusions" leading to stupidity. The clichés are a system of classification through which life in all its complexity is forced. This anonymous voice of culture expounds a rigid system of meaning, whether in its old wives' tales or its scientific formulae. It is not that these "conclusions" are always untrue but that they pretend they are the only possible truth. They organize the world in terms of type and generalization that belie the contingency of individual fact.

If in the style of scrupulous meanness Joyce tried to pare away the numerous associations of words, in "Eumaeus" he deliberately decided to let the linguistic memory loose on the page to devour the individual style. If the style of scrupulous meanness was in part a defense against a lapse into the stupidity of language, the style of "Eumaeus" suggests that no one is exempt from this stupidity. For by the time we reach "Eumaeus," we realize that everyone is implicated in it. Wayne Booth's "stable irony" is no longer possible, for no one, no writer or reader, can remain outside the ring of stupidity that Joyce draws. The condescending irony of Flaubert to his characters in *Madame Bovary* and of Joyce to the "submerged population" in *Dubliners* and in "Nausicaa" is obsolete. The narrative of "Eumaeus" embodies, with gross exaggeration, our inescapable stupidities; no one, Joyce seems to be saying, even the most "scrupulous" writer, can prevent the presence of at least some cliché in his writing.

But if he abandoned the defense against stupidity available in the style of scrupulous meanness, Joyce substituted another defense. On one level, the writing of "Eumaeus" functions like the parodies of "Cyclops": it attempts to disarm criticism through self-mockery. There is something redemptive about conceding one's stupidity. Both the writer's and the reader's implicit defense against stupidity is to recognize it. We recognize a cliché as a cliché—a reader who does not would not be the one for whom the book was created (and only someone like Gerty MacDowell or a cliché expert like Joyce could produce such a thorough list of received locutions). The attempt to outdo a Gerty Mac-Dowell in producing clichés is a strategy that can be used after stable irony is obsolete. But there is a greater sense of defensiveness about the writing in "Eumaeus," for in turning his writing over to cliché, Joyce asserts his own consciousness over the kind of inadvertent slips into cliché displayed by even the best writers. The compulsiveness and comprehensiveness of the catalogue of clichés in "Eumaeus" makes one sense that Joyce felt the worst thing that he could do was to accidentally include a cliché without recognizing it as such. There is a driven quality to the writing, as if by including all possible clichés, Joyce could prove himself their master. Instead of mocking eloquence and emotion by rewriting it in parodic form (as in "Cyclops"), Joyce subjects all writing to "stupidity" right away. In this sense, the writing takes no risks. It is like lying down to prevent a fall.

But on the other hand, the writing of "Eumaeus" is a virtuoso display of what a writer can do once he accepts the inadequacy of language: it is both a demonstration of the problems of language and a linguistic performance. If everybody succumbs to cliché some of the time, no one but Joyce would think of writing in cliché for a whole chapter. By intensifying the use of clichés, by making them come at the reader so thick and so fast at every comma, Joyce exposes their absurdity. He destroys the context in which clichés might appear natural (as in a nineteenth-century sentimental novel, for example, in which some cliché is permissible and, indeed, expected). But Joyce also asserts his own ability to tell a story using only this execrable language, to put more of an obstacle in his way than any other writer, and then to proceed to keep our attention by showing us just how wonderfully bad the style is. In fact, what is startling about the clichés in "Eumaeus" is that Joyce deliberately does nothing to revitalize them in the way he does in "Cyclops," for example, or in *Finnegans Wake*. In "Language of/as Gesture in Joyce," David Hayman shows effectively how Joyce often cleverly returns the language of cliché to gesture (for example, by turning the expression "I could eat you up" into "We could ate you, par Buccas, and imbabe through you, reassuranced in the wild lac of gotliness" in *Finnegans Wake* [p. 378]).[8] Conversely, in "Eumaeus," he gives us the narrator's deliberately feeble attempts to revive cliché in expressions like "the horse at the end of his tether," which applies to a literal horse. A phrase like "gone the way of all buttons" is the kind of phrase that would become a pun in *Finnegans Wake* (one can imagine that the substitution of "buttons" for "flesh" in the phrase "gone the way of all flesh" would at least produce "gone the way of all buttoms"). The performance in "Eumaeus" consists of Joyce's *refusal* to revitalize cliché, his insistence on using the worn-out style to tell the story.

The enormous confidence behind the writing and the "risk" that Joyce really does take in "Eumaeus" is most apparent when we realize the chapter's place in the book. In "Eumaeus," what could have been the dramatic and allegorical climax of the plot coincides with the nadir of the writing. "Eumaeus" represents the recognition scene between Stephen (Telemachus) and Bloom (Odysseus), and this has a special place in the plot of the story. The "Eumaeus" chapter is Joyce's deliberate "sabotage" of both style and the dramatic climax. The coming together of Stephen and Bloom is rendered entirely in vacuous clichés and vague phrases: "Side by side," "tête-à-tête," "with a certain anal-

---

[8] David Hayman, "Language of/as Gesture in Joyce," in *Ulysses: cinquante ans après: Témoignages franco-anglais sur le chef-d'oeuvre de James Joyce*, ed. Louis Bonnerot (Paris: Didier, 1974), p. 221n.

ogy," Joyce's Odysseus and Telemachus are united. What other writer would render this climax in the following way?

> The queer suddenly things he popped out with attracted the elder man who was several years the other's senior or like his father. . . . Though they didn't see eye to eye in everything, a certain analogy there somehow was, as if both their minds were travelling, so to speak, in the one train of thought. (P. 656)

and

> —Yes, Stephen said uncertainly, because he thought he felt a strange kind of flesh of a different man approach him, sinewless and wobbly and all that. (P. 660)

Almost everything possible is done to the language here to destroy the emotion and eloquence of the dramatic climax. In the first quotation, for example, the succession of clichés, the vagueness, and the comic literalization of the metaphor "train of thought" all serve to deflate the language and the event. It is possible to imagine certain parts of the second quotation written "straight" in another novel: "He felt a strange kind of flesh . . . sinewless." But characteristically in the chapter, Joyce deliberately overwrites the phrase, making it redundant ("a strange kind of flesh of a different man") and mocking Stephen's important perception and the temporary eloquence of the writing with the sloppy "and all that." Similarly, the phrase "the elder man who was . . . like his father" is conceivable in another novel, but the insertion of the phrase "several years the other's senior" deliberately sabotages the simile (and thus the allegorical unity of Odysseus and Telemachus). The eloquence of the writing and the significance of the drama are deflated: both style and climax are revealed to be clichés—one linguistic, the other dramatic.

And yet, somehow, by "sacrificing" the moment of climax, Joyce gets something back. The clichéd writing is an artistic strategy to allow emotion and inarticulate eloquence to enter the narrative obliquely. In language that deliberately claims very little, he finds a way to suggest emotion while avoiding sentimentality, and significance while avoiding dramatic climax. Somehow the very lameness and incompetence of the writing creates the proper significance of the moment of meeting: displaying neither the solemnity of myth nor the neat doubleness of the "mock-heroic," the moment possesses, to use Joyce's idiom, "a certain sort of significance." By destroying eloquence, he allows emotion to be felt. The climax of the story is transcribed in the language of cliché because there is no other narrative means available that has not been "scorched." The clichés are, in effect, both the sabotage of style and a means of allowing the narrative to continue.

In "Cyclops," the exposure of the book's limitations allows the book to continue and expand. One can view the destruction of "literature" in "Eumaeus" in the same paradoxical way: literature is destroyed as the book expands. I have charted a movement away from "literature" in *Ulysses*, in the introduction of the subliterary text of the newspaper in "Aeolus" and the subliterary clichés of "Cyclops." The inclusion of the subliterary is, however, a part of a larger enterprise of the book, which is to expand its borders to include what is outside of it. The intrusion of the headings in "Aeolus" signifies not only the usurpation of narrative authority and the appearance of the public language of journalism but also the book's incorporation of something it had excluded. If the headings displace the narrative, it is because the narrative, in a sense, displaced journalism in its original narrative contract. It implicitly agreed to exclude it. In *Ulysses*, Joyce progressively incorporates in the novel what has been banished from it previously: other forms (for example, drama, catechism, newspaper) and other styles.

The text, like the self, is a circle that excludes everything outside itself. Through the devices of interruption and displacement, Joyce has dramatized what Stephen learned in

"Proteus," that what is outside is "there all the time without you."[9] Now in "Eumaeus," the total displacement of the literate narrative by cliché expands the limits of the book as literature *and* the limits of the "self" (both the narrative "self" and the "self" of the characters), for the language is both subliterary and transpersonal (in contrast, allegory, for example, is transpersonal but not subliterary).

"He is a purely literary writer," T. S. Eliot observed of Joyce to Virginia Woolf. "He is founded upon Walter Pater with a dash of Newman."[10] The clichéd style of "Eumaeus" (unlike the pastiche in "Oxen of the Sun") can be regarded as Joyce's deliberate refusal of this kind of mantle. In "Ithaca," he rejected "literature" in a different way: by pretending to use the "neutral" language of the sciences. By the close of "Eumaeus," he had taken both his indictment of the "anonymous voice of culture" and his use of it as far as it could go in *Ulysses.*

[9] I am using Stephen's words metaphorically. As I said in my discussion of "Nausicaa," he refers to material reality in the chapter. But the point is that what is outside the self is always there; it does not depend upon the existence of the self.

[10] Quoted in *A Writer's Diary: Being Extracts from the Diary of Virginia Woolf*, ed. Leonard Woolf (New York: Harcourt, Brace and Company, 1953), p. 49.

VIII

"Ithaca": The Order of Things

"Ithaca" represents the climax of the book's movement away from "literature," a movement initiated in the subliterary headings of "Aeolus." The narrative of the chapter dons the antiliterary mask of science. Its technical, denotative language, like the prose advocated by Thomas Sprat's Royal Society, represents science's "answer" to metaphor and fine writing. But Joyce's use of this kind of language in a book that began as a novel is subversive to literature in a more profound way: no other modern novel works quite as hard to dispense with most of the beauties of style. Joyce called "Ithaca" the "ugly duckling" of *Ulysses*,[1] but in a book that he called his "damned monster-novel,"[2] the ugly duckling is likely to be the favorite child. In reading "Ithaca," one senses that a page has been turned in literary history. From now on, it would seem, the most interesting creative project for the modern writer is to create ugly ducklings rather than swans. If the style of scrupulous meanness was Joyce's early answer to the fine writing and purple prose of his contemporaries, the language of "Ithaca" mounts a far more radical attack on the idea of literary style.

The chapter that deliberately dispenses with the beauties of style dispenses with other niceties of novel writing as

[1] Quoted in Frank Budgen, *James Joyce and the Making of Ulysses* (1934; reprint ed., Bloomington: Indiana University Press, 1960), p. 258. Joyce did tell Budgen that "Ithaca" was his favorite episode.

[2] See the translation of Joyce's letter to Carlo Linati, 21 September 1920, in *Selected Letters of James Joyce*, ed. Richard Ellmann (New York: The Viking Press, 1975), pp. 270-271.

well. In it, Joyce plays with our conceptions of narrative as well as style. "Ithaca" is an anatomy of a chapter: it offers us an outline of events. Instead of the suspense of a linear plot, it advances direct questions and answers; instead of the human voice of a narrative persona, it offers a catalogue of cold, hard facts. The book seems to interrogate itself in the catechism, implicitly promising to fill in the blanks by telling us the present and past perceptions, actions, and feelings of the characters. Joyce wrote to Budgen that in the "mathematical catechism" of "Ithaca," all events would be "resolved into their cosmic, physical, psychical etc. equivalents," so that the reader would "know everything and know it in the baldest and coldest way."[3]

Both the coldness and the mechanical cataloguing in "Ithaca" are anticipated in "Wandering Rocks." The mind represented in the narrative of "Ithaca" resembles the alienated, "lateral" imagination found in the earlier chapter: it meticulously strings together facts without establishing any sense of priority among them. This narrative mind amasses facts with no regard for normal conventions of significance and relevance. In an exaggerated form of inductive observation, the lateral imagination of "Ithaca" peruses the world, exhaustively cataloguing its contents, whether they are objects in a drawer, books on a bookshelf, or thoughts in someone's mind. In "Wandering Rocks," characters are treated as physical objects moving in space; in "Ithaca," the equation of people and objects is evidence of a general tonal and emotional leveling that surpasses anything in the early

[3] Letter to Frank Budgen, end February 1921, in *Letters of James Joyce*, Vol. 1, ed. Stuart Gilbert (New York: The Viking Press, 1957), pp. 159-160. Critics have argued about whether the source of the catechism is the Christian catechism that Joyce recited as a child or the secular catechisms that he read in school, such as Mangnall's *Historical and Miscellaneous Questions*. They have argued persuasively for each of these catechisms as the "source" of the form of "Ithaca." See A. Walton Litz, "Ithaca," in *James Joyce's Ulysses: Critical Essays*, ed. Clive Hart and David Hayman (Berkeley: University of California Press, 1974), pp. 385-405, and Harry C. Staley, "Joyce's Catechisms," *James Joyce Quarterly* 6 (Winter 1968): 137-153.

chapters. The real strangeness of the writing is described beautifully by Frank Budgen: "It is the coldest episode in an unemotional book. . . . The skeleton of each fact is stripped of its emotional covering. One fact stands by the other like the skeletons of man and woman, ape and tiger in an anatomical museum at twilight, all their differences of contour made secondary by their sameness of material, function and mechanism."[4]

There is a curious sense of displacement about the writing, as if one story were being written, while another, more important story were taking place. Instead of human feelings, we are given a scientific record of phenomena. For example, Bloom's awareness of Stephen's potential significance as an adopted son and Stephen's awareness of Bloom's potential meaning as an adopted father are recorded in terms of auditory and visual sensations: "He heard in a profound ancient male unfamiliar melody the accumulation of the past" and "He saw in a quick young male familiar form the predestination of a future" (p. 689). One has only to compare some of these passages with earlier passages in the book to see how the emotions and situations of the characters are now transcribed in the language of mathematics and statistics: "Reduce Bloom by cross multiplication of reverses of fortune, from which these supports protected him, and by elimination of all positive values to a negligible negative irrational unreal quantity" (p. 725). We strain for signs of human characters and are told of physical objects; we try to understand the relationship among characters and encounter mathematical tangents and algebraic equations.

There seems to be a mechanism of avoidance in the narrative that resembles Bloom's sudden scrutiny of his fingernails at the mention of Blazes Boylan in "Hades." In that chapter, Bloom psychologically displaces his anxieties onto a physical object; in "Ithaca," it is as if the story were displaced onto objects, as if the mechanisms of avoidance char-

---

[4] Budgen, *James Joyce and the Making of Ulysses*, p. 257.

acterized the behavior of the text. This narrative displacement, in fact, sometimes dovetails with Bloom's own
mechanism of avoidance, as in the answer to the question
"By what reflections did he, a conscious reactor against the
void incertitude, justify to himself his sentiments?" (p. 734).
The answer includes a disquisition on everything from the
"frangibility of the hymen" to the "apathy of the stars." A.
Walton Litz has observed, rightly I believe, that this answer
"is a reflection of Bloom's thought as he strives for equa-
nimity by sinking his own anxieties in the processes of nature."[5] Bloom's strategy for dealing with his domestic situation merges with the narrative strategy. The rational
organization of the catechetical form seems to shade into
Bloom's habit of rationalizing. The contiguous relationships
catalogued throughout the narrative seem like psychological
sidling, a way of not reaching a destination or climax, a
means of avoiding a final realization.

I would like to be as clear as possible about the "minds"
represented by the writing in "Ithaca." On one level, it is
Joyce, of course, who deliberately "resolves" the events into
their physical equivalents. One can imagine Joyce delight-
ing in the creation of this obstacle to his writing—to fashion
the end of the plot in this language and form is itself a tour
de force. Joyce thus sets the task for himself of sabotaging
the climax (as he did in "Eumaeus"), and yet, in his own
way, of creating the "right" ending for the book. To abandon
the arsenal of literature's weapons, like dramatic climax,
tone, style, and linear narration, and still to tell the story
is the kind of challenge Joyce enjoyed. The "lateral imagination" is the psyche represented in the text. Although I
occasionally use the term "narrator" for ease of reference,
I prefer the concept of the consciousness or mind of the text,
since Joyce does everything possible in "Ithaca" to destroy

[5] Litz, "Ithaca," p. 397. Litz goes on to say, however, that in "Ithaca" "Joyce
did not renounce his interest in 'the romantic heart of things,' but simply found
new means for expressing it." This view of what occurs in "Ithaca" is itself
a romanticizing of the text. I will discuss this in more detail shortly.

our sense of a narrating, human voice. To say that the text avoids or displaces is not to psychoanalyze Joyce but to describe the behavior of the text. One of the conventions of this particular stylistic mask in "Ithaca" is that we are told too much and not enough; the book performs a gesture of disclosure and withholding. Lastly, the habit of mind represented in "Ithaca" resembles the mind of Leopold Bloom in its displacement: at certain specific points in the text when the narrative catalogues objects or focuses on nature, it is paraphrasing the thoughts of Leopold Bloom.

Empirical reality is not totally obscured in this process— what actually happens in the chapter can be determined. As Budgen maintains, it is the emotional drama of the characters that is obscured by the writing. Yet, paradoxically, one of the effects of the disparity between the emotion we expect and the intellectualization that we find is that the chapter *is* touching in its own way.[6] It is through the intellectualizing and the coldness in "Ithaca" that Joyce is able to communicate the loneliness of Leopold Bloom, just as it is through cliché in "Eumaeus" that he is able to convey the sense of Bloom and Stephen's relationship. Somehow its coldness and its ostensible lack of interest in the emotional drama of the characters allows the narrative to be moving in certain places without immediately turning parodic, as it does in the "Cyclops" chapter, for example.

So, in the midst of the fussy, almost scholastic description of "What rendered problematic for Bloom the realisation of these mutually selfexcluding propositions," two short pairs of questions and answers appear. The preceding lengthy passage has described Bloom's experience with the "clown in quest of paternity" and his gesture of marking a florin to see if it would be returned. Now we come upon the

[6] In *Anatomy of Criticism: Four Essays* (Princeton: Princeton University Press, 1957), Northrop Frye describes the disparity as part of the "novel-anatomy combination": "In the novel-anatomy combination, too, found in the 'Ithaca' chapter, the sense of lurking antagonism between the personal and intellectual aspects of the scene accounts for much of its pathos" (p. 314).

following: "Was the clown Bloom's son? No. Had Bloom's coin returned? Never" (p. 696). The simplicity of these questions and answers is striking—the contrast in the writing brings the reader up short. He feels that he is confronting an important passage in the text. The starkness of the statement, telling us of the frustration of Bloom's desire, elicits our understanding of the depths of Bloom's loneliness. The complete avoidance of sentimentality here allows for the entrance of the reader's sympathy.

Even within one sentence, the punctilious, denotative style will suddenly give way to a short, fragile phrase of beauty. The question is asked, "Alone, what did Bloom feel?" The answer is: "The cold of interstellar space, thousands of degrees below freezing point or the absolute zero of Fahrenheit, Centigrade or Réaumur: the incipient intimations of proximate dawn" (p. 704). The soft, Latinate sounds of the final phrase surprise us after the preceding barrage of facts. In "Ithaca," lyrical passages of the type parodied in other chapters of *Ulysses* are left to stand without becoming parodic. In the midst of the scientific jargon, we come upon the following line in one of the answers: "The heaventree of stars hung with humid nightblue fruit" (p. 698). The one statement we can make about this line is that no matter what it is supposed to mean, we know from the sounds, the verbal compression, the images, and the allusion to *The Divine Comedy* that this is poetry. The line is not, however, a parody of lyricism, although one can imagine something like it on the lips of one of the "eloquent" speakers parodied during the course of *Ulysses*.[7] Somehow, it is as

[7] What significance we are supposed to attribute to this line is another matter. The two main characters have just moved out of obscurity in the direction of light—the Dantesque stars seem to offer resonance and meaning as a symbol. And yet, to call this line symbolic would be to act as if it were in another context. It is more like an allusion to symbol than a functioning symbol in the text. Because the narrative immediately returns to the language of mathematical calculation, the symbol ("the heaventree") seems to be only one type of "translation" among many possible translations, a way of perceiving that is quickly replaced by another, as it has itself replaced "the apathy of the

if the coldness and ugliness of the rest of the narration have earned the narrative the right to this lyricism without parody, as, in a different way, the scrupulous meanness of the early Joyce allowed the lyricism at the end of "The Dead" to exist. No prior context of stylistic hyperbole undermines the significance of these isolated lines as it does in "Cyclops" and "Nausicaa," no surrounding sentimentality turns this line "namby-pamby." The coldness of the narration in "Ithaca" functions to clear the air of phrases like "Love loves to love love." The writing represents a way to tell the story using the English language without parody.

But the disparity between the human story and the writing in the narrative leads to comedy as well as pathos and has important philosophical implications for the reading of the text as well. The reader finds himself bombarded with a wealth of data. If, as Joyce said in his letter, the reader is told everything, it seems as if he is told everything that he does not really need to know. The text's implicit promise to supply all the details of the plot is overzealously fulfilled. The most exhaustive answers respond to the simplest of questions.[8] What constitutes an answer becomes problematical, even in the case of the simplest questions of plot. For example, the question "What did Bloom do at the range?" receives the following response: "He removed the saucepan to the left hob, rose and carried the iron kettle to the sink in order to tap the current by turning the faucet to let it flow" (p. 670). The process of making tea is anatomized into a series of smaller actions, as details of information are given in the text that one would normally assume rather than state. The carrying of the kettle to the sink and

---

stars." This is the kind of line every student of *Ulysses* would automatically circle, without having a definite idea of what the phrase actually signifies in the text.

[8] An element of comedy is added here if one compares these questions and answers to those in the Christian catechism: the long, convoluted answers to simple questions in "Ithaca" are funny if one remembers the "simple," rotelike answers in the catechism to questions like "What is sin?"

the motive for this action ("in order to tap the current . . . to let it flow") are details that are usually taken for granted. It is not only the wealth of detail that makes this answer so strange and unexpected but also the type of information included. A similar description of Bloom's domestic ritual in "Calypso," for example, is almost as detailed: "He scalded and rinsed out the teapot and put in four full spoons of tea, tilting the kettle then to let water flow in" (p. 62). But this description is unified by the aura of domesticity that surrounds Bloom; the details of the description mirror Bloom's delight in the trappings of his domestic activity. The later description suggests instead that the narrator and the reader are unfamiliar with the act of making tea.

Similarly, the description of certain common events like a handshake, a sunrise, and a bump on the head, are documented with such precision that they are almost unrecognizable. The action of Bloom and Stephen shaking hands is not named as such; rather, their geometric relationship is described. They are described as "standing perpendicular at the same door and on different sides of its base, the lines of their valedictory arms, meeting at any point and forming any angle less than the sum of two right angles" (pp. 703-704). This is, of course, another example of the resolution of the characters into their mathematical equivalents, but to analyze a common action so scrupulously is to make the narrative very strange. Like Zeno Cosini in Italo Svevo's *Confessions of Zeno*, who thinks of the twenty-six movements necessary to the action of walking, the narrator does not take anything for granted, even the relative position of two people shaking hands. Like the narrator in "Wandering Rocks," he amasses an abundance of facts without classifying them in the conceptual categories on which both literary and nonliterary discourse generally rely. He plows through a mass of facts laboriously, as if a name were a labor-saving device of which he had never heard.

The laboriousness of this kind of description is comic; as in "Cyclops" and in the final paragraphs of "Wandering

Rocks," the writing becomes an obvious performance, an exhibition of excess. The particular comic quality of much of the narration in "Ithaca" derives from a sense of the extravagance of the writing (this is different, of course, from actual *stylistic* hyperbole). Here Freud's analysis of the comedy of the clown is applicable, for he says that we laugh at a clown because his actions "seem to us extravagant and inexpedient. We are laughing at an expenditure that is too large."[9] The term "burlesque" applies to the excessive expenditure of energy in the writing, not only in its meaning as a literary technique that employs a grand style to describe a trivial matter but in its associations with physical comedy.[10] For if one reads the description of the handshake between Stephen and Bloom, the description itself begins to seem like a Rube Goldberg invention—a ludicrously elaborate mechanism with pretensions to efficiency and accuracy, a dogged, meticulous effort with small results. The description comically perverts the fundamental law of science, which is economy, and offers a comic translation of the epic impulse to go the long way around.

In its overprecision, the narration engages in what Stephen Heath has called a transgression of "the threshold of functional relevance below which things are taken for granted," a threshold that "divides the narratable from the non-narratable."[11] This transgression is a form of what the Russian formalists have called the "defamiliarization" or

[9] Sigmund Freud, *Jokes and Their Relation to the Unconscious*, trans. James Strachey (1905); reprinted in *Theories of Comedy*, ed. Paul Lauter (New York: Doubleday & Company, Inc., 1964), p. 402.

[10] See David Hayman's discussion of farce in the "Cyclops" chapter in his article "Cyclops," in *James Joyce's Ulysses: Critical Essays*, ed. Clive Hart and David Hayman (Berkeley: University of California Press, 1974), pp. 243-275. In "Cyclops," the exuberant energy of the writing leads to a more farcical performance.

[11] Stephen Heath, "Structuration of the Novel-Text: Method and Analysis," in *Signs of the Times: Introductory Readings in Textual Semiotics* (Cambridge, Eng.: Granta, 1971), p. 75.

making strange of the text (the type of thing we saw in "Wandering Rocks"). This kind of overprecision can serve varied functions in a literary text. For instance, in *Gulliver's Travels*, the purpose of the microscopic perspective is primarily satiric; it throws into relief the absurdity of human society. But this is not the purpose of the defamiliarization in "Ithaca." Rather, the overprecision shows what the stream-of-consciousness suggested in the early chapters: that reality is infinitely expansible by being infinitely divisible. A clue to this view of reality is found in one of the answers of the catechism. The response to the question "Were there obverse meditations of involution increasingly less vast?" ends with a tongue-twisting disquisition on the infinite number of microscopic organisms

> of the universe of human serum constellated with red and white bodies, themselves universes of void space constellated with other bodies, each, in continuity, its universe of divisible component bodies of which each was again divisible in divisions of redivisible component bodies, dividends and divisors ever diminishing without actual division till, if the progress were carried far enough, nought nowhere was never reached. (P. 699)

This examination of the Chinese box of the world represents another point in the chapter where Bloom's obsessive calculations merge with the overprecision of the narrative. But it describes also the divisibility of reality that is implied in the narrative. The narrative promise to fill in the gaps of the plot is fulfilled surprisingly in a microscopic notation of reality that threatens to continue forever.

This demonstration of the infinite divisibility of reality tells us something about the relationship between writing and the reality it represents. The "threshold of functional relevance," transgressed in the answers of "Ithaca," pertains to the conventions of discourse. As Heath says, it refers to the narrative choices made in the text. The microscopic notation in "Ithaca" transforms even the smallest detail of reality into a "narratable" fact. But it is the breakdown of the plot into discrete questions and answers that is the primary model of the infinite divisibility of experience and the expansibility of writing. Ironically, no answer is definitive because it has the potential to generate another, more specific question, which leads to another answer, and so on.

The narrative of "Ithaca" also demonstrates that events are infinitely expansible into larger sequences of which they are a part. Again, the precision of the writing leads to an expanding answer. (And again, a specific answer in the catechism represents this expansibility. See Bloom's "meditations of evolution increasingly vaster" [p. 698].) For example, the running of tap water is "explained" by tracing the water back to its source; the action of turning on the water is seen as a stage in a physical process that begins with the reservoir. Similarly, in a parody of the scientific investigation of causes and effects, the boiling of water is traced back to the coal that heats it, to the "decidua" of the forest that became the coal, to the energy of the sun that formed the coal (pp. 673-674). The details of the plot move outward from the actions of the characters, as the narrative spins a web of actions and reactions, antecedents and causes.

The narrative traces the antecedents of cognitive as well as physical events. Perceptions have a "history" that can be traced in the text. Bloom's perception of the gaslight spawns a description of a prior identical perception. Similarly, the sight of Bloom lighting the fire leads to a list of the previous actions of this sort that Stephen remembers. It is as if the stream-of-consciousness of the early chapters were turned inside out, as "remembrances of things past," both the characters' and the book's, are inventoried. Each event narrated can be seen as a point in a chain of events; each event has a potential relationship with another. "Really, universally, relations stop nowhere," says Henry James in his Preface to *Roderick Hudson*, "and the exquisite problem of the artist is eternally but to draw, by a geometry of his own, the circle within which they shall happily *appear* to do so."[12] "Ithaca" is a demonstration that "relations stop nowhere" and a refusal to limit the representation of experience in a personal "geometry." The lateral imagination sweeps backwards and forwards both in time and in space.

In "Ithaca," as in the last passages of "Wandering Rocks," plot and digression are almost synonymous, as the conventions of relevance are undermined. The "facts" included in the answers seem increasingly arbitrary: the answer to the question "Did it [the water] flow?" (p. 671) includes the record of steps taken by one Mr Spencer Harty to prevent a worsening drought as well as Mr Harty's hypothetical solution, recorded parenthetically, to the contingent possibility of the drought's becoming severe.[13] Logically, of course, the details of Mr Harty's plans are less relevant to the plot than the actions of Stephen and Bloom. But the idea of plot, based on the concepts of relevance and closure, are parodied, as the surplus of data makes the separation of the relevant from the irrelevant more problematical. Our progress towards the book's end is impeded as the narrative goes off in all directions; we are overwhelmed by the excess of information and are unable to organize the data into patterns of significance. Joyce plays with our desire to organize the material of the book—the parentheses in the above answer seem to be a wink from the author: What can a parenthetical thought be in a sentence so full of random associations?[14]

---

[12] *The Art of the Novel: Critical Prefaces by Henry James* (New York: Charles Scribner's Sons, 1962), p. 5.

[13] "The borough surveyor and waterworks engineer, Mr Spencer Harty, C. E., on the instructions of the waterworks committee, had prohibited the use of municipal water for purposes other than those of consumption (envisaging the possibility of recourse being had to the impotable water of the Grand and Royal canals in 1893) particularly as the South Dublin Guardians, notwithstanding their ration of 15 gallons per day per pauper . . . had been convicted of a wastage of 20,000 gallons per night" (p. 671).

[14] It is difficult to assign these irrelevant details either empirical or thematic significance, that is, to regard them as salient details of the plot or the theme.

Just as we are hoping for the resolution of the plot, then, the narrative opens up to include almost everything imaginable. In addition to the exhaustive tracing of the causes and effects of events in the plot, the narrative increasingly speculates on potential causes and effects of hypothetical events. Joyce expands the realm of relevant "fact" by including the conditional tense as well as the past and present; conjecture and hypothesis enter the narration. Early in the chapter the narrator asks, "For what personal purpose could Bloom have applied the water so boiled?" and the answer "To shave himself" generates other questions related to the desirability of shaving at night.[15] In the midst of its "progress" to limit indeterminacy, the narrative begins to entertain (and I stress this word) various kinds of possibilities and potentialities: "If he had smiled why would he have smiled?" "What various advantages would or might have resulted from a prolongation of such extemporisation?" "Why might these several provisional contingencies between a guest and a hostess not necessarily preclude or be precluded by a permanent eventuality of reconciliatory union between a schoolfellow and a jew's daughter?" (p. 695).

In certain passages, Bloom's daydreams occasion the narrative journey into the hypothetical. The prime example of this convergence is the three-page description of Bloom's

---

The detail is a red herring that leads nowhere in particular; we have no ready method for interpreting it. Roland Barthes, in an essay called "L'effet de réel," has called this kind of detail a sign of "the real"—it exists, he says, for purely referential purposes, to give a sense of facticity to the narrative (see *Communications*, no. 11 [1968], pp. 84-89). It seems to me that the mimetic status of these details is less important than their irrelevance to established categories; they represent both the literary "fact" that resists "recuperation" by our systems of literary criticism and the contingent "fact" that refuses to be assimilated to literary purposes.

[15] That is, "What advantages attended shaving by night?" "Why did absence of light disturb him less than presence of noise?" (p. 674).

suburban dream house.[16] Bloom's obsessiveness and the obsessiveness of the narrative come together to produce the most detailed of descriptions of a nonexistent place. Bloom's psychic energy and the narrator's descriptive energy are lavished on this dream house—again, one has the sense of an extravagant expenditure of energy. The specificity of the description is funny: "What additional attractions might the grounds contain?" "What improvements might be subsequently introduced?" "What facilities of transit were desirable?" (p. 713), asks the narrator, offering us one of the most exhaustive anatomies of desire in literature.[17]

Not only do the questions investigate the real and hypothetical details of plot, but they also conduct a search for the *relationship* between events or objects. Especially in the first half of the chapter, many of the questions seek to organize the world of facts into a series of relationships. This demand for comparison in the catechism is the second major means by which Joyce shows us that "relations stop nowhere." Throughout the catechism, the questions of the inquirer induce the respondent to make comparisons (this is not to suggest that they are two different personae, but to differentiate between functions). Almost every question includes words of comparison. In some, these comparative words are applied in heaping portions. The comparative question that begins the chapter, "What parallel course

[16] One is reminded of a statement James Boswell was reported to have made, that there are many people who build castles in the air but that he was the first to attempt to move into one.

[17] The passages on Bloom's dream house are reminiscent of Bouvard and Pécuchet's exhaustive efforts to improve their lot, to live out the Utopian bourgeois dream. At some point in reading the three-page description of the dream house, I felt that the obsessiveness of Bloom and the narrator were supplemented by Joyce's own desire to be able to use the quaint, faintly archaic vocabulary associated with the English country house, that is, to actually include words like "tumbling rake," "dovecote," "grindstone," et cetera, in the narrative. It is as if in a particularly palpable way, Bloom's desire for a house and Joyce's desire to write these pages were both being expressed.

... ?" is followed by many others, which inquire about "common facts of similarity between reactions," "common study," "points of contact," "previous intimations," and "glyphic comparisons," to name a few. The major comparisons requested in the questions pertain to the relationship of Stephen and Bloom. The leading questions of the catechism promise to structure a final sorting out of their relationship.

And so, the various points of contact are outlined according to the principle of identity and difference. The ways in which Stephen and Bloom are similar and dissimilar are catalogued: their opinions, their ages, their temperaments, their ancestors' languages, their drinking speed, the trajectory of their urination. They are substituted linguistically for one another ("Substituting Stephen for Bloom, Stoom ..."), charted geometrically ("Standing perpendicular ..."), their thoughts are "reduced to their simplest reciprocal form." The inquirer conducts a search for their common denominator.[18]

Again, the "lateral imagination" of the narrator is apparent, as he ranges over a set of facts, drawing connections. The most unlikely analogies are made: it seems that everything can potentially be compared to everything else (for example, Milly Bloom and the cat). Conversely, two entities (like Stephen and Bloom) can be compared and contrasted in a number of ways: every detail of the characters' biography and behavior can be potentially assimilated to the comparison. The questions encourage an analytical exercise in constructing binary oppositions. They seem more like theoretical constructs imposed than natural congruences discovered. The binarism of the narrator allows anything to be classified, and the comedy of the comparisons, in many cases, derives from their sheer irrelevance. As Hugh Kenner

---

[18] Bloom and Stephen are, to use a line from *Finnegans Wake*, "traduced by their comedy nominator, to the loaferst terms for their aloquent parts" (p. 283). (In fact, the catechism and the "resolution" of the characters into their physical and mathematical equivalents in "Ithaca" anticipate Book II, Chapter 2 of *Finnegans Wake*.)

observes of the mind of the narrator, it "loses nothing, penetrates nothing, and has a category for everything."[19]

Kenner discusses the analytic enterprise of the chapter as a kind of parody of "metaphysical intuition, or of allied aesthetic modes of knowledge." "Ithaca" does indeed parody the attempt to find an intelligible pattern, religious or secular. In *The Order of Things*, Michel Foucault has written brilliantly of Don Quixote's attempt to transform his own world into the Renaissance world of resemblance and similitude—it seems to me that the same kind of semiotic hope is parodied in "Ithaca." In attempting to connect the dots, the narrator becomes a kind of comic Thomas Browne, searching high and low for quincunxes. The desire for an intelligible pattern overwhelms the search.

What the catechism of "Ithaca" parodies is not the idea of relationship but the idea of a system that purports to halt the play of potential relationships. All sorts of relationships *do* exist in unexpected places—coincidences, repetitions, puns—but these "facts" cannot be reduced to a schema. Critics have had difficulty in agreeing on the particular system parodied in "Ithaca" (for example, the Christian catechism, nineteenth-century books of knowledge, or nineteenth-century science) because it is the *idea* of a taxonomic system itself, not any particular system, that is parodied. Science, logic, mathematics, theology, and literary criticism are all implicated in the parody, for they are all systems of ordering and containing knowledge. In fact, almost any kind of criticism that has been revered at one time or another ("new," old, structural, exegetical) is in some way represented or anticipated in the parody in "Ithaca." For example, the binary divisions classifying Milly Bloom and the cat (pp. 693-694) can be thought of as a perfect parody of structuralist criticism. It is, perhaps, particularly ironic to think of the Christian catechism behind the form of the

[19] Hugh Kenner, *Dublin's Joyce* (1956; reprint ed. Boston: Beacon Press, 1962), p. 167. Kenner believes, however, that this mind represented in "Ithaca" "epiphanizes" the machinelike mind of the book.

chapter: the book adopts the mask of dogma and belief in order to reveal a radical skepticism of order and authority.[20]

The questions and answers of the catechism offer various suggestions for ordering the world of facts—by similitude, by hypothesis, by causality, and so on. Facts are classified into categories, categories dispersed, new categories formed. Despite the prominence of the catechetical form, the underlying impulse for the movement of the chapter is rhetorical. In "Ithaca," Joyce employs the rhetorical topoi of "inventio," the first part of classical rhetoric. The narrative proceeds by ingenious "arguments" from analogy, difference, contraries, cause and effect, example.[21] Some examples of topoi used in "Ithaca" are: "If he had smiled why would he have smiled?" (hypothesis, p. 731); "What past consecutive causes . . . did Bloom . . . recapitulate?" (causes and effects, p. 728); "Prove that he loved rectitude . . ." (proof by example, p. 716). Analogy and difference are found, of course, throughout.[22] The performance of the catechism is really a school performance in the rhetorical classification of facts. For the Ciceronian orator, these rhetorical topoi represented the machinery for an investigation of a subject— they were the means of generating true statements about something. Using these topoi for comic purposes, Joyce plays with the idea of the human wish to arrive at truth. Like the system of nineteenth-century positivism, the system of rhetoric was originally a testimony to man's belief in his capacity for wisdom. However, in "Ithaca," the topoi

[20] Justifiably, one could point to the various structural schemas that Joyce was so fond of dispensing as evidence of his belief in structural organizations. To me, however, the "Ithaca" chapter represents Joyce's basic skepticism about order and schemes of order. It is possible that as a critic of his book he desired to be able to reduce it to the kind of schema he subverted within the writing. But in this case, I would prefer to trust Joyce the fiction writer rather than Joyce the letter writer and critic.

[21] I am indebted to Betsy Seifter for pointing this out to me.

[22] For a list of rhetorical arguments, see Richard Lanham's *A Handlist of Rhetorical Terms: A Guide for Students of English Literature* (Berkeley: University of California Press, 1969), p. 110.

ordinarily used in the service of investigation do not include or prove anything. If each of the book's last chapters is an experiment in ordering experience, "Ithaca" is the climax and the microcosm of this enterprise. It shows the arbitrariness of any system of classification, either of the book or, by implication, of the world. Instead of "truth" about his subject, Joyce offers us an exercise in the many ways in which the subject can be discussed.

The real subversion of the comprehensive classification of knowledge is implied, then, in the questions themselves. The series of comparative questions reveals that a line can be drawn between any two points, but it is impossible to connect all the dots. Each pair of questions and answers carves up a segment of reality but tells us nothing about the whole of the universe of the book. If "reality" and the meaning of it are investigated in each pair of questions and answers, there is always another question to be asked, another comparison to be explored. One can imagine an infinite series of questions and answers. René Girard, in discussing the "conversion" at the end of certain novels, says that "the conclusion must be considered as a successful effort to overcome the inability to conclude."[23] "Ithaca" is a parody of such closure; the book's "inability to conclude" is emphasized rather than overcome. If, as Hugh Kenner suggests, the catechism is like a huge filing system,[24] it is a system that has no necessary final entry.

In fact, by the end of the chapter, the connections made by the narrative mind become looser and looser. Instead of forging connections between characters, the respondent sinks into a spasm of verbal association, in a realm of imagination that fuses the child's world with the mythic. The answer to the question of the identity of Bloom's companions is "Sinbad the Sailor." The answer generates, however, a

[23] René Girard, *Deceit, Desire, and the Novel: Self and Other in Literary Structure*, trans. Yvonne Freccero (Baltimore: The Johns Hopkins University Press, 1965), p. 308.

[24] See Kenner, *Dublin's Joyce*, p. 167.

series of alliterative names that rhyme with Sinbad (Tinbad the Tailor and Jinbad the Jailer), and finally, the principle of alliteration itself gives way to the final reply "Xinbad the Phthailer," as the association becomes freer (p. 737). This kind of language looks back to the "moo-cow" story that begins *A Portrait* and forward to the language of *Finnegans Wake*. Although the final answer is a paraphrase of Bloom's response to Molly, its implication is that the book has now embarked on a course of generating all sorts of linguistic connections from this fertile medium of dream language. The mind that peruses the world, cataloguing and making connections, could conceivably continue in its effort forever, in a language even more unlikely to encourage a halt in the play of connections than that of the rest of the chapter. The chapter stops, as if the mind went to sleep or the power of the machine were cut off, but it doesn't really end.

In "Ithaca," we see that the wealth of possible connections can never be catalogued completely. There is no system that can include or account for them all. Among other things, "Ithaca" is about ordering: the way characters order their world, the way authors order their texts, the way readers order their interpretations, and the way people order the world they live in. The chapter incorporates Joyce's ideas about making sense of the world and about making sense of a literary text. Just as the wealth of life exceeds the book's representation of it, so the surplus of meanings in the book exceeds the reader's interpretation of it.

The "roles" of interrogator and respondent in the cate-chism represent both the characters trying to make their way through the world and the reader trying to make his way through the book. In playing "twenty questions" with itself, the chapter makes explicit the questions and answers usually embedded in the linear narrative. During the course of the chapter, these narrative questions and answers have converged at certain points with Leopold Bloom's attempt to solve his personal problems. The questions that they ask and answer are questions that Bloom asks himself (indeed, the language of logic is used to underline this problem-solving activity). At the end of the chapter, it is Bloom's dialogue with Molly that now converges with the narrative, and the narrator's role as a kind of substitute or surrogate for the characters is explicitly noted. Molly's questions to Bloom are actually referred to by the narrator as "the catechetical interrogation," Bloom is called the "narrator" and Molly the "listener," who sometimes interrupts to ask questions. The slackening pace of the narration is observed in the narrative itself, as the interrogator asks "What limitations of activity and inhibitions of conjugal rights were perceived by listener and narrator concerning themselves during the course of this intermittent and increasingly more laconic narration?" (pp. 735-736). The dialogue of the characters and the dialogue of the chapter become one.

But the reader too is represented in the catechism, for the interrogation in the text parodies the kind of activity we ourselves usually perform. Both the characters and the reader go through the book trying to solve enigmas. It is the central irony of the chapter that despite the exhaustiveness of the interrogation process, fundamental questions remain unanswered, both for the characters and for the reader. Just as Bloom reminds himself of all his unfinished business and the "unsolved enigmas" (p. 729), we too recognize that everything has not been resolved in the chapter. The pedagogical "mask" of the chapter, in fact, has interesting implications for the notion of the "ideal reader," who, like the ideal student, tries to arrive at a vision of truth. What we understand from this final simulated educational exercise in "Ithaca" is that there are no ideal readers for the text, no perfect students who can arrive at a definitive reading of the book. It is not surprising that the conception of the ideal reader has a religious source: it originated in St. Augustine's "On Christian Doctrine" and applied to the Christian who had the "preunderstanding" necessary to read and interpret scriptures. The notion of this "ideal reader" and the student of the Christian catechism dovetail in "Ithaca": the "mysteries" of the text cannot be taught or learned in any absolute way; there is no privileged position from which to arrive at "truth" or knowledge.[25] That the book is about writing and reading fiction as well as the characters in Dublin is something I have tried to demonstrate throughout—but "Ithaca" shows us that the play of the text will always exceed the reader's attempt to grasp it.

The multiple possibilities of meaning in *Ulysses* and a parody of the attempt to arrive at a *conclusive* reading are comically presented in an hermeneutic metaphor within the chapter. The narrator's question "What in water did Bloom, waterlover, drawer of water, watercarrier returning to the range, admire?" (p. 672) is answered in a Rabelaisian catalogue of Bloom's thoughts on the meaning of water: "Its universality: its democratic equality and constancy to its nature in seeking its own level . . . its infallibility as paradigm and paragon." In one sense, the catalogue of Bloom's thoughts on the "potency of water as a symbol" can be seen as a projection of his desire to mean something to somebody. But the catalogue also represents a "reading" of water—the book, in this instance, like Stephen in "Proteus," attempts to read a "signature" in the material world. We recognize in this kind of reading a parody of the basic activity of symbol making and deciphering, the kind of activities engaged in by everyone, but by writers and readers especially. Indeed, one has only to think of Joyce's statement to Budgen that Odysseus is "the complete man" (representing son, father, husband, and warrior)[26] to realize how writers, as well as characters and readers, are represented in this disquisition. On the one hand, the passage is a parody of the

---

[25] The attractiveness of a final understanding of the text's mysteries can be seen in an essay as recent as M.J.C. Hodgart's "Aeolus," in *James Joyce's Ulysses: Critical Essays*, ed. Clive Hart and David Hayman (Berkeley: University of California Press, 1974): "The whole of *Ulysses* is a parable, for him who heareth the word and understandeth it; he indeed beareth fruit" (p. 119).

[26] See Budgen, *James Joyce and the Making of Ulysses*, pp. 15-17).

writer's attempt to create symbolism and the reader's attempt to exhaust the significance of what he reads. The passage parodies the desire for epiphany, as it catalogues the "whatness" of the object. Any one of these interpretations of water, serving as the basis of a metaphor in a poem, for example, would not be comic; it is the completeness and ingenuity of these multiple readings that parody the search for significance and the creation of symbolism.

But on the other hand, the passage offers a range of potential meaning, that is, a surplus of meanings, and this is, in fact, what *Ulysses* itself offers to the reader. The meditation on water, to quote William Gass, an expert meditator, shows how things "become concepts": somewhere between the perceiver and the object, significance resides.[27] For after all, water, like Homer's Odysseus, *is* a perfect paradigm. If the passage parodies the desire for the exhaustion of meaning, for a final, conclusive interpretation, it reveals a surplus rather than a dearth of meanings.

Despite the representation of events in what Joyce called "the coldest, baldest way," a sense of possibility mitigates the alienation of the cosmic perspective. The abstract record of events somehow confirms the richness of the story. The leveling of experience that derives from the form and style of "Ithaca" ultimately does not feel like an aggressive cancellation of possibilities or a ruthless satire of belief but imparts instead a sense of the various possibilities that exist in life. *Ulysses* is full of meaning, but this is not to say that its final meaning is the affirmation of life. It is a book that is beyond what we generally mean by affirmation or negation; it shows us all kinds of truths about life but doesn't sum it up in any one statement of meaning. The overabundance of details and styles invites the reader to pare away the excess until he arrives at some kind of interpretation. The history of Joyce criticism reveals how personal

[27] William H. Gass, *On Being Blue: A Philosophical Inquiry* (Boston: David R. Godine, 1975), p. 31.

this winnowing process is. As Arnold Goldman pointed out in *The Joyce Paradox*, *Ulysses* allows us to see the progression of the style toward the computerlike abstractions of "Ithaca" as life denying, the triumph of mechanism (as Kenner does in *Dublin's Joyce*), or we can see the characters' survival in spite of the stylistic progression as ultimately life affirming (as does S. L. Goldberg, for example).[28]

My own feeling is that while *Ulysses* is skeptical about meaning and belief, it is not "pyrrhonic" (to use Hugh Kenner's recent term for it[29]): anyone as concerned with life as Joyce is in *Ulysses* cannot be as much of an eternal pessimist as Kenner makes him sound in his brilliant but ultimately too dark readings of the book. Neither, however, is *Ulysses* a "self-consuming artifact" by which the reader is led to a vision of truth.

[28] See Arnold Goldman, *The Joyce Paradox: Form and Freedom in His Fiction* (London: Routledge & Kegan Paul, 1966), pp. 113-114.

[29] See "Myth and Pyrrhonism" in Hugh Kenner, *Joyce's Voices* (Berkeley: University of California Press, 1978), pp. 39-63.

IX

"Penelope": A Coda

"The Ithaca episode . . . is in reality the end as Penelope has no beginning, middle or end," Joyce wrote to Harriet Shaw Weaver.[1] The only chapter not assigned a specific hour in the time scheme of the book, "Penelope" seems like a coda to the main progression of the book's styles and plot. And yet, we are faced with something of a paradox in the relationship between the final two chapters. "Ithaca," with its seemingly closed form of question and answer, actually fades out into a dream language of inexhaustible possibilities. The inventory of events has no necessary final entry. "Penelope," with its seamless web of past and present and its apparent formlessness, is, nevertheless, much more self-contained and, in its own way, conclusive. Joyce wrote to Frank Budgen: "The last word (human all-too-human) is left to Penelope."[2] It is worth pondering the difference between the "real ending" in "Ithaca," the parody of closure, and the formless, flowing monologue that provides the "last word" of the book.

The "increasingly more laconic narration" in "Ithaca" prepares the way for the meandering prose of "Penelope." Bloom, answering Molly's questions about the day, drifts off to sleep and the dialogue gives way to Molly's monologue. In writing on the "autonomous monologue," of which "Penelope" is her paradigm, Dorrit Cohn points to the "anti-

---

[1] Letter to Harriet Shaw Weaver, 7 October 1921, *Letters of James Joyce*, Vol. 1, ed. Stuart Gilbert (New York: The Viking Press, 1957), pp. 172-173.

[2] End February 1921, *Letters*, Vol. 1, pp. 159-160.

narrative" nature of the chapter. The voice of Molly "totally obliterates the authorial narrative voice throughout an entire chapter."[3] "Penelope" is first-person narration that does shut out a third-person narrative voice. But some narrative presence transcribes the sound of the train whistle (pp. 754, 762, 763) and, if it performs this act of transcription, it is also scribe for Molly's monologue as well. Even in "Penelope," Joyce never totally lets us forget the narrative context of the book.

Upon first encounter, "Penelope" seems very unconventional: the absence of third-person narration, the unpunctuated, unbroken "sentences," and the representation of thought as if it were continuous speech distinguish it from the earlier chapters of interior monologue. But however radical the monologue first appears on the page, its underlying conventionality becomes apparent. First, in reforging the link between character and style in "Penelope," Joyce returned to one of the stylistic conceptions that dominates the early chapters of the book. And, second, once we learn how to read the continuous rhythms of the prose, the style seems much less radical than it first appears—linguistic play such as we find in "Sirens," for example, is almost nonexistent. As A. Walton Litz says, "Penelope" "does not contribute to the sequence of styles which is one of our chief interests in *Ulysses*."[4]

The technical reversion contributes to our sense of return and closure: even though we have never heard this voice before, we return to the sound of one mind thinking, a type of sound we heard throughout the first part of the book. Despite the fact that Joyce saw the chapter as a kind of nonending for the book—a chapter with no beginning, middle, or end—and despite its existence outside the main progression of styles, "Penelope" does give the reader a sense

[3] See Dorrit Cohn, *Transparent Minds: Narrative Modes for Presenting Consciousness in Fiction* (Princeton: Princeton University Press, 1978), p. 218.

[4] A. Walton Litz, "Ithaca," in *James Joyce's Ulysses: Critical Essays*, ed. Clive Hart and David Hayman (Berkeley: University of California Press, 1974), p. 404.

of closure, different from the kind of "ending" we found in "Ithaca." This sense of coming home is sanctioned by symbol, technique, and structure. We have reached the *nostos* of our Homeric journey: Odysseus comes home to Penelope, the male to the female, and the wanderings of the narrative to a point of origin, a single consciousness, a single voice. After the stark abstractions and cold "precision" of "Ithaca," the breakdown of grammatical and syntactic categories into lush, emotional rhythms provides a release of tension in the narrative, soothing to the beleaguered reader.

The chapter's strategic location at the end of the book and the dominance of one voice over our attention seem to give "Penelope" a privileged position. After the succession of styles, this single voice rising up out of the narrative brings with it a special authority. As Kenner says, it is as if we finally hear the solitary voice of the Muse.[5] Joyce's resolution to end the monologue with "the female word Yes"[6] further enhances this authority—Molly does indeed have "the last word." Again, one finds a paradoxical relationship between the chapter as privileged "last word" and the nonending Joyce projected.[7]

The meaning of Molly's climactic assent at the end of the chapter has been much debated. Most critics have seen in it an affirmation of life; others insist that this indiscriminate acceptance of life renders life meaningless.[8] But despite the disagreement, critics have looked to "Penelope" to provide

[5] Hugh Kenner, *Joyce's Voices* (Berkeley: University of California Press, 1978), p. 98.

[6] Letter to Frank Budgen, 16 August 1921, *Letters*, Vol. 1, pp. 169-170.

[7] In *Transparent Minds*, Dorrit Cohn says: "If the introductory moment of an autonomous monologue appears most natural when it is least introductory, its concluding moment appears most natural when it is least conclusive" (p. 243). "Penelope" does begin *in medias res* but ends climactically (in at least two senses). Cohn goes on to say that the least conclusive ending of an autonomous monologue would be to have the characters drift off to sleep. Interestingly, then, it is "Ithaca" that best fulfills Cohn's requirements for the ending of an autonomous monologue.

[8] See S. L. Goldberg, *The Classical Temper: A Study of James Joyce's Ulysses* (London: Chatto and Windus, 1961), p. 298.

a message or truth. James Maddox says that *"Ulysses,* an extensive critique of false sentiment, ends on a moment of true sentiment: Molly is reviving those dear dead days not yet beyond recall precisely in order to reenact them tomorrow."[9] And in an interesting essay, *"Ulysses:* The Exhaustion of Literature and the Literature of Exhaustion," Seamus Deane calls the "Penelope" chapter a "new resolution." According to Deane: "By parody, the novel exhausts its own possibility of resolution. Then, amazingly, out of that exhaustion, it creates a new resolution—Molly's monologue—which gains a new access of energy for the whole work by its specifically non-literary character."[10] Even those interpretations that see in Molly's amoral, undiscriminating view of life the epitome or emblem of potentiality itself, still regard the thematic content of the chapter as providing the *key* to the book.

I would like to suggest that regardless of the specifics of these interpretations, the idea of a natural resolution is precisely what is undermined in the book as a whole. Because my own reading of the book depends upon the notion that *Ulysses* presents possibilities instead of conclusions, the "Penelope" chapter seems to me to be regressive, to present something denied by the rest of the book. If Molly's monologue contains the truth or resolution, hasn't the book implicitly suggested that we cannot trust messages or any version of the truth? All along it has played with and subverted its own momentary climaxes and seeming resolutions. As a result, it has sharpened our suspicion of any "last word." "Penelope" *does* seem to give us a symbol of the life force, but the rest of the book has shown us that same protean life force in its varied manifestations and dramatic

---

[9] James H. Maddox, Jr. *Joyce's Ulysses and the Assault upon Character* (New Brunswick: Rutgers University Press, 1978), p. 230.

[10] Seamus Deane, *"Ulysses:* The Exhaustion of Literature and the Literature of Exhaustion," in *Ulysses: cinquante ans après: Témoignages franco-anglais sur le chef-d'oeuvre de James Joyce,* ed. Louis Bonnerot (Paris: Didier, 1974), p. 270.

possibilities. Finally, *Ulysses* represents the complexity in addition to the wealth of life that defies summation: Molly's chapter symbolizes the wealth but not the complexity; it ignores the distinctions and discriminations formed and re-formed in the book.

Perhaps it makes sense to say that in "Penelope" Joyce provides a powerful ending for one "story" in *Ulysses* and not another: he completes the archetypal plot of the *Odyssey* by giving us Penelope, and he fleshes out the naturalistic plot as well by showing us the very human Molly Bloom, whom we have waited to see throughout the day. Joyce called "Penelope" the "indispensable countersign to Bloom's passport to eternity"[11]—he felt the chapter was necessary to provide thematic and structural balance. But the other "story" in *Ulysses* that I have traced, the story of the writing of a novel, is somehow falsified by this kind of final chapter. "Penelope" does exist outside the sequence of styles, but it has the whole weight of that sequence behind it. The whole book has cautioned us not to trust any one version of things more than another, even one so apparently formless or "natural" as this one.

Instead, it is in the type of myth and language found at the end of "Ithaca," rather than in the symbolism and style of "Penelope," that Joyce found a way to end his novel without creating a sense of the necessity of closure. It took another book, *Finnegans Wake*, for him to explore the direction he had taken at the end of "Ithaca." It is not the single voice and "nonliterariness" of "Penelope" that provided Joyce's fiction with a new direction; it is, instead, the artifice and the curious blend of dream, culture, myth, and nursery rhyme at the end of "Ithaca" that was to be the most open-ended for Joyce—both in terms of *Ulysses* and *Finnegans Wake*. However beautifully and powerfully Joyce presented the return to a single voice in "Penelope," he

[11] Letter to Frank Budgen, end February 1921, *Letters*, Vol. 1, pp. 159-160.

gives us a kind of closure that the rest of the book seems to subvert.

Ulysses is a set of fictions that reveals the inconclusiveness of all "fictions," a compendium of schemes of order that implies that there is no absolute way to order experience, either in life or in literature. The elaborate schematization in *Ulysses* does not represent, as many critics have contended, an absolute and closed symbolic order. One gets a sense of spillage in the text: despite the many aesthetic patterns offered in the book (rhetorical, allegorical, symbolic), there is always something left over, something that transcends order and criticism. The excess of details and styles makes us pare away what we cannot assimilate to our critical statements about the book, but the surplus remains to remind us of what cannot be incorporated in one scheme or interpretation. To describe the kind of book *Ulysses* represents one must account for the compulsive ordering *and* the ongoing experimentation in the work, for the tidiness of its forms and the sprawling richness of detail.

In abandoning the norm with which the book begins and substituting instead a succession of stylistic experiments, Joyce reveals how style is always an interpretation of reality, a choice among many possibilities. In the direction of the style, from the breakdown of narrative, to the borrowing of styles, to the new mode beyond parody that he created in "Ithaca," Joyce signaled the end and the reconstitution of the form of the novel. The exercises of style are not extrinsic to a central meaning; rather, they create the meanings in the book.

The provisional nature of the styles and the structure of anticlimax they create reflects something about Joyce's view of life as well as literature. Unlike most modernists, Joyce did not believe in crisis as the model of the age. The characters survive tense moments; it is as if the moments we saw in *Dubliners* were lived beyond. The reader, too, passes from a dramatic version of an event to a less intense, often deflationary version. If *Ulysses* contains certain moments when pace quickens and meaning is shaped into aesthetic pattern, it also shows us how provisional and evanescent these moments are. When direct statements of meaning or belief are made by the characters, they are likely to be parodied; when direct expression of feeling or belief is given in the narrative, the text is apt to print some kind of retraction. "A heaventree" is likely to vanish in a double take and become "the apathy of the stars." The story of the characters and the story of the writing unfold and there is energy in both processes. Joyce's skepticism about language and things such as resolution, change, and crisis in life does not lead to a sense of a dead end.

Instead, Joyce's skepticism about the "drama" of life leads to a picture of a survivor and an appreciation of the stamina it takes to get through the excesses of even one day's experience. And if *Ulysses* reflects Joyce's skepticism about any one mode of order and about the limitations of language, it nevertheless reflects his enormous confidence in what a writer can do with the resources available. It gives us a sense of the possibilities both in literature and in life.

BIBLIOGRAPHY

JOYCE TEXTS

The Critical Writings of James Joyce. Edited by Ellsworth Mason and Richard Ellmann. New York: The Viking Press, 1959.

Dubliners. 1914. Edited by Robert Scholes in consultation with Richard Ellmann. New York: The Viking Press, 1967.

Dubliners: Text, Criticism, and Notes. Edited by Robert Scholes and A. Walton Litz. New York: Viking Critical Library-The Viking Press, 1969.

The James Joyce Archives. Ulysses vols. Edited by Michael Groden. New York: Garland Publishing, Inc., 1978.

James Joyce Ulysses: The Manuscript and First Printing Compared. Annotated by Clive Driver. New York: Farrar, Straus and Giroux, 1975.

Joyce's Notes and Early Drafts for Ulysses: Selections from the Buffalo Collection. Edited by Phillip F. Herring. Charlottesville: University Press of Virginia, 1977.

Joyce's Ulysses Notesheets in the British Museum. Edited by Phillip F. Herring. Charlottesville: University Press of Virginia, 1972.

Letters of James Joyce. Vol. 1. Edited by Stuart Gilbert. New York: The Viking Press, 1957. Vols. 2 and 3. Edited by Richard Ellmann. New York: The Viking Press, 1966.

A Portrait of the Artist as a Young Man. 1916. Text corrected by Chester G. Anderson and edited by Richard Ellmann. New York: The Viking Press, 1964.

Selected Letters of James Joyce. Edited by Richard Ellmann. New York: The Viking Press, 1975.

Stephen Hero. 1944. Rev. ed. Edited by Theodore Spencer. New York: New Directions, 1963.

Ulysses. 1922. Rev. ed. New York: Modern Library-Random House, 1961.

Bibliography

SECONDARY SOURCES ON JOYCE

Adams, Robert M. *James Joyce: Common Sense and Beyond.* New York: Random House, 1967.

———. *Surface and Symbol: The Consistency of James Joyce's Ulysses.* New York: Oxford University Press, 1962.

Atherton, J. S. "The Oxen of the Sun." In *James Joyce's Ulysses: Critical Essays*, edited by Clive Hart and David Hayman, pp. 313-339. Berkeley: University of California Press, 1974.

Beck, Warren. *Joyce's Dubliners: Substance, Vision, and Art.* Durham, N.C.: Duke University Press, 1969.

Beebe, Maurice. "*Ulysses* and the Age of Modernism." In *Ulysses: Fifty Years*, edited by Thomas F. Staley, pp. 172-188. 1972. Reprint. Bloomington: Indiana University Press, 1974.

Bennett, Arnold. "James Joyce's 'Ulysses'." In *Things That Have Interested Me: Second Series*, pp. 185-194. New York: George H. Doran Co., 1923.

Blamires, Harry. *The Bloomsday Book: A Guide through Joyce's Ulysses.* London: Methuen & Co., Ltd., 1966.

Bruns, Gerald L. "Eumaeus." In *James Joyce's Ulysses: Critical Essays*, edited by Clive Hart and David Hayman, pp. 363-383. Berkeley: University of California Press, 1974.

Budgen, Frank. *James Joyce and the Making of Ulysses.* 1934. Reprint. Bloomington: Indiana University Press, 1960.

Burgess, Anthony. *Joysprick: An Introduction to the Language of James Joyce.* London: André Deutsch, 1973.

———. *Re Joyce.* New York: W.W. Norton & Co., Inc., 1965.

Cohn, Alan M. "Supplementary James Joyce Checklist, 1971." *James Joyce Quarterly* 11 (Winter 1974): 150-164.

Cope, Jackson. "Sirens." In *James Joyce's Ulysses: Critical Essays*, edited by Clive Hart and David Hayman, pp. 217-242. Berkeley: University of California Press, 1974.

Deane, Seamus. "*Ulysses*: The Exhaustion of Literature and the Literature of Exhaustion." In *Ulysses: cinquante ans après: Témoignages franco-anglais sur le chef-d'oeuvre de James Joyce*, edited by Louis Bonnerot, pp. 263-274. Paris: Didier, 1974.

Deming, Robert H. *A Bibliography of James Joyce Studies.* Lawrence, Kans.: University of Kansas Libraries, 1964.

Edel, Leon. *The Modern Psychological Novel.* Rev. ed. New York: Universal Library-Grosset and Dunlap, 1964.

Bibliography

Eliot, T. S. "Contemporanea." *The Egoist* 5 (1918): 84-85.

———. "Lettre d'Angleterre: Le Style dans la prose anglaise contemporaine." *La Nouvelle Revue Française* 19 (July-Dec., 1922): 751-756.

———. "Ulysses, Order and Myth." *The Dial*, Nov. 1923. Reprinted in *James Joyce: Two Decades of Criticism*, edited by Seon Givens, pp. 198-202. New York: Vanguard Press, 1948.

Ellmann, Richard. *The Consciousness of Joyce.* New York: Oxford University Press, 1977.

———. *James Joyce.* New York: Oxford University Press, 1959.

———. *Ulysses on the Liffey.* New York: Oxford University Press, 1972.

Fiedler, Leslie. "Bloom on Joyce; or, Jokey for Jacob." In *New Light on Joyce from the Dublin Symposium*, edited by Fritz Senn, pp. 195-208. Bloomington: Indiana University Press, 1972.

Frank, Joseph. "Spatial Form in Modern Literature." *Sewanee Review* 53 (1945). Revised in *The Widening Gyre: Crisis and Mastery in Modern Literature*, pp. 3-62. Bloomington: Indiana University Press, 1963.

French, Marilyn. *The Book as World: James Joyce's Ulysses.* Cambridge, Mass.: Harvard University Press, 1976.

Friedman, Melvin. *Stream of Consciousness: A Study in Literary Method.* New Haven: Yale University Press, 1956.

Garrett, Peter K. *Scene and Symbol from George Eliot to James Joyce: Studies in Changing Fictional Mode.* New Haven: Yale University Press, 1969.

Gifford, Don, and Seidman, Robert J. *Notes for Joyce: An Annotation of James Joyce's Ulysses.* New York: E. P. Dutton Co., Inc., 1974.

Gilbert, Stuart, *James Joyce's Ulysses: A Study.* Rev. ed. New York: Vintage Books-Random House, 1952.

Goldberg, S. L. *The Classical Temper: A Study of James Joyce's Ulysses.* London: Chatto and Windus, 1961.

———. *Joyce.* Edinburgh, 1962. Reprint. New York: Capricorn Books, 1972.

Goldman, Arnold. *The Joyce Paradox: Form and Freedom in His Fiction.* London: Routledge & Kegan Paul, 1966.

Gottfried, Roy K. *The Art of Joyce's Syntax in Ulysses.* Athens: University of Georgia Press, 1980.

Bibliography

Groden, Michael. *Ulysses in Progress*. Princeton: Princeton University Press, 1977.

Gross, John. *James Joyce*. New York: The Viking Press, 1970.

Hanley, Miles L. *A Word Index to James Joyce's Ulysses*. Rev. ed. Madison: University of Wisconsin Press, 1951.

Hart, Clive. "James Joyce's Sentimentality." *Philosophical Quarterly* 46 (Oct. 1967): 516-526.

———. *James Joyce's Ulysses*. Sydney: Sydney University Press, 1968.

———. "Wandering Rocks." In *James Joyce's Ulysses: Critical Essays*, edited by Clive Hart and David Hayman, pp. 181-216. Berkeley: University of California Press, 1974.

Hawks, Terry. "Joyce and Speech." *James Joyce Review* 1 (Dec. 1957): 33-37.

Hayman, David. "Cyclops." In *James Joyce's Ulysses: Critical Essays*, edited by Clive Hart and David Hayman, pp. 243-275. Berkeley: University of California Press, 1974.

———. "Language of/as Gesture in Joyce." In *Ulysses: cinquante ans après: Témoignages franco-anglais sur le chef-d'oeuvre de James Joyce*, edited by Louis Bonnerot, pp. 209-221. Paris: Didier, 1974.

———. *Ulysses: The Mechanics of Meaning*. Englewood Cliffs, N.J.: Prentice-Hall, Inc., 1970.

Hendry, Irene. "Joyce's Epiphanies." *Sewanee Review* 54 (1946): 449-467.

Hodgart, M.J.C. "Aeolus." In *James Joyce's Ulysses: Critical Essays*, edited by Clive Hart and David Hayman, pp. 115-130. Berkeley: University of California Press, 1974.

Hoffmann, Frederick J. "The Authority of the Commonplace: Joyce's Bloomsday." *Kenyon Review* 22 (Spring 1960): 316-323.

Humphrey, Robert. *Stream of Consciousness in the Modern Novel*. Berkeley: University of California Press, 1954.

Iser, Wolfgang. *The Implied Reader: Patterns of Communication in Prose Fiction from Bunyan to Beckett*. Baltimore: The Johns Hopkins University Press, 1974.

———. "Indeterminacy and the Reader's Response in Prose Fiction." In *Aspects of Narrative: Selected Papers from the English Institute*, edited by J. Hillis Miller, pp. 1-45. New York: Columbia University Press, 1971.

Bibliography

Joyce, Stanislaus. *The Dublin Diary of Stanislaus Joyce*. Edited by George Harris Healey. London: Faber and Faber, 1962.

———. *My Brother's Keeper: James Joyce's Early Years*. Edited by Richard Ellmann. London: Faber and Faber, 1958.

Kain, Richard M. "The Cosmic View in *Ulysses*." In *Ulysses cinquante ans après: Témoignages franco-anglais sur le chef-d'oeuvre de James Joyce*, edited by Louis Bonnerot, pp. 275-286. Paris: Didier, 1974.

Kellogg, Robert. "Scylla and Charybdis." In *James Joyce's Ulysses: Critical Essays*, edited by Clive Hart and David Hayman, pp. 147-179. Berkeley: University of California Press, 1974.

Kenner, Hugh. "Circe." In *James Joyce's Ulysses: Critical Essays*, edited by Clive Hart and David Hayman, pp. 341-362. Berkeley: University of California Press, 1974.

———. *Dublin's Joyce*. 1956. Reprint. Boston: Beacon Press, 1962.

———. "Joyce and Pyrrhonism." *Boston University Journal* 25, no. 1 (1977): 12-21.

———. *Joyce's Voices*. Berkeley: University of California Press, 1978.

———. "Molly's Masterstroke." In *Ulysses: Fifty Years*, edited by Thomas F. Staley, pp. 19-28. 1972. Reprint. Bloomington: Indiana University Press, 1974.

———. "The Rhetoric of Silence." *James Joyce Quarterly* 14 (Summer 1977): 382-394.

———. *The Stoic Comedians: Flaubert, Joyce, and Beckett*. Berkeley: University of California Press, 1962.

———. *Ulysses*. London: Allen & Unwin, Ltd., 1980.

Kimpel, Ben D. "The Voices of *Ulysses*." *Style* 9 (Summer 1975): 283-319.

Levin, Harry. *James Joyce: A Critical Introduction*. Rev. ed. New York: New Directions, 1960.

The Little Review. Oct. 1918.

Litz, A. Walton. *The Art of James Joyce: Method and Design in Ulysses and Finnegans Wake*. New York: Oxford University Press, 1964.

———. "The Genre of *Ulysses*." In *The Theory of the Novel: New Essays*, edited by John Halperin, pp. 109-120. New York: Oxford University Press, 1974.

———. "Ithaca." In *James Joyce's Ulysses: Critical Essays*, edited by Clive Hart and David Hayman, pp. 385-405. Berkeley: University of California Press, 1974.

McBride, Margaret. "Watchwords in *Ulysses*: The Stylistics of

Suppression." *The Journal of English and Germanic Philology* 77 (July 1978): 356-366.

Maddox, James H., Jr. *Joyce's Ulysses and the Assault upon Character.* New Brunswick: Rutgers University Press, 1978.

Magalaner, Marvin, and Kain, Richard M. *Joyce: The Man, the Work, the Reputation.* New York: New York University Press, 1956.

Manso, Peter. "The Metaphoric Style of Joyce's *Portrait.*" *Modern Fiction Studies* 13 (Summer 1967): 221-236.

Mayoux, Jean-Jacques. "Parody and Self-Mockery in the Work of James Joyce." In *English Studies Today.* 4th ser. Edited by G. I. Duthie, pp. 187-198. Edinburgh: University of Edinburgh Press, 1964.

Mercier, Vivian. *The Irish Comic Tradition.* Oxford: Oxford University Press, 1962.

Modern Fiction Studies. James Joyce Special Number 15 (Spring 1969).

Morse, J. Mitchell. "The Unobtrusive Rhetoric of *Ulysses.*" *James Joyce Quarterly* 13 (Winter 1976): 202-207.

Murillo, L. A. *The Cyclical Night: Irony in James Joyce and Jorge Luis Borges.* Cambridge, Mass.: Harvard University Press, 1968.

Naremore, James. "Style and Meaning in *A Portrait of the Artist.*" *James Joyce Quarterly* 4 (Summer 1967): 331-342.

New Ireland: A Weekly Literary and Political Review. May 15, 1915.

Norris, Margot. *The Decentered Universe of Finnegans Wake: A Structuralist Analysis.* Baltimore: The Johns Hopkins University Press, 1974.

Oates, Joyce Carol. "Jocoserious Joyce." *Critical Inquiry* 2 (Summer 1976): 677-688.

O'Connor, Frank. *The Lonely Voice: A Study of the Short Story.* Cleveland: The World Publishing Company, 1962.

Peake, C. H. *James Joyce: The Citizen and the Artist.* Stanford: Stanford University Press, 1977.

Peter, John. "Joyce and the Novel." *Kenyon Review* 18 (Autumn 1956): 619-632.

Ridgeway, Ann. "Two Authors in Search of a Reader." *James Joyce Quarterly* 1 (Summer 1964): 41-51.

San Juan, Epifanio, Jr. *James Joyce and the Craft of Fiction: An Interpretation of "Dubliners."* Rutherford: Fairleigh Dickinson University Press, 1972.

Bibliography

Schechner, Mark. *Joyce in Nighttown: A Psychoanalytic Inquiry into Ulysses.* Berkeley: University of California Press, 1974.

Scholes, Robert. "*Ulysses:* A Structuralist Perspective." In *Ulysses: Fifty Years,* edited by Thomas F. Staley, pp. 161-171. 1972. Reprint. Bloomington: Indiana University Press, 1974.

Senn, Fritz. "Nausicaa." In *James Joyce's Ulysses: Critical Essays,* edited by Clive Hart and David Hayman, pp. 277-311. Berkeley: University of California Press, 1974.

————. "The Rhythm of *Ulysses.*" In *Ulysses: cinquante ans après: Témoignages franco-anglais sur le chef-d'oeuvre de James Joyce,* edited by Louis Bonnerot, pp. 33-43. Paris: Didier, 1974.

Solomon, Margaret C. "Character as Linguistic Mode: A New Look at Streams-of-Consciousness in *Ulysses.*" In *Ulysses: cinquante ans après: Témoignages franco-anglais sur le chef-d'oeuvre de James Joyce,* edited by Louis Bonnerot, pp. 111-130. Paris: Didier, 1974.

Staley, Harry C. "Joyce's Catechisms." *James Joyce Quarterly* 6 (Winter 1968): 137-153.

Stanzel, Franz. *Narrative Situations in the Novel: Tom Jones, Moby Dick, The Ambassadors, Ulysses.* Translated by James P. Pusack. Bloomington: Indiana University Press, 1971.

Steinberg, Erwin R. "Characteristic Sentence Patterns in Proteus and Lestrygonians." In *New Light on Joyce from the Dublin Symposium,* edited by Fritz Senn, pp. 79-98. Bloomington: Indiana University Press, 1972.

————. *The Stream of Consciousness and Beyond in Ulysses.* Pittsburgh: University of Pittsburgh Press, 1973.

Sultan, Stanley. *The Argument of Ulysses.* Columbus: Ohio State University Press, 1964.

————. "The Sirens at the Ormond Bar: *Ulysses.*" University of Kansas City Review 26 (Winter 1959): 83-92.

Thornton, Weldon. *Allusions in Ulysses: A Line-by-Line Reference to Joyce's Complex Symbolism.* 1961. Reprint. New York: Simon and Schuster, 1973.

Tindall, William York. *James Joyce: His Way of Interpreting the Modern World.* New York: Charles Scribner's Sons, 1950.

————. *A Reader's Guide to James Joyce.* New York: Farrar, Straus & Giroux, 1959.

Toynbee, Philip. "A Study of James Joyce's *Ulysses.*" In *James Joyce:*

Two Decades of Criticism, edited by Seon Givens, pp. 243-284. New York: Vanguard Press, 1948.

Trilling, Lionel. *The Opposing Self: Nine Essays in Criticism*. New York: The Viking Press, 1955.

Van Ghent, Dorothy. *The English Novel: Form and Function*. New York: Harper & Row, 1953.

Wilds, Nancy G. "Style and Auctorial Presence in 'A Portrait of the Artist as a Young Man'." *Style* 7 (Winter 1973): 39-55.

Wilson, Edmund. *Axel's Castle: A Study in the Imaginative Literature of 1870-1930*. New York: Charles Scribner's Sons, 1959.

GENERAL BACKGROUND

Barthes, Roland. "Flaubert et la phrase." In *Le Degré zéro de l'écriture suivi de nouveaux essais critiques*, pp. 135-144. Paris: Seuil, 1972.

―――. "L'effet de réel." *Communications*, no. 11 (1968), pp. 84-89.

―――. "Literature and Discontinuity." In *Critical Essays*, translated by Richard Howard, pp. 171-183. Evanston, Ill.: Northwestern University Press, 1972.

―――. "Littérature et discontinu." In *Essais critiques*, pp. 175-187. Paris: Seuil, 1964.

―――. *Mythologies*. Translated by Annette Lavers. New York: Hill and Wang, 1972.

―――. "Style and Its Image." In *Literary Style: A Symposium*, edited by Seymour Chatman, pp. 3-10. New York: Oxford University Press, 1971.

―――. "Writing and the Novel." In *Writing Degree Zero*, translated by Annette Lavers and Colin Smith, pp. 29-40. 1967. Reprint. New York: Hill and Wang, 1968.

Benjamin, Walter. *Illuminations*. Translated by Harry Zohn. 1968. Reprint. New York: Schocken, 1969.

Bersani, Leo. "Proust and the Art of Incompletion." In *Aspects of Narrative: Selected Papers from the English Institute*, edited by J. Hillis Miller, pp. 119-142. New York: Columbia University Press, 1971.

Bloom, Harold. *The Anxiety of Influence: A Theory of Poetry*. New York: Oxford University Press, 1973.

Booth, Wayne C. *The Rhetoric of Fiction*. Chicago: The University of Chicago Press, 1961.

———. *A Rhetoric of Irony*. Chicago: The University of Chicago Press, 1974.

Carreter, Fernando Lazaro. "The Literal Message." *Critical Inquiry* 3 (Winter 1976): 315-332.

Chatman, Seymour. "New Ways of Analyzing Narrative Structure." *Language and Style* 2 (1969): 13-36.

Cohn, Dorrit, *Transparent Minds: Narrative Modes for Presenting Consciousness in Fiction*. Princeton: Princeton University Press, 1978.

Culler, Jonathan. *Flaubert: The Uses of Uncertainty*. London: Elek, 1974.

———. *Structuralist Poetics: Structuralism, Linguistics, and the Study of Literature*. Ithaca: Cornell University Press, 1975.

Derrida, Jacques. "Signature Event Context." Translated by Samuel Weber and Jeffrey Mehlman. *Glyph* 1: 172-197. Baltimore: The Johns Hopkins University Press, 1977.

Erlich, Victor. "Roman Jakobson: Grammar of Poetry and Poetry of Grammar." In *Approaches to Poetics: Selected Papers from the English Institute*, edited by Seymour Chatman, pp. 1-27. New York: Columbia University Press, 1973.

Fish, Stanley E. *Self-Consuming Artifacts: The Experience of Seventeenth-Century Literature*. Berkeley: University of California Press, 1972.

Fletcher, Angus. *Allegory: The Theory of a Symbolic Mode*. Ithaca: Cornell University Press, 1964.

Foucault, Michel. *The Order of Things: An Archaeology of the Human Sciences*. New York: Pantheon-Random House, 1971.

Frank Joseph. "Spatial Form: An Answer to Critics." *Critical Inquiry* 4 (Winter 1977): 231-252.

———. "Spatial Form: Some Further Reflections." *Critical Inquiry* 5 (Winter 1978): 275-290.

Frye, Northrop. *Anatomy of Criticism: Four Essays*. Princeton: Princeton University Press, 1957.

Gass, William H. "The Medium of Fiction." In *Fiction and the Figures of Life*, pp. 27-33. New York: Alfred A. Knopf, 1970.

———. *On Being Blue: A Philosophical Inquiry*. Boston: David R. Godine, 1975.

Genette, Gérard. "Time and Narrative in *A la recherche du temps perdu*." Translated by Paul de Man. In *Aspects of Narrative: Selected Papers from the English Institute*, edited by J. Hillis

Miller, pp. 93-118. New York: Columbia University Press, 1971.

Gibson, Walker. *Tough, Sweet and Stuffy*. Bloomington: Indiana University Press, 1966.

Girard, René. *Deceit, Desire, and the Novel: Self and Other in Literary Structure*. Translated by Yvonne Freccero. Baltimore: The Johns Hopkins University Press, 1965.

Goodman, Nelson. "The Status of Style." *Critical Inquiry* 3 (June 1975): 799-811.

Gurewitch, Morton. *Comedy: The Irrational Vision*. Ithaca: Cornell University Press, 1975.

Hardy, Barbara. *The Appropriate Form: An Essay on the Novel*. London: The Athlone Press, 1964.

———. "Towards a Poetics of Fiction: An Approach through Narrative." *Novel* 2 (Fall 1968): 5-14.

Hartman, Geoffrey H. *Beyond Formalism: Literary Essays 1958-1970*. New Haven: Yale University Press, 1970.

———. Letter. *PMLA* 92 (March 1977): 307-308.

———. "Literary Criticism and Its Discontents." *Critical Inquiry* 3 (Winter 1976): 203-220.

Heath, Stephen. "Structuration of the Novel-Text: Method and Analysis." In *Signs of the Times: Introductory Readings in Textual Semiotics*, pp. 52-75. Cambridge, Eng.: Granta, 1971.

Hill, Leslie. "Flaubert and the Rhetoric of Stupidity." *Critical Inquiry* 3 (Winter 1976): 333-344.

Hirsch, E. D., Jr. *Validity in Interpretation*. New Haven: Yale University Press, 1976.

Hough, Graham. *Style and Stylistics*. New York: Humanities Press, 1969.

Jakobson, Roman. "Linguistics and Poetics." In *Style in Language*, edited by T. Sebeok, pp. 350-377. Cambridge, Mass.: M.I.T. Press, 1960.

James, Henry. *The Art of the Novel: Critical Prefaces by Henry James*. New York: Charles Scribner's Sons, 1962.

Jameson, Fredric. "Metacommentary." *PMLA* 86 (Jan. 1971): 9-18.

———. *The Prison-House of Language: A Critical Account of Structuralism and Russian Formalism*. Princeton: Princeton University Press, 1972.

Kermode, Frank. "Novel, History and Type." *Novel* 1 (Spring 1968): 231-238.

Bibliography

————. "Novels: Recognition and Deception." *Critical Inquiry* 1 (Sept. 1974): 103-122.

————. "Reply to Joseph Frank." *Critical Inquiry* 4 (Spring 1978): 579-588.

————. *The Sense of an Ending: Studies in the Theory of Fiction.* London: Oxford University Press, 1966.

Kierkegaard, Søren. *The Point of View for My Work as an Author: A Report to History and Related Writings.* Translated by Walter Lowrie; edited by Benjamin Nelson. New York: Harper & Brothers, 1962.

Lane, Michael, ed. *Introduction to Structuralism.* New York: Basic Books, Inc., 1970.

Lanham, Richard A. *A Handlist of Rhetorical Terms: A Guide for Students of English Literature.* Berkeley: University of California Press, 1969.

————. *The Motives of Eloquence: Literary Rhetoric in the Renaissance.* New Haven: Yale University Press, 1976.

Lang, Berel. "Space, Time, and Philosophical Style." *Critical Inquiry* 2 (Winter 1975): 263-280.

Lauter, Paul, ed. *Theories of Comedy.* New York: Doubleday & Company, Inc., 1964.

Levin, Harry. *Contexts of Criticism.* Cambridge, Mass.: Harvard University Press, 1957.

Lévi-Strauss, Claude. "The Structural Study of Myth." *Journal of American Folklore* 68 (1955): 428-444.

Lodge, David. *Language of Fiction: Essays in Criticism and Verbal Analysis of the English Novel.* New York: Columbia University Press, 1966.

Lubbock, Percy. *The Craft of Fiction.* New York: The Viking Press, 1957.

Lukács, Georg. *Realism in Our Time: Literature and the Class Struggle.* Translated by John and Necke Mander. New York: Harper & Row Publishers, 1964.

————. *The Theory of the Novel: A Historico-Philosophical Essay on the Forms of Great Epic Literature.* Translated by Anna Bostock. Cambridge, Mass.: M.I.T. Press, 1971.

Lutwack, Leonard. "Mixed and Uniform Prose Styles in the Novel." In *The Theory of the Novel,* edited by Philip Stevick, pp. 208-219. New York: The Free Press, 1967.

Macksey, Richard, and Donato, Eugenio, eds. *The Structuralist Con-*

Bibliography

troversy: The Languages of Criticism and the Sciences of Man. Baltimore: The Johns Hopkins University Press, 1970.

Meyer, Leonard. *Emotion and Meaning in Music*. Chicago: University of Chicago Press, 1956.

Meyerhoff, Hans. *Time in Literature*. Berkeley: University of California Press, 1955.

Miller, J. Hillis. "Ariadne's Thread: Repetition and the Narrative Line." *Critical Inquiry* 3 (Autumn 1976): 57-77.

Miner, Earl, ed. *To Tell a Story: Narrative Theory and Practice*. Papers read at a Clark Library Seminar, February 4, 1972. Los Angeles: University of California Press, 1973.

Mink, Louis O. "History and Fiction as Modes of Comprehension." *New Literary History* 1 (Spring 1970): 541-558.

Mudrick, Marvin. *Jane Austen: Irony as Defense and Discovery*. Princeton: Princeton University Press, 1952.

Ohmann, Richard M. "Prolegomena to the Analysis of Prose Style." In *Style in Prose Fiction: English Institute Essays, 1958*, edited by Harold C. Martin, pp. 1-24. New York: Columbia University Press, 1959.

Ong, Walter J. "The Writer's Audience Is Always a Fiction." *PMLA* 90 (1975): 9-21.

Poletta, Gregory. "The Place and Performance of Criticism." In *Issues in Contemporary Criticism*, edited by Gregory Poletta, pp. 1-27. Boston: Little, Brown & Co., 1973.

Said, Edward. *Beginnings: Intention and Method*. New York: Basic Books, Inc., 1975.

Schapiro, Meyer. "Style." In *Aesthetics Today*, edited by Morris Philipson. Cleveland and New York: The World Publishing Co., 1961.

The Selected Letters of Gustave Flaubert. Translated and edited by Francis Steegmuller. Excerpts reprinted in *Madame Bovary*, edited by Paul de Man. New York: W.W. Norton—Norton Critical Edition, 1965.

Smith, Barbara Herrnstein. "On the Margins of Discourse." *Critical Inquiry* 1 (June 1975): 769-798.

Sontag, Susan. "On Style." *Partisan Review* 32 (fall, 1965): 543-560.

Sypher, Wylie. *Loss of the Self in Modern Literature and Art*. New York: Vintage Press, 1962.

Tillotson, Kathleen. *Novels of the Eighteen-Forties*. London: Oxford University Press, 1956.

Bibliography

Todorov, Tzvetan. "Comment lire." In *Poétique de la prose*, pp. 241-253. Paris: Seuil, 1974.

———. "The Origin of Genres." Translated by Richard M. Berrong. *New Literary History* 8 (Autumn 1976): 159-170.

Ullmann, Stephen. *Style in the French Novel*. New York: Barnes & Noble, 1964.

Woolf, Virginia. *A Writer's Diary: Being Extracts from the Diary of Virginia Woolf*. Edited by Leonard Woolf. New York: Harcourt, Brace and Company, 1953.

INDEX

Index

Index

Index

Index

"Telemachus," 13, 41, 44-48, 62, 97-98, 150
Thorton, Weldon, 105
Tindall, William York, 5, 58n

Ullmann, Stephen, 19n, 23, 26, 67-68
Ulysses. *See* Odysseus.

Van Ghent, Dorothy, 10, 12

"Wandering Rocks," 54, 82-90, 104, 120, 147-50, 188-89; arbitrariness in, 84, 86-90; discontinuity in, 83, 87; "lateral imagination" in, 83-87, 181, 187; plot in, 84, 87-88, 191
Woolf, Virginia, 9, 179

Library of Congress Cataloging in Publication Data

Lawrence, Karen, 1949-
    The odyssey of style in Ulysses.

    Bibliography: p.
    Includes index.
    1.   Joyce, James, 1882-1941   Ulysses.
2.   Joyce, James, 1882-1941—Style.   I.   Title.
PR6019.O9U6743   1981   823′.912   81-47142
ISBN 0-691-06487-3   AACR2